She Won the Vote for Women

The Life and Times of Lillian Beynon Thomas

Robert E. Hawkins

GREAT PLAINS
PRESS

Great Plains Press
320 Rosedale Ave
Winnipeg, MB, R3L 1L8
www.greatplains.mb.ca

Great Plains Press gratefully acknowledges the financial support provided for its publishing program by the Government of Canada through the Canada Book Fund; the Canada Council for the Arts; the Province of Manitoba through the Book Publishing Tax Credit and the Book Publisher Marketing Assistance Program; and the Manitoba Arts Council.

Design & Typography by Relish Ideas Inc.
Printed in Canada by Friesens

Library and Archives Canada Cataloguing in Publication

Title: She won the vote for women : the life and times of Lillian Beynon Thomas / Robert E. Hawkins.
Other titles: Life and times of Lillian Beynon Thomas
Names: Hawkins, Robert E. (Law professor and historian), author.
Description: Includes bibliographical references and index.
Identifiers: Canadiana (print) 20240388372 | Canadiana (ebook) 20240388410 | ISBN 9781773371283 (softcover) | ISBN 9781773371290 (EPUB)
Subjects: LCSH: Thomas, Lillian Beynon, 1874-1961. | LCSH: Suffragists—Manitoba—Biography. | LCSH: Women—Suffrage—Manitoba—History. | LCSH: Manitoba—Biography. | LCGFT: Biographies.
Classification: LCC HQ1455.T48 H39 2024 | DDC 324.6/23092—dc23

ENVIRONMENTAL BENEFITS STATEMENT

Great Plains Press saved the following resources by printing the pages of this book on chlorine free paper made with 100% post-consumer waste.

TREES	WATER	ENERGY	SOLID WASTE	GREENHOUSE GASES
11	870	5	37	4,660
FULLY GROWN	GALLONS	MILLION BTUs	POUNDS	POUNDS

Environmental impact estimates were made using the Environmental Paper Network Paper Calculator 4.0. For more information visit www.papercalculator.org

Canadä

FSC
www.fsc.org

MIX

Paper | Supporting responsible forestry

FSC® C016245

Dedication
Dr. Peter F. Neary
Newfoundlander/Scholar/Friend

Peter Neary, professor emeritus, was, from 1965 to 2005, a member of the Department of History, and from 1995 to 2002, Dean of the Faculty of Social Science, at the University of Western Ontario. He authored books on the history of Newfoundland, paying particular attention to the pre- and post-Confederation periods, and on the artists who painted that province's rugged landscapes. He also wrote of a "Relief Stiff" who rode the rails as he sketched his way across Depression-era Canada and of the public servants who devised policy for Canadian veterans returning from the Second World War. Peter was a compelling teacher, and storyteller, who introduced generations of undergraduate students to their country's past and supervised numerous graduate students as they worked their way through their theses. This book owes its existence to his wise advice and constant friendship.

TABLE OF CONTENTS

INTRODUCTION

An Historical Gap

Lillian Beynon Thomas was a woman who valued self-determination for herself, as a pioneering journalist, activist, and author; for women, as settlers on an unforgiving prairie; and for Canada, as a country striving to establish a unique cultural identity. Despite her significant accomplishments, she has been almost completely overlooked by history. The question is why, despite her many lifetime accomplishments, and with only occasional references to her leadership role in winning suffrage for Manitoba women, has she not received the recognition that is her due? This biography seeks to answer that question.

This gap in the historical record was discovered while researching why, in 1917, Manitoba restored dower, a wife's right to an interest in her husband's property acquired during marriage, after having abolished it in 1885.[1] One possible explanation is that Beynon Thomas has been overshadowed by her more charismatic allies. Another possibility is that her initial focus on specific legal, economic, and social reforms, such as dower, that benefit defined categories of women, masked the importance of her subsequent advocacy for a broader voting reform that benefit women in general.

Even apart from winning suffrage, the grassroots campaign that led to that success was itself a significant landmark in encouraging broad engagement in the democratic process. Some of the techniques that

Beynon Thomas employed to achieve that mobilization, such as having delegations visit the Premier, were familiar but, as in the past, proved ineffective. Others, such as the collection of petition names, were also familiar; however, this time they were undertaken on a different scale, most notably in their pan-provincial deployment and in their use of door-to-door canvassing. Still, other techniques were new. She founded the Political Equality League, an organization initially made up of delegates drawn from cities, and subsequently from across the province, to direct the campaign. Catherine Cleverdon, an early historian of the suffrage movement, observed that Manitoba "was the only one of the three [Prairie provinces] in which final victory was mainly attributable to the efforts of a well-organized suffrage society. In the other provinces, the prime agitators were powerful farmers' organizations and their women's auxiliaries."[2]

There were other organizational innovations. Beynon Thomas established a bureau that trained and dispatched speakers to communities big and small throughout the province. She used her newspaper columns to keep supporters informed of suffrage arguments and campaign progress, to boost supporters' morale, and to urge them to greater canvassing and pamphleteering efforts. She reached out across class lines to connect with women in the labour movement. She was an invited platform speaker at the 1914 provincial Liberal Party convention and actively campaigned in support of the Liberal pro-suffrage platform in two provincial elections. This was the first time in Canada that a suffrage organization had intervened directly in partisan political electoral activity. Her presence as the founder of the Saskatchewan Homemakers' Clubs at its meetings, and as a speaker at Manitoba Home Economics Society gatherings drew powerful attention from farm women to the suffrage cause even though both organizations, supported by government, nominally felt the need to be apolitical.[3]

There are other reasons for telling Beynon Thomas's story. Her biography nuances insights that can be gleaned from the extensive body of feminist literature that exists on Canadian women's suffrage. That literature draws distinctions between different eras, or "waves," in the fight for equality.[4] The first wave, including Beynon Thomas, focused on legal inequalities and mostly culminated by 1920 with successful suffrage movements. The second wave, which covered the 1960s to the 1980s, focused on breaking down female role stereotypes and institutional barriers to equality and was marked by progress in areas such as reproductive rights and pay equity. The third wave broadened the analysis, focusing on intersectionality to show how gender oppression intersects with race, sexual orientation, and other individual differences to create unique kinds of oppression. The fourth wave, still being defined, extends the intersectional analysis to account for the impact of the internet, social media, and popular mass movements.

Some historians have categorized first-wave suffragettes according to their motivation in championing women's rights.[5] One group of these suffragettes, perhaps the largest, were principally motivated by their deeply held philosophic belief in women's inherent human right of equality with men. They maintained that social and economic reform would only follow as a consequence of winning the vote. For a second group, more pragmatic than philosophic, it was the other way around. Their main motivation in demanding suffrage grew out of their frustration after finding it impossible to gain specific legal, economic, and social reforms by working through existing political channels. A third group, women who made up a variety of professional, political, class, religious, or advocacy organizations and social clubs, only became suffrage supporters when their organizations or clubs became convinced to endorse suffrage.

Beynon Thomas's motivation combined all three of these elements. At the outset, she championed specific reforms favouring women, including dower and other "kindred rights"[6] such as homesteads for women, fair intestacy laws, equal guardianship laws, improved factory working conditions, fairer wages, better public schooling, rural nursing, local libraries, community rest rooms, assistance for immigrants, scientific urban planning, and an end to corruption in government. Her inability to win these reforms led her to conclude that the vote was a prerequisite to advancing equality for women. She saw that it was time for a new suffrage campaign.

In order to launch such a campaign, she began recruiting allies among her extensive personal network of contacts within a variety of women's organizations to which she belonged and about which she had reported in her newspaper columns. In some cases, as with the local Council of Women, which hesitated to support suffrage for fear of endangering the careers of its members' husbands, she was able to overcome their reluctance through her advocacy. By the end of the campaign, her thinking had evolved to the point where she frequently cited equality as the main reason for winning the vote.

Other historians have categorized first-wave suffragettes using descriptive labels such as agrarian feminists, urban feminists, maternal feminists, professional feminists, liberal feminists, socialist feminists, evangelical feminists, secular feminists, working or middle-class feminists, imperial feminists, and temperance feminists.[7] Beynon Thomas's biography shows that she straddled these distinctions as well. She grew up on a rented pioneer farm, taught in one-room schoolhouses, and corresponded with rural wives through her newspaper columns. She moved to the city as a college-educated journalist and founded or joined organizations that grouped middle-class, professional women who shared common attitudes that favoured family stability, religious Protestantism, access to education, and British institutions. She maintained close contact with the leaders of the social gospel movement, volunteered with organizations assisting immigrants, campaigned for labour candidates, and championed scientific ideas and government regulation as a way of dealing with such urban problems as poverty, overcrowding, and ill health. She rejected arguments favored by suffrage opponents suggesting that distinct spheres of activity belonged to women, particularly domestic activity inside the home, whereas other spheres of activity, those outside the home, belonged to men. At the core of Beynon Thomas's thinking was the idea that women deserved legal security and equal opportunity, whether as caregivers inside the home or as wage earners outside of it. Here too, when viewed through the lens of an individual protagonist in the suffrage movement, classification categories used to describe different types of feminists become blurred, making it difficult to apply any one label.

Beynon Thomas's biography matters for another reason. Like many of the first-wave suffragettes, her accomplishments were many and varied; her life story is not one dimensional. Her career in journalism provided a role model at a time when women were entering the profession in greater numbers. As historian Marjory Lang has observed, "The aura of power and influence that clung to the world of journalism in the late nineteenth century and early twentieth rendered women's participation in the print media something of a flagship for advancing the status of women."[8] Her career as the principal political architect of the suffrage campaign was key to the first successful provincial or federal drive to enfranchise women. Her career as a short story writer and playwright, reflecting as it did her deeply held rural and small-town Canadian values, was widely recognized in its own time. Her efforts later in life as a public advocate for cultural nationalism put her in the vanguard of a movement that continues to the present. Her biography is a reminder not to overlook the diverse contributions, beyond the political, made by other early Canadian feminists.[9]

A "Champion of Prairie Womanhood"

Early photographs of Beynon Thomas show a serious person, someone not to be taken lightly. This characterization might be dismissed as a by-product of the style of photography of the era except that it also accords with descriptions by her contemporaries. Florence Lediard (Dame Durden), who edited the woman's page of the *Farmer's and Home Journal*, and who reported on the 1911 Regina Homemakers' convention at which Beynon Thomas spoke, wrote: "She was so alert, so tactful, so businesslike, so self-possessed and so well groomed."[10] Two years later, the *Canadian Courier* described Beynon Thomas as a "very quiet person," adding, however, that there was "force behind her unassuming, still exterior."[11] Blanche Ellinthorpe, a journalist who interviewed Beynon Thomas for a "personal sketch" that was published in 1953 in *Country Guide Magazine*, described her when she was first employed in the early twentieth century as the woman's page editor of the *Manitoba Weekly Free Press and*

Prairie Farmer: "She had the courage of her convictions and a persistence in maintaining her ideals."[12]

Beynon Thomas was indelibly marked by the hardships that she faced as a child and young adult. In 1889, at age 14, she moved from southern Ontario to southwestern Manitoba where her family took up a rented homestead. There they discovered that Prairie winters were among the harshest in the world. Drafty buildings, crudely constructed, were insulted only with mud to keep out bone-chilling temperatures reaching minus 40 Celsius. The sweltering heat of summers ran in the opposite direction to plus 40. Shoulder seasons were astonishingly abrupt. The moment the frost was out of the ground, farmers rushed to plant their crops, praying that flood or drought did not prevent germination, that early summer grasshoppers did not devour the young shoots, that late summer hail did not knock down the ripening grain, and, hoping against hope, that an early fall frost did not beat them to the harvest. The Prairies were known as "tomorrow country." E. Cora Hind, agricultural editor of the *Free Press*, and Beynon Thomas's friend and journalistic mentor, explained why the Beynon's farm in Hartney, Manitoba failed: "Her people struck the bad years of the middle [eighteen] eighties, and she knows from personal experience what it meant to have frozen crops and all that that means in the way of deprivation on prairie farms."[13]

Beynon Thomas's home life was difficult. At five years old, she developed a tubercular hip that left her with a lifelong limp.[14] Her mother raised seven children before succumbing to cancer at age 50. Her restless father chased his will-o'-the-wisp dreams with ill-starred undertakings as farmer, merchant, hotelier, and well-digger. He was barely able to support his family and was eventually incapacitated by deteriorating health.

These rural roots created in Beynon Thomas a strong empathy for pioneer settlers, especially farm women. All her life, she retained a "great love of the Prairies," and a "great likening for small towns."[15] It was E. Cora Hind who observed that Beynon Thomas, "knows pioneer life in all its phases, and having seen the struggle which her own mother had with small and inconvenient homes and lack of help, she has been able to sympathize very keenly with the thousands of women who, in the Canadian west, are similarly circumstanced."[16] The time that Beynon Thomas spent as a young woman billeting with local families while teaching in rural, one-room, southwestern Manitoba elementary schools, as well as the time she later spent travelling throughout Manitoba, contributed to her understanding of rural life.[17] So, too, did the letters that she received from lonely rural women seeking her advice as editor of the "Home Loving Hearts" women's page in the *Prairie Farmer*.

Florence Lediard, Women's Editor of the *Farmer's Advocate and Home Journal*, reporting on Beynon Thomas's speech to the January 1917 Manitoba Grain Growers' Convention, held in Brandon, Manitoba, stated that Beynon Thomas had, "become established in the minds of the people as one of the foremost among the champions of prairie womanhood."[18]

A Pragmatic Reformer

In 1906, Beynon Thomas left the rural countryside for Winnipeg at a time when the city was going through what Manitoba historian W.L. Morton has called, without exaggeration, "The Great Boom."[19] The underbelly of that boom, however, was economic disparity and ethnic and linguistic tension that divided the impoverished, immigrant, and working classes living in the city's north end from the wealthy Anglo-Saxon elite living in the south. This divide created activist movements ranging from social gospelers to temperance crusaders. Beynon Thomas actively championed many of these causes while maintaining her focus on improving the lot of rural farm women.

Beynon Thomas was a change agent in that changing time. She transformed her woman's page in the weekly *Prairie Farmer* from one that featured such topics as recipes, fashion society news, and household tips to one that debated such issues as dower, guardianship, homestead laws, and suffrage. In a 1914 article, she coined the phrase "practical idealist" to describe J.S. Woodsworth, leader of the Winnipeg social gospel movement, and his fact-based, scientific approach for finding solutions to pressing urban social issues.[20] She could have been describing herself. Just as the Methodist church, by following the precepts of the Gospels, aimed to achieve "Heaven on Earth" in the here and now, Beynon Thomas, by legislative reform, aimed to achieve greater social justice in her immediate settler surroundings. She changed forever how politics in Manitoba was done by organizing the Political Equality League and by spearheading the novel grassroots campaign that made Manitoba, in 1916, the first provincial or federal jurisdiction to enact women's suffrage. For her, the ballot was not just an abstract matter of fairness and equity. It was a workable response to the urgent need to ameliorate the physical and material lives of women and their children. Writing in 1957, W.L. Morton credited these accomplishments as follows:

> And the vigorous Political Equality League not only pushed the cause of women's suffrage and legal emancipation hard in these years, but gave further impetus to the whole reform movement, in the various aspects of which women were deeply interested, and especially in temperance. A generation of able women, led by Lillian Beynon Thomas and inspired by the fighting spirit of Nellie McClung, was thrusting to the front. Their action ensured the triumph of the reform movement and changed the character of Manitoba's public life.[21]

A "Custodian of Words"

Beynon Thomas's "intellectual approach"[22] relied upon logic, not confrontation; evidence, not emotion. Only rarely did she display anger, and even then, the anger was cool and usually reserved for dismissive politicians. In 1913, E. Cora Hind wrote: "An unbounded sympathy with women and a very kindly toleration of the limitations and prejudices of both men and women were two of the strongest features of her character. She holds radical views on the subject of the economic independence of the women, but although she is radical, she is never rabid and for that reason she can speak to mixed audiences on votes for women and similar subjects without antagonising them."[23] In a 1944 letter to historian

Catherine Cleverdon, Beynon Thomas commented on the late 1911/early 1912 visits to Winnipeg and Saskatchewan of the militant British suffragettes Emmeline Pankhurst and Barbara Wylie. She wrote: "We had not yet used peaceful methods and we refused to do anything violent until we had. We did not need anything like that."[24]

Words, both written and spoken, were her primary tool. World War II was already on the horizon when she made the opening speech at the Canadian Women's Press Club's 1938 triennial convention in Winnipeg. She told delegates, "Words are more powerful than armies, navies or aeroplanes. You are the custodians of words. Remember this when you are facing the big problems of today, and perhaps even bigger problems later on."[25] Writing dialogue was a genre that she particularly favoured. In her 1946 play, *As the Twig is Bent*, Beynon Thomas had a young Abe Lincoln end a feud with a neighbour through talk. Her script had the future president say: "Words do something that fighting can't do."[26] Beynon Thomas honed her speaking ability by addressing women's groups on the benefits of establishing homemaker's clubs and on the advantages of suffrage. A 1914 newspaper article, quoted by Nellie McClung in her 1945 autobiography *The Stream Runs Fast*, referred to Beynon Thomas as, "A speaker of well-known earnestness and power."[27] When announcing that Beynon Thomas would be speaking to both the women's meetings and the main convention of the 1916 Saskatchewan Grain Growers' Association, the *Free Press* observed that, "Her deep insight into the hearts of prairie women makes her a speaker of great worth."[28]

Beynon Thomas's written works were voluminous. Her topics included fishing on the Pacific coast, late nineteenth- century Ontario political feuding, the arrival of the first Methodist minister in Winnipeg, travelogues detailing summer car trips through Manitoba, and the impact of the development of the atomic bomb. Her newspaper columns dealt with women's property rights, divorce and child custody, abused and impoverished women, and the need to curb the liquor trade. Among the formats she adopted were newspaper columns and articles, learned papers, political pamphlets, speeches, short stories, plays, radio and TV dramas, and a novel. In her time, Beynon Thomas was widely read by the public; one book reviewer wrote of her popularity: "Canadians generally, Manitobans and Winnipeggers in particular, are proud of her as people must be when one of their very own makes a success of a chosen field."[29]

CHAPTER 1

The Hardscrabble Prairie

Arrival

In 1819, Lillian Beynon Thomas's paternal great-grandfather, John Bannon, a farmer, departed with his family from King's County, Ireland, for York (now Toronto), Upper Canada.[30] He left to avoid the death threats that he had been receiving because of his position as master of the local Orange Lodge, an Irish Protestant order engaged in sectarian conflict with their Catholic countrymen. Upon their arrival in Canada, the family changed its surname from Bannon to Beynon. John and his two eldest sons—Thomas, born in 1803, and James Barnes, born in 1805—speculated in farm properties that were being opened just to the north in Upper York County in the early nineteenth century.[31]

James Barnes, known informally as Barnes, was Lillian's grandfather. He obtained title to a homestead property in King Township, York County, not far north of present-day Toronto. The property fronted on King Sideroad just west of where the road intersected with Bathurst Street.

James Barnes Beynon Homestead, King Sideroad, Lot 5,
Concession 2, King Township, York County – Birthplace of Lillian
Beynon Thomas. SOURCE: LIBRARY AND ARCHIVES CANADA

The small village of Love's Corners, named after the settler Love family, was located at that intersection. Later, the village would be renamed Temperanceville. Barnes married one of the Love family daughters, Lydia 'Lily' Love, Lillian's grandmother. Barnes built a log family home on the property, which he eventually replaced with a frame house.[32] He and Lily had eight children. Their fourth child, James Barnes Beynon, Jr., Lillian's father, was born in 1835. In 1843, Barnes passed away at the age of 38 of bilious colic. Lydia, along with members of the extended family, carried on the Barnes family homestead until James Jr. was old enough to take over.

In October 1872, James Jr., then 37, married Rebecca Manning, then 25, a resident of Tecumseth Township, Simcoe County, the neighboring county to the north of York County.[33] Like the Beynons, the Manning family were devout Wesleyan Methodists. James Jr. brought his Grit political allegiance to the marriage; Rebecca brought her family's strong Methodist and temperance convictions.[34] James Jr. and Rebecca had their first child, James Henry Manning Beynon (known as Manning) on June 26, 1873. Their daughter Lilly Kate was born just over a year later, on September 4, 1874.[35] Lilly was named after her father's mother Lily and her father's youngest sister Catherine 'Kate' Beynon. In her professional life, however, Lilly used the name Lillian.[36] She was born in the same frame family home that had been constructed by her grandfather Barnes at Temperanceville.[37]

Lillian was constantly uprooted as her father sought an ever more elusive fortune in a variety of different places and occupations. In 1876, while she was still a toddler, her family moved from Temperanceville to Streetsville, just west of Toronto. Her father established a retail business there, but it enjoyed little success. Four more children, two brothers and two sisters, joined Manning and Lillian as the family grew. When Beynon Thomas's younger sister, by nearly ten years, was born, her parents registered her with the name Francis, spelled in the masculine way with an "i," likely after the American temperance crusader Frances E. Willard, who often spelt her first name with an "i."[38] Francis would grow up to share Lillian's passion for writing, journalism, social activism, and women's suffrage.

In 1889, James Jr. again pulled up stakes, this time heading west with a view to becoming a pioneering homesteader. He stopped on the bald prairie in the southwest corner of Manitoba near where the town of Hartney would later be founded. The Souris River was close by, and the community of Brandon was fifty miles to the northeast. At the time of the family's move to Manitoba, James Jr. had two relatives living in the area. His cousin, Thomas Beynon, was a Methodist minister who had settled in Souris in 1881 and had missions initially at Meglund, near Hartney, subsequently at Rapid City, and finally at Virden, where he eventually took ill and died in 1901.[39] Another of James Jr.'s cousins, Thomas's younger brother George, established a lucrative law practice in Minnedosa, Manitoba, north of Hartney, in the 1880s.

James Jr. preceded his family west by six weeks, presumably to prepare the way. Decades later, Lillian wrote about the rest of the family's
trek by sleigh across the prairie in the early spring of 1889.[40] She told of
seeing the previous fall's ruined wheat crop standing frozen in place by a
winter that came too soon, and crocuses blooming in icy water left by the
now retreating spring snow. So began what Lillian described as the "great
adventure of making our living in a strange, wild part of the country."[41]
"Wild" was not an exaggeration. The first two settlers only arrived in the
area in 1881, constructing a shack in what was then unorganized territory and sowing a few acres to grain.[42] Upon arrival, the Beynons rented
James Hartney's homestead on land Hartney had purchased from the
CPR in 1881. He tackled the problem of crops lost to frost by becoming
the first farmer in the West to import early ripening Red Fife wheat. In
1883, he established a rural post office on his homestead. He employed
Lillian's mother as the postmistress despite her refusal to give out mail
on the Sabbath, such was the strength of her Methodist convictions.[43]
Much later, Lillian wrote of the day when they heard that the railroad
was coming: "We all wanted it. ...It meant change."[44] Shortly thereafter, Hartney drove through the homestead with Cornelius Van Horne,
president of the CPR, in tow.[45] A survey for the railroad was made and
a townsite was chosen just north of the homestead. The first CPR train
arrived from Brandon on Christmas Day 1890. The Beynons hosted a
party at the homestead to mark the great occasion.[46] The new townsite,
just a short distance to the northwest of the homestead, quickly grew into
the village of Hartney. Fifteen years on, in 1905, Hartney was incorporated as a town. The town's population in 1906 was 653; a decade later
it was 659; after that it declined steadily in numbers.[47]

When the family went west, Lillian was exposed to the challenges of
pioneer farming on the harsh and sparsely populated prairie. Initially, her
father had to transport grain by horse team twenty miles to the railroad so
that it could be marketed.[48] Her mother struggled to raise her children with
little money and few amenities.[49] Her youngest sister Francis remembered
"our paper box of a country home" where, "houses were so cold that one
ached from the weight of quilts on the bed and the hair felt as if it were

freezing to the scalp,"[50] and where "many a time," her feet were, "covered with chilblains from the cold floor.[51] Lillian's limp caused her difficulty in walking, particularly during the long trek to the rural schoolhouse.[52]

Life for the Beynons on the Hartney homestead fell into a routine. Rebecca and several neighbours started rotating prayer meetings on Sunday evenings, the first held at the Beynons. Lillian recalled this: "That first prayer meeting people came walking, or on horseback, or driving in buckboards, buggies, and lumber wagons. One family came on a rake drawn by an ox."[53] The men did the Bible readings and there were prayers and hymns. Later, on January 15, 1897, it was reported in the *Hartney Star* that, "Mrs. Beynon's Sunday School class assembled at her residence and surprised their teacher by presenting a handsome album as a token of their esteem."[54]

Discipline in Lillian's home was strict. Years later, in an October 28, 1914 "Country Homemakers" column in the *Grain Growers' Guide*, Francis described how, at different times, each of her parents would administer corporal punishment, often for trivial matters, with the scolding parent then being criticized by his or her spouse for administering cruel discipline.[55] In another column, she told of how her parents would threaten to withdraw permission from the children to attend the yearly Sunday school picnic for even a trifling misdemeanor.[56]

These early hardships and the struggles to overcome them may have resulted in the lofty goals and demanding standards that Lillian later set for herself, and for others, including the characters in her short stories and plays. They may account for Lillian's determination, curiosity, and confidence in her own ability. They may also explain the strong empathy that she developed for oppressed women, particularly for those struggling on isolated homesteads, and why she focused on the need for practical reforms.

Tragedies

The 1890s was a time of increasing difficulty for the Beynons. In March 1891 the *Free Press* reported that, "Mr. J.B. Beynon launched the enterprise of erecting, furnishing and managing a first-class temperance hotel," with a bountiful opening dinner for 200 invitees put on by the local branch of the Dominion Alliance for the Total Suppression of Liquor Traffic.[57] A year later, however, he advertised "for sale or exchange for a good farm, the largest and best situated hotel in the rising town of Hartney."[58] Hotels regularly went out of business in Hartney owing to the ban on liquor sales as a result of local referenda triggered by temperance crusaders.[59] On January 27, 1893, Lillian's youngest sibling Reuben was born. He may have come as a surprise. His father was 57 years old when this seventh child entered the world; Rebecca was 45.[60] Farming continued to be perilous. The 1894-95 season was, "dry and the frost came early."[61] Lillian's father was forever seeking other sources of income to support his family. Earlier, on March 1, 1895, he had even written to Manitoba Premier Thomas Greenway to offer his services as an underground water finder. In his letter he wrote: "I claim that with copper wire I can locate veins of water at any depth under the ground; and you can easily see the great advantage it would be to the farmer to be able to strike water every time."[62]

Tragically, Lillian's mother died of cancer on the morning of April 14, 1898, when she was only 50 and her youngest child only 5. The next day, the *Hartney Star* eulogized:

> There have been few women readier to help in times of sickness and trouble in any home than Mrs. Beynon, and her bright smile, cheerful countenance and happy disposition, together with her rich Christian experience, ever made her a welcome visitor, while her ever ready helpful hand and thoughtful mind not only relieved many a physical sufferer but also helped those who were perplexed in mind as the best course to pursue. Though loyal to her own church (the Methodist) she was prompt to recognize the spirit of Christ in any, and to show the Christ-like spirit to all, especially those in trouble or sickness.[63]

The report added: "She was a willing worker in the cause of God, gladly using her talents, even in the midst of difficulties and misunderstandings, for the good of humanity." It was not clear whether the "difficulties and misunderstandings" referred to her personal domestic circumstances or whether they referred to the challenges faced by the Hartney settler community as a whole.

Rebecca's death coincided with a decline in the physical and mental health of her husband, James Jr. Their eldest son, Manning, took over the farm. Money must have been scarce because, over the next four years, Manning also acted as a real estate agent. He frequently solicited business by placing "Farms Wanted" ads in the local paper. He placed ads offering building lots and houses for sale in Hartney, loans at 6% and 7%, farm equipment such as Norwegian Plows and Scotch Diamond Chip Harrows, and insurance.[64]

Tragedy struck again when Lillian's father's cousin, Thomas Beynon, the Methodist minister with missions in southwestern Manitoba, died in Virden on May 11, 1901.[65] This was followed by the sudden death from pneumonia of Thomas's brother, George, the lawyer land registrar, in Portage la Prairie on May 28, 1902.[66] At this time, Lillian's father's and brother's entrepreneurial endeavours, along with the family farming efforts, came to naught and the family scattered. On July 18, 1902, as they departed, the Beynons were honoured by their friends in the Hartney Epworth League.[67] James Jr. was given a "handsome easy chair" and Manning a gold watch chain. Upon receiving the gifts, the recipients expressed, "surprise, pleasure and pain that showed the regard to be mutual and the parting 'a sweet sorrow'."[68] Lillian was already living in Winnipeg.

Things went from bad to worse. On May 19, 1902, James Jr. made a last, ill-fated attempt at homesteading near Antler, Saskatchewan, in the southwest corner of that province.[69] Manning was already homesteading nearby.[70] During the summer months over the next five years, except for an absence in 1904 due to illness, James Jr. lived alone and cleared about 80 acres, or one-half of the 160-acre homestead. During the winter months he lived in Regina and Winnipeg. On November 20, 1906, he applied for a homestead patent[71] which he received on February 22, 1907.[72] The process was completed on March 20, 1907 when he was granted title giving him ownership of the farm.[73] Shortly afterwards, he left for St. Catharines, Ontario, probably to be near relatives.[74] There, he worked as a fruit grower,[75] soon fell ill, and died of "paralysis," on June 21, 1907.[76] He was 72 years old, although his death notice incorrectly listed him as 73.[77] Nine days before his death, he transferred the farm to Manning for $1,200 or approximately $25,000 in today's dollars.[78]

Two months after that, on August 22, 1907, a short obituary appeared in the *Manitoba Free Press* announcing the death of Reuben Beynon, the orphaned son of James Jr. and Rebecca Beynon.[79] Reuben had been living with his brother William in Estevan, Saskatchewan, when he suddenly took ill with severe throat trouble. After five days, he died on August 14, 1907, at the young age of 14. He left behind his three brothers, of whom Manning was the most senior, and three sisters, of whom Lillian was the eldest.

Teaching

When Lillian first arrived in Manitoba in 1889, she and her siblings attended Webb School, a one-room, rural school, a mile and a half from the family's rented Hartney homestead.[80] Although her siblings had no trouble walking to school, it proved too much for Lillian because of her tubercular hip. As a result, her parents sent her to live with relatives and attend school at the newly opened Harbord Collegiate Institute in Toronto.[81] Upon her return west, Lillian continued her high school education in Portage la Prairie[82] and at the Winnipeg Collegiate Institute.[83] The Institute offered three curriculum streams: teaching, commercial, and university. Lillian graduated from the university stream. Nellie McClung spent six months in the Institute's teaching stream around this time, graduating in 1894 with a First-Class Teaching Certificate.[84]

During this period, a majority of rural schoolteachers were young, single, and female. Teachers could start their career with third-class teaching certificates if they had not yet completed Grade 12.[85] From January 2 to March 15, 1893, Lillian attended teacher training at the Local Normal School in Brandon. She placed in the middle of her class in the professional

TOP Webb School – Rural one-room school built in 1884 briefly attended by the young Lillian Beynon after moving west in 1889.
SOURCE: HAZEL MCDONALD PARKINSON, *THE MERE LIVING*, 245.

BOTTOM East Railway Street, Hartney, circa 1902, looking northwest. In the upper right corner, at number 2, is the new Hartney school where Lillian Beynon was one of the first teachers. Note the horse hitching posts along the left side of Railway Street.
SOURCE: HAZEL MCDONALD PARKINSON, *THE MERE LIVING*, 104.

examinations for third-class teachers, doing particularly well in Grammar and Composition (85/100) and in School Management (55/75).[86] This was perhaps indicative of developing skills that would serve her well throughout her future career. Following the examinations, the students did several months of practice teaching in the classroom. All were judged to have performed "satisfactorily."[87] Lillian graduated on April 5, 1893, with a Third-Class Normal School Diploma.[88] From August to December 1896, Lillian attended Provincial Normal School in Winnipeg in order to earn her Second-Class Normal School Diploma. That qualified her to receive her Non-Professional Second-Class Teaching Certificate.[89] Seven years earlier, in 1889, Nellie McClung had attended the same Normal School where she had earned her Second-Class Teaching Certificate.[90]

By the end of the 1890s, Lillian had decided that she wanted to earn a university degree. To that end, on December 6, 1899, she enrolled in the Collegiate Division of Wesley College, a Methodist college that had affiliated with the University of Manitoba in 1888. She took a language course required for university admittance.[91] She entered the undergraduate Arts program in the fall of 1901. Finally, in the spring of 1905, at a time when women were only 11% of all college graduates,[92] Lillian, then 30 years old, graduated with four other women in a class of fifteen.[93] She graduated with a 'First-Class' Bachelor's degree, majoring in philosophy, with high marks in Plato, Aristotle, and Mill.[94] The University student newspaper commented that she had, "closed her university course in very competent fashion."[95]

Lillian then took the final step in her formal teacher training. In July 1905, she passed the Special Professional Examination for First-Class Teachers. On August 31 of that year, she was awarded her Professional First-Class Certificate, Grade 'A.' This was the highest teaching qualification, "good until recalled." The Certificate was available only to those who had earned a university degree, who had obtained a 67% average in the required professional teaching examination subjects, and who had taught for a year. For good measure, lest she not find a teaching job in Manitoba, on June 30, 1905, Lillian applied for and received an Interim Second-Class Certificate from the neighboring North-West Territories.

"Naughty Five:" Lillian Beynon Thomas and the four other
women graduates of the class of 1905, Wesley College,
University of Manitoba SOURCE: UNIVERSITY OF WINNIPEG ARCHIVES

This would have permitted her to teach for one year in what was to become, in two months, the province of Saskatchewan. However, she need not have bothered looking further afield. Soon after receiving her First-Class Teaching Certificate, she obtained a position at the Morden High School, south of Winnipeg, for the 1905–1906 academic year.[96]

Teaching was one of the few occupations open to women in the 1890s.[97] During this time, Lillian interspersed periods of teaching with periods of teacher training. The teaching enabled her to pay for her education and support her struggling family. With her help, all four of her younger siblings earned teaching certificates and several went on to hold positions in rural schools. In January 1894, Beynon Thomas took charge of the primary classes at the Webb school, which had moved from its rural location into the growing settlement at Hartney in 1892.[98] At other times she found employment as an elementary schoolteacher in one-room schools at communities surrounding Hartney.[99] These included schools at Pelican Lake,[100] Grand Bend,[101] Arden,[102] Lauder,[103] and at Chain Lakes.[104] where the Inspector wrote that she was "an excellent teacher" and that her school was "above the average of rural schools."[105] In the summer of

1904 she taught at Ochre River, north of Hartney on the other side of Riding Mountain.[106] The Presbyterian Minister in charge of that school told how her influence had produced a marked improvement in the manners and knowledge of her students and wrote, "Miss Beynon loves her work and infuses a like feeling into her scholars."[107]

Something of Beynon Thomas's teaching philosophy was revealed in a short story that she wrote in 1913. The editor of *The Canadian Courier* magazine had called for stories that would, "depict the men and women of today at their tasks."[108] "Banking on Sam," a submission by Beynon Thomas, was accepted for publication.[109] It described, "humorously and naively" in the editor's opinion, how a young schoolteacher in a small town, one-room school succeeded in winning the good will of a bullying gang of teenage school boys. Instead of assuming that the boys were all bad and discipling them, the teacher trusted them with a variety of important tasks which they carried out responsibly. To reward them, she persuaded the town to build a skating rink as an alternative to the distractions provided by the local pool hall. Reason proved more effective than force in achieving the desired result.

Lillian's year in Morden, after graduating from Wesley College and obtaining her first-class teaching certificate, was the last year that she spent in the classroom. She had long held a "cherished determination" to become a journalist.[110] One evening, in the spring of 1906, the legendary editor of the *Winnipeg Free Press*, John Wesley Dafoe, came to town to give a talk. The next morning, Lillian was waiting on the Morden train station platform hoping to meet him before he boarded the return train to Winnipeg. She struck up a conversation. The two found that they had much in common. Dafoe had a rural upbringing and had also taught school before taking a job as a reporter at a Montreal paper.[111] By the time that Lillian and Dafoe finished their conversation, he had offered her a page in the *Prairie Farmer*, the weekly rural publication of the *Free Press*. When her classes in Morden finished in June, Lillian quickly packed her bags and headed for the big city, a new career, and a different life.

That said, even as she moved out of the schoolhouse, Beynon Thomas never stopped being a teacher. She went on to help rural homemakers through her newspaper columns, offer advice to her fellow journalists, instruct suffragettes on organizing campaigns, provide adult education to aspiring writers and, in later life, to educate the public on the value of developing a uniquely Canadian literary culture.[112] In 1913, Violet McNaughton turned in desperation to Beynon Thomas for advice on speechmaking. Recalling that event some thirty-seven years later, McNaughton wrote to Beynon Thomas expressing her gratitude for the instruction that she had received: "I shall never forget what I owe to you in giving me confidence for that first speech that I ever made as provincial president of the WGGA [Women's Grain Growers' Association of Saskatchewan] and all the other encouragements that followed."[113] Following the publication of her book in 1946, one reviewer wrote, "Many an aspiring writer has been dealt with kindly by Mrs. Thomas and the sympathetic touch of her deep understanding."[114]

During the years from 1890 to 1905, when Beynon Thomas was getting her education, teaching in rural communities, and boarding with farm families, she would return home to Hartney for holidays and vacations. Her exposure to her own family's hardships, and those of the other rural families with whom she came in contact through her teaching, gave her first-hand knowledge of the poverty, isolation, lack of medical care, and challenges faced by Prairie homesteaders.[115] This is evident in an address that Beynon Thomas made to a meeting of The Lord Selkirk Chapter of the Daughters of the Empire at the YWCA in Winnipeg. The talk, entitled "Pioneer Women of the West," was covered in the *Grain Growers' Guide (GGG)*, the official newspaper organ of the two main Grain Gowers associations with the highest circulation of any farm newspaper in Manitoba and Saskatchewan. Mary Ford, the women's page editor prior to Francis Beynon taking over, reported that Beynon Thomas described the conditions under which farm women laboured:

> 'With the thought of the pioneer women comes to me some conception of the loneliness that is hers to bear. It is something of which city dwellers can never know, for it is the longing for the sight of human faces and the sound of human

voices.' ... Speaking further, Mrs. Thomas told of the sacrifice of the pioneer woman in seeing her children growing up uneducated, for often the homestead was far from a school. ... Sickness was a horror to homes 20 to 65 miles from a doctor and nurse. 'We may not feel our cold,' she said, 'but the strenuous climate drives people. Prairie dwellers wear out young.' ... Mrs. Thomas scored the educational system which sends women out ignorant of the cares of a home or children. Her work on the *Free Press* had brought her into touch with the women of the far places, and often their hardships had root in ignorance.[116]

In 1914, a fellow journalist wrote: "From these early experiences of agricultural life and conditions Lillian, being of a ruminating, observant turn of mind, absorbed an immense store of well digested impressions which, later, were to prove of great value in her work as journalist, organiser and feminist."[117]

CHAPTER 2

The Fourth Estate

Pressroom Barriers

In the early days, as professor of history Marjory Lang has written, journalism was not an easy field for interested women to enter: "The would-be woman writer had to try some other career first. The first generation of newspaper women had, almost to a woman, been fugitives from teaching."[118] Lillian Beynon Thomas was one of those women. She had worked long and hard to gain top qualifications as a teacher, often in the face of considerable hardship. She liked young people and was very good at her job.[119] Why, then, did she leave her profession only one year after having obtained a permanent position at Morden High School? In part, she may have been looking for a fresh start after her family's struggles making a living in Hartney and the gradual scattering of family members following the death of her parents. In part, at 30 years of age, she may have decided that it was time to pursue her lifelong interest in writing, especially given that women were starting to be hired as journalists.[120]

There was another possibly overarching reason why journalism beckoned. In a 1912 *Saturday Night* column, Lady Gay (Grace Denison) captures the restless, transformative spirit that led pioneering women journalists like Beynon Thomas to the pressroom:

> The girl who is too enterprising to turn to nursing, too independent to long for marriage, too full of strength and life and curiosity and a certain devil-may-care daring and faith in her lucky star, to accept sports and the conventional pursuits as an adequate outlet for her eager spirit, turns to journalism as a flower to the sun. She wants to jump into the interests that sweep along in the river of life, not to wade or paddle upon the shore; she goes in up to her neck, and also, alas, sometimes, over her head.[121]

That description may explain Beynon Thomas's motivation. When she first met John Dafoe, editor of the *Free Press*, on the Morden train station platform, Beynon Thomas told him that, "she'd like a position on the newspaper, 'because in a few more years I am going to start looking like a typical school teacher'."[122] She may have found teaching tedious. As she said, she had, "the urge to do something 'different'"[123] and was "extremely interested in everything."[124] By nature, Lillian was a practical person, a doer. She realized that she was a woman of the world, not a woman of the classroom.

Marjory Lang has described the profession of journalism in the late nineteenth and early twentieth centuries as very much a man's world.[125] The pressroom was a place of cussing, boozy male comradery made up of hard-living men full of risqué stories who pounded the urban beat, ferreting out real-world accounts of devious politicians, ruthless capitalists, and petty idlers who haunted the city's bars.[126] Newspaper bosses considered the pressroom no place for gentle womenfolk more suited to homemaking or perhaps those professions that more closely resembled traditional women's work, such as teaching, nursing, social work, or stenographic office jobs. This attitude reflected a 'separate sphere' notion of society in which women and men occupied different spaces, women handling domestic responsibilities inside the home while men supported the family outside of it.[127]

There were other differences in the ways in which men and women journalists were treated. Women reporters were encouraged to adopt a pen name that would project their personalities in a way that would establish a close relationship with readers[128] and that would appeal to editors and advertisers.[129] These were not exigencies imposed on male newspaper reporters. Editorial bosses paid little heed to women journalists. They "occupied the borderlands of the press world, whose barons tolerated but barely acknowledged their presence."[130] While the aspiring woman journalist might have hoped to find herself in the main section of the paper reporting on 'hard' news, or on the editorial page expressing her opinion on the public affairs, as often as not she found herself "cloistered discretely"[131] in the center pages of the newspaper reporting on such 'soft news' items as fashion, social events, and household hints or, if she was able to comment at all, editorializing on topics considered appropriate for female readers.[132]

Male journalist colleagues tended to hold in contempt the academic credentials of new female recruits. On-the-job training, earned on the streets, was what mattered.[133] Curiously, given her academic background, Beynon Thomas seemed to share this view. E. Cora Hind painted the picture this way:

> 'Lillian Laurie' has a good sense of humor, and a most enjoyable thing is to hear her tell of her experiences in joining the Free Press staff. Newspaper folk are proverbially lacking in reverence for titles and degrees. She had come fresh from a scholastic atmosphere and while her early days of teaching had left her with less vanity in the possession of a college degree than is common among those who go straight from school to the University, still she was conscious that she had the degree. She declares that a month on the Free Press convinced her that a college degree was less than nothing, and vanity, was something that was to be carefully concealed. The beautiful unconsciousness with which the various members of the staff rubbed this idea in, robbed it of any sting and she saw only the humorous side.[134]

Benyon Thomas's rejection of the importance of a college degree might be dismissed as an early attempt on her part to fit into her new surroundings except that five years later she confirmed her point of view. The minutes of a meeting of the Winnipeg branch of the Canadian Women's Press Club on May 11, 1911, record a talk that Beynon Thomas gave to its members:

> Miss Beynon spoke of the attitude of girls in other professions toward the girl in journalistic work, speaking more particularly of the point of view of the college girl in regard to the newspaper girl, remarking that the woman of the world is the strong woman rather than the college woman, who has little practical knowledge. She closed her remarks by saying that one is much more natural and broader in newspaper work than in that of teaching, where one is constantly trying to be an example.[135]

Journalism may have been a man's world, but it was a world in transition. This was partly because women were needed as editors of the women's pages that carried the lucrative advertising on which newspapers were coming to depend for their survival. It was also because increasing numbers of women were entering journalism and were, by their presence, changing the culture of the pressroom. This was particularly true in the West. The evolving attitude towards hiring women journalists was evident in Beynon Thomas's case. John Dafoe may have been a leading "newspaper baron" but he was also an intellectual giant, a man who, prior to taking his first job in journalism in Montreal, had been a teacher, and who was prepared to give Beynon Thomas, with her university degree, the wider world opportunity that she sought. She became not only an employee of his newspaper, but a friend of his family.[136]

Beynon Thomas was not isolated in her new profession.[137] In 1914, E. Cora Hind estimated that there were twenty columns in Canadian newspapers devoted to women's work and problems.[138] Beynon Thomas networked extensively with the journalists who wrote these columns through regular weekly meetings of the Winnipeg Branch of the Canadian

Women's Press Club.[139] E. Cora Hind, fast becoming one of the world's leading agricultural journalists for her crop reports, was her mentor at the *Free Press* and an ideal guardian angel. Beynon Thomas also networked with a group of prominent male journalists in Winnipeg who shared her liberal views, including George Chipman, editor of the *Grain Growers' Guide*, and Vernon Thomas, a fellow *Free Press* reporter whom she subsequently married.

At the start of her employment, Dafoe did not give Beynon Thomas the position on the editorial staff of the daily paper as she had hoped.[140] Instead, he gave her a job as the editor of the women's page of the weekly *Prairie Farmer*,[141] the rural publication of the *Free Press* and the most widely circulated farm weekly in Canada.[142] In 1906, soon after Beynon Thomas began editing her Home Loving Hearts page in the weekly paper, Kate Simpson Hayes (Mary Markwell), the editor of the women's page in the daily *Free Press*, left her job to move to England to promote, on behalf of the Canadian Pacific Railway, the immigration of women to Western Canada.[143] Beynon Thomas took over Hayes's position in the daily paper while retaining her editorship of the Home Loving Hearts page in the weekly rural paper. Very often articles that she wrote and letters that she published appeared in both papers. There is nothing to suggest that Beynon Thomas felt constrained by Dafoe when taking reformist editorial positions, although she was cautious about discussing peace issues, especially in wartime, something that she knew would upset her boss. Privately, she was a pacifist.[144]

Unlike some of her contemporaries who found that marriage either limited or put an end to their promising journalistic careers, Beynon Thomas was able to devote herself almost entirely to her new occupation. In one of her columns, she described how her adult brothers and sisters, with whom she lived at the time, had the advantage of a housekeeper who was also responsible for meal preparation. "I do not do any of the housekeeping," she wrote, "perhaps not as much as many men do, and, like the average man, I expect my meals to be ready at the proper time."[145] Beynon Thomas, an unmarried, middle-class, professional woman with a housekeeper, a college degree, and a career outside of the home, may have had a deep understanding from her past of the hardships faced by the isolated farm women for whom she wrote, but she had, through her own efforts, come a long way and those kinds of hardships were no longer part of her current situation.

In the column in which she described the kind of housekeeper she liked to employ, Beynon Thomas, unmarried at the time, took the opportunity to lecture her female readers on the kind of wife a husband would want in his home: "In the first place we desire a woman who is cheerful. A woman who is always talking about her woes depresses any home, and only those who have worked hard away from home all day know the pleasure of going home to a smiling woman." However, the cheerful wife was not meant to be passive. Beynon Thomas continued, "I have taught school for years, and I have lived in other people's homes for years and from what I have seen I think that everyone [every husband] will be a bully if he gets the chance. And women, instead of bearing it in martyred silence should insist on their rights, and they would get them."[146] Beynon Thomas may have been less idealistic than some of her contemporaries, but her advice, based on her personal experience, was meant to connect women so that they could support each other. This practical approach was a hallmark of her journalism and later, her political career.

Letters from the Countryside

Beynon Thomas's women's page, at first unsigned, appeared on August 29, 1906, under the heading "Home Loving Hearts—A Page Especially for Them."[147] In an October 22, 1913, column, Beynon Thomas reminisced about the origins of her page:

> My memory wanders back to the autumn of 1906, when in a small office I sat and pondered on the advisability of having a page in the paper [*The Prairie Farmer*] for the women on the farm. Up to that time all the material that was put on the 'Woman's Page' was just transferred from the daily paper to the weekly. ... In those days women

```
HOME LOVING HEARTS
A PAGE ESPECIALLY FOR THEM
```

M. B. A.

Home Loving Hearts headline. *PRAIRIE FARMER*, JUNE 24. 1908, PAGE 14

were supposed to be chiefly interested in 'beauty hints' and 'dress'. Pages were devoted to telling women how to appear young, keep slight, prevent grey hair, and furnish and run a house on nothing a week. ... It seemed to me that women had too much sense, on the whole, to be wholly interested in such matters. At least I gave the country women credit for having too much sense to want a weekly diet of such reading matter. ... It seemed to me that the day for such articles for intelligent women was passing. It seemed time for the women to come out and say what they really wanted, and in our Home Loving Hearts page we have tried to give them a chance to do so.[148]

From the beginning, Beynon Thomas set out to give women a voice. The topics and tone of her columns came to reflect this with more and more intensity as time went on. In an early column titled "A Society Of Helpful Hearts," dated December 19, 1906, Beynon Thomas, aka "Lillian Laurie," proposed the following: "We want all the women and girls who read this page to combine for mutual benefit. There are very many ways in which women on the prairie could only help each other if they only knew what to do." Proposing to launch a new club, she wrote, "Our first duty will be to choose a name for ourselves." After suggesting a few ideas, she invited the women and girls reading her column to send in their ideas. The name of the club would be "whatever the majority wish."[149] It appears that no suggestions were submitted as the name ultimately chosen resembled very much one that Beynon Thomas had initially suggested as an example. In her column on January 9, 1907, she announced that the club would be called "Mutual Benefit Association" or "The M.B.A." for short.[150] Its purpose, she explained in 1911, was for members to help each other in whatever way they could: "Any help that one can give another is what we mean. It may be advice about house-keeping, the care of children, the work of clubs, or something else of that nature. Or it may be a cheerful letter, that makes everyone feel better, or a letter dealing with the philosophy of life and the problems that the intellectual must meet and face some day."[151]

Anyone who expressed an interest in belonging to the M.B.A. could write a "friendly letter" to Lillian Laurie and become a member. The symbol of the M.B.A. was a fountain pen with the letters M.B.A. appearing on the barrel of the pen. A sketch of the pen appeared at the start of the letters section of every Home Loving Hearts column. Club members could send Lillian Laurie fifty cents and receive an M.B.A. pin that they could wear to identify themselves to other country women whom they happened to meet in their communities.[152] Beynon Thomas was at pains to point out that you did not need to purchase the pin to belong to the Association and that the fifty-cent charge simply covered the cost of the pin.

At first, Beynon Thomas received no letters. Then, early in 1907, the first letters came in under the pseudonyms "Meadow Rue," "Marie Bluebell," "Primrose," "Daisy" and "Hopeful."[153] After that, the letters came in so thick and fast that on December 25, 1907, Beynon Thomas, looking back over the year, wrote in her column that, "almost three hundred letters from women engaged in the active struggle of life, have been published and sent out a word of cheer and comfort to all the readers of this paper."[154] Beynon Thomas was not being entirely frank in her description on the origins of the first letters. On June 1, 1960, a correspondent to the *Free Press Weekly Prairie Farmer*, the successor weekly to the original *Prairie Farmer*, wrote that it "would be hard for mothers today to realize or understand the true meaning of what the Home Loving

Hearts page meant to the women of those early days."[155] She explained that many years after the first two M.B.A. letters were published, Lillian Laurie confessed that she had "primed the pump" by writing those first two letters herself, "just to get it started."[156]

Beynon Thomas was not the first women's page editor to invite women settlers to write a "Letter to the Editor" with their comments and suggestions or seeking advice. In addition to Beynon Thomas's Home Loving Hearts page in the *Prairie Farmer*, such columns appeared, usually weekly, in the *Grain Growers' Guide* ('The Country Homemakers,' edited by Francis Marion Beynon), the *Western Home Monthly*, the *Nor'-West Farmer* ('From a Woman's Standpoint,' edited by Mary S. Mantle aka Margaret Freestone), the *Farmer's Advocate* ('The Ingle Nook,' edited by Florence Lediard, aka Dame Durden, and May Clendenan aka Dame Dibbins), all published in Winnipeg, and the *Family Herald and Weekly Star* ('Prim Rose at Home'), published in Montreal. Historian Norah Lewis, in an anthology of those letters, identified the following four major themes raised by their authors: "their desire to share recent adventures and experiences with others; their loneliness and isolation; their lack of traditional support groups and networks; and the need for laws to protect their own personal and property rights and those of their children."[157] To this list can be added two other themes: their difficulty farming in a harsh and unpredictable climate and the fragility of their subsistence living.

Most of these letters were similar in tone: polite, proud of their homesteading accomplishments, appreciative of the grandeur of the western countryside, and grateful for the opportunity to correspond through the newspaper. Most letters were also similar in content. Farm women wrote of having to travel up to 40 miles in horse-drawn buggies to get their grain to the railway, to shop in town, to attend church, or even to visit a neighbour. Still others spoke of barely surviving because of successive crop failures caused by drought, flooding, hail, frost, or insects. In some cases, crop failure meant husbands sought work in town during the winter months, leaving their wives at home alone to cope with large families. Other wives struggled to raise their children after their husbands deserted them, sometimes for younger women, sometimes tempted by excessive drink, often having sold their homesteads without the consent of their wives. Other wives told of disease, aggravated by the lack of rural nurses, and sickness that frequently resulted in the death of a spouse or a child. Migrant women told of the isolation caused by their difficulty communicating in English, and by discrimination. Lonely women wrote that they never received mail and asked that reading material be passed along to help them battle their isolation. New wives sought advice on domestic challenges such as food preparation and preservation, family health and discipline, home decorating and cleaning, making garments and mending used clothing, and gardening. In addition, they looked for suggestions on coping with farm chores including poultry tending and egg collection, cow milking and butter churning, and field work, particularly in the busy seasons. For most women on the farm, life, while not without rewards, was hard. There appear to have been no letters from Indigenous women, although the use of pseudonyms may have disguised this, and literacy may have posed a barrier.[158]

Like the letters printed in other agricultural publications, Beynon Thomas's Home Loving Hearts column at first focused on home-making hints, recipes, child-rearing advice, clothing patterns, society news, magazine exchanges, suggestions on how to do farm chores, health and nutrition information, and the like. Using a pseudonym, a letter writer would ask Lillian Laurie questions, or make suggestions for her other readers, or ask her to coordinate a trade of goods such as clothing or reading material between the letter writer and the column's readers. The letter writer would include a stamped, self-addressed envelope. Lillian Laurie would print the letter in her Home Loving Hearts column using the letter writer's pseudonym. She would often include her own advice, instructions, suggestions, or editorial comments with the letter. A reader wishing to respond directly to a writer whose letter had been published could do so by sending in the response to Lillian Laurie, who would then forward the response on to the original letter writer in the stamped, self-addressed envelope they had provided.

In 1960, four decades after Lillian Laurie's time, the Home Loving Hearts page was still publishing letters from farm women in the

Prairie Farmer, by then known as *Free Press Weekly Prairie Farmer*. On April 10, 1960, a letter using the pseudonym "Ashnola, B.C." was printed under the headline, "Looking back on the good old days—Home Loving Hearts 1912."[159] Ashnola told of how she had discovered among her mother's sheet music four well-worn pages of the Magazine Section of the Wednesday April 10, 1912, edition of the *Free Press*. One page contained Lillian Laurie's Home Loving Hearts column. Ashnola outlined the contents of that column. She told of how Lillian Laurie was trying to get the government to provide maternity nursing for rural districts. Lillian asked that women of various districts write with cases where lack of nurses had caused suffering. Ashnola then described the many letters from farm women that Lillian had reproduced. "Hyacinthe" provided a recipe for Oak Cakes; "Shorty" wrote that you could cure heartburn by chewing a coffee bean; "Head of Wheat" put out an appeal for used baby clothing for a neighbour who was expecting a baby after having lost a child the year previous; "Marigold" wrote that a mix of honey, goose oil, and callum given a little at a time would cure colds in children; "Nyosothis" suggested hanging a pail of hot coals in the chicken house to keep the birds warm; "Baby Dodds" wrote that she was lonely. Her new husband had taken her four hundred miles west of Winnipeg and settled her into a "bachelor's shack." Their crop had been hailed and frozen out for the last two years. On it went. Ashnola reflected on that earlier time: "As I read the letters, I could sense the lonely stretches of the prairies as these home loving hearts reached out a helping hand or appealed to other kind souls for assistance with their problems."

The M.B.A. set out to help settler women like "Baby Dodds" by putting them in contact with each other through the Home Loving Hearts page.[160] Just before Christmas 1911, under the heading "A Pathetic Story," one woman who signed herself "Tired" sought help from M.B.A. club members who were giving away clothes. "I have seven children, five girls and two boys," she wrote. "The crop has been spoiled year after year, dried out, hailed and frozen. Last year it looked good but was black with smut but this year is worst of all, everything is frozen, even the potatoes and they have always been good till this time. Two of the horses are dead and the blackleg is in the cattle. I myself have been sick. I am a little better, but my hands and feet are so swollen that I can hardly do anything, least of all knit, and that is what I have done before to get money to buy clothes for the little ones. May God help me."[161] In a note below the letter, Beynon Thomas responded by saying that she was sure that some of the members would write with suggestions. They did. After the holidays, Beynon Thomas reported that, "A dozen or more wrote to the member who signed herself 'Tired' in the Dec. 6th issue." [162] In a subsequent letter to Beynon Thomas, "Tired" gratefully acknowledged the help: "The members are kind and I cried over those letters. I could not help it; I was so glad. I was so lonely, nobody to say a kind word. Then my letter appears on the page with your kind words, and yesterday there came those blessed letters, six from members and one from you."[163]

The letters from Prairie women had an intimate quality about them. They took the place of phone calls before there were phones.[164] English "Tea Rose" wrote that the page seemed "to bind us together."[165] "Hawk Eye" wrote, "I lie down for a few minutes rest, I read the letters and it seems as if I were talking to you [Lillian Laurie] and I have my say between the lines."[166] Violet McNaughton, who became the first president of the Saskatchewan Women Grain Growers' Association in 1914, reminisced in her 1952 column in the *Western Producer*, "How many of us from down east or overseas, new to prairie isolation and hardship, watched for Lillian Laurie's weekly message? How many of us shared our joys and sorrows with her, through her page or by personal letters?"[167] Perhaps the best summary of Beynon Thomas's influence as a journalist was written by one of her contemporaries, Pearl Richmond Hamilton, editor of the Women's Department in the monthly *The Canadian Thresherman and Farmer*. In 1912, she wrote that Benyon Thomas:

> who edits the department for women and girls in the *Weekly Free Press* is regarded as a friend in nearly every western home. Under the pen name of Lillian Laurie she touches the very heart of women's affairs and her readers regard her advice and help as most practical. Her correspondence department

brings letters from hundreds of women who ask her assistance on every problem pertaining to women and in many cases she has by her contributions from the pen saved lives. She not only helps with her pen but she is a gifted speaker concerning women, before large audiences at conventions and other gatherings throughout the western provinces. She is a very popular speaker and presents her arguments in a most convincing manner.[168]

Broadening Horizons

Beynon Thomas was in the vanguard of an evolution in the content of the women's pages. In a 1972 retrospective article, the *Free Press* explained that at the turn of the century coverage of women's issues was "spotty" with most of the space being filled with advertising purchased by major department stores. However, it continued, by the end of the century's first decade, "women wanted to read about more serious topics," including coverage of club meetings of such organizations as the Imperial Order Daughters of the Empire and the Women's Christian Temperance Union and coverage of the right to vote campaign.[169] In a 1910 opinion piece entitled "The Woman's Page of Yesterday, Today and Tomorrow," Francis Beynon, Beynon Thomas's sister, provided more detail:

> It was only yesterday that women's pages used to be filled with prescriptions for making furniture out of boxes, beauty hints and instructions for the young girl as to the words in which she should bid adieu to her gentleman caller. ... Within the last few years we have advanced a revolution or two. Housekeeping has been discovered to be a science and the proper sanitary care of our homes and children, the intelligent up-bringing of the growing generation, the woman's right to take up land and have a voice in the affairs of the nation have crept into the woman's page... The woman's page of tomorrow will be filled, I hope, with broader

questions… The time is coming, I am convinced, when
the interest of women will have broadened out from the
narrow confines of their own family life to include the life
of that larger family—the nation. We can't shut our children up inside of our own four walls and keep them from
the contamination of the life outside. They will be obliged
to face it sooner or later and the only way to protect them
is to clean up the civic and national life by which they are
surrounded.[170]

Beynon Thomas summarized this evolution well in her final column
before leaving her journalism career on May 2, 1917:

You remember we started with special attention to our inner
selves and devoted much space to recipes, home remedies
and suggestions for making furniture out of boxes and
covering it with flour sacks to look like the real thing. …
Then we took up the question of the rights of women—and
a dower law… The next step was—but there have been too
many steps to enumerate them all. But the jump has been
made, from a page devoted to recipes, home remedies, and
grievances, to a page where taxes, trade, and laws, sociology and kindred subjects are intelligently discussed. Four
walls no longer bind the minds of our women. They have
reached out to the district, then to the nation, and now, it is
with the great international problems they are wrestling.[171]

In an earlier 1913 editorial, Beynon Thomas told her readers that
she thought that they "had too much sense, on the whole, to be wholly
interested in such matters" as "hints on beauty, dress and how to win
and keep a man's heart." It was her hope that her page would, "reflect
the mental life of our women as it has never done before." She continued,
"I hope the mental life of our women is on such a high plane that it will
be an inspiration to all."[172] She evidently felt that she had accomplished
her goal, for in April 1914 she wrote, "It is interesting to note that more

and more of our members are becoming interested in public questions."[173] As if to prove her point, between May and July 1914, she published a twelve-instalment feature intended to educate women readers who had, "come from different countries, where the laws and conditions [were] different," and who, "for the first time [were taking] an interest in public questions."[174] These historical-political articles dealt with everything from the Canadian constitution to the issue of homelessness, to property ownership and child guardianship, to women's suffrage.

The analysis of "public questions," and all other advice to homemakers, was briefly interrupted at the outbreak of World War I. On September 9, 1914, in a "note to say farewell," Beynon Thomas wrote: "You all know that the nation in which we live is at war, and although we are far from where the battles are raging, we are feeling the effects. One is the great scarcity of paper. The newspapers are using less paper, lest there should be a great shortage. ... But during this time of stress, it is thought best to cut out most of the special departments, one of which is our 'Home Loving Hearts' department. It is unnecessary for me to say I am sorry."[175] The hiatus, however, was short lived. Six months later, on March 10, 1915, under the familiar banner "Lillian Laurie's Page For Women and Girls," the Home Loving Hearts section reappeared and, along with it, the M.B.A. column. Beynon Thomas opened with the words, "Here I am back at my desk again."[176]

Public questions continued to be the order of the day. They fell under the rubric of "kindred rights"[177]—kindred because the proposed reforms had in common the emancipation of women by reversing laws that placed them in a legal, social, political, and economic positions inferior to men.[178] Beynon Thomas's causes included a campaign that would prevent a husband from disinheriting his wife; a campaign for a homesteading law that would enable a woman to acquire homesteading rights equal to those available to men; a campaign for equal child custody rights upon the dissolution of marriage; a campaign for maintenance and alimony laws that would compel deserting husbands to provide for their families left destitute; a campaign for the establishment of rural women's clubs for companionship, mutual assistance, and civic involvement; a campaign for better provision of rural health services, particularly nursing services; and a temperance campaign. The two closely related causes that stood out, however, were the dower campaign, which would prevent a husband from selling his property acquired during marriage without the consent of his wife, and the suffrage campaign, which was aimed at giving women the vote.

The Dower Campaign

The dower campaign ignited Beynon Thomas's passion, honed her advocacy technique, and ultimately led to her suffrage drive. On June 17, 1908, she published a letter signed "An Old Woman" in her *Prairie Farmer* M.B.A. column.[179] The author of the letter had moved with her husband from Ontario to a homestead in BC. She was writing to express her "consternation" upon discovering that, unlike in Ontario, there was no dower law in the western provinces. She told of witnessing a situation in which a man and his wife had worked hard to build up their homestead only to have the husband take to drink when a town with a saloon grew up nearby. The farm work was left to his wife and sons. A neighbour, coveting the farm for his own son, encouraged the reprobate husband in his drunken ways until finally convincing him, while partly inebriated, to sell the farm. Beynon Thomas recounted how the situation ended badly: "This poor woman found that she could do nothing but take her children and walk out, which she did and they are now scattered all over, while the husband still hangs around the hotel spending the money as he gets it by installments, but the poor wife got nothing."

This letter, which was reprinted in the daily *Free Press* on February 15, 1910,[180] "certainly did," in Beynon Thomas words, "start a big campaign, but not before one was needed."[181] Between June 1908 and September 1909, Beynon Thomas published, mostly in their entirety, 442 letters that dealt with dower.[182] Of these, fifty-seven indicated that they were convinced by "Old Woman's" letter or other letters that had recounted "sad cases." Sometimes the correspondents wrote from personal experience; other times they recounted sad stories that they had heard about in their local rural areas. Twenty of the letters expressed anger in words such as "shame" or "disgrace" to describe the lack of a dower law. There were sixty-five letters from men which ran 2:1 in favour of a dower law. Women journalists writing in other farm newspapers picked up the campaign. Florence Lediard (Dame Durden), editor of the women's page in the *Farmer's Advocate*, argued for a dower law. She cited a case, very much like the one told by "Old Woman," of a wife left homeless after a husband sold the farm out from under his family.[183]

Beynon Thomas developed four arguments in favour of a dower law. First, married women with no property rights were at the mercy of, and so needed protection from, wayward, unscrupulous, or violent husbands who might be tempted to sell the homestead without their wives' consent, leaving the family destitute. Second, the groom in his marriage vow promised his bride, "with all my worldly goods I thee endow." Third, the wife earned her fair share of the farm through her hard work in helping to build and operate it. Fourth, like "Old Woman," many wives had followed their husbands west on the reasonable expectation that they would find dower as it existed in the east, or in the homeland, or in many of the prairie states of the United States.

The men who wrote into the Home Loving Hearts page feared the re-introduction of any form of dower law. A requirement that a husband obtain his wife's consent before selling or mortgaging land, which is a requirement for her to 'bar her dower,' would hinder such transactions that took place frequently during settlement times. Some farmers objected that they had come into their marriage with property to which their wives had contributed nothing and so felt she should be entitled to no interest in the land. As Lillian Laurie repeatedly pointed out, these husbands misunderstood dower, which would only apply to property acquired during the marriage. Other farmers felt that they were being singled out as a dower law would not apply to husbands with property in town, another misapprehension. Still others argued that their wives did not contribute to the heavy work on the farm sufficient to earn them a share of the property and some even suggested that was not just husbands but wives as well who were inclined to run off and leave their partners

"Lillian Laurie" at her desk at the *Prairie Farmer* circa 1913
SOURCE: *CANADIAN COURIER WOMAN'S SUPPLEMENT*, FEBRUARY 24, 1924,
AND ARCHIVES OF MANITOBA, LILLIAN BEYNON THOMAS FONDS

destitute. Lillian Laurie answered all of these objections insisting that men educate themselves in the meaning of a dower law, frequently providing that guidance herself through her columns often indicating that she had consulted lawyers who were experts in the field.[184]

Fact, reason, and words, not sentiment, intuition and charisma, were the tools of persuasion that Beynon Thomas preferred to employ.[185] She believed that if she presented her points, whether on dower, suffrage, or any other issue, calmly and rationally, her listeners would come to see the validity of her positions. "I think all new ideas," she once told an interviewer, "have an impact on life, gradually changing people."[186]

The methods that Beynon Thomas developed to lobby the provincial government on dower reform became the blueprint that she would later use for her suffrage campaign. She triggered the dower agitation by publishing letters in her newspaper columns from women who lacked property rights. These letters were often accompanied by her own, rather didactic, commentary further elucidating the arguments in favour of dower. Beynon Thomas's readers were urged to write to their local newspapers, and to their local legislative assembly representatives, with a "plain statement" of the injustice of the dower situation. They were told to illustrate their position, if possible, with examples like the "Old Woman" example.[187] She encouraged her followers to send her clippings of any such letters published in local newspapers. She also asked them to send her any replies to their letters that they received from elected politicians. In the future, she hoped to use these letters and replies to remind the politicians of the strength of public opinion in favour of dower and of the promises that they had made in their responses.[188] She preferred letter writing to petitioning campaigns. Both E. Cora Hind and Nellie McClung had told her that petitions were not treated seriously by elected representatives.[189]

Beynon Thomas urged her readers to "work up public feeling" in favour of dower reform. She told them that "public opinion, the greatest force of all ages, must be educated"; that in the end no government would be able to "stand against public opinion."[190] When a form of dower was eventually passed into law in Saskatchewan and Alberta, she commented, "So does education change people when taken in small doses, with plenty of time for it to assimilate."[191] She regularly reminded her letter writers that their efforts were creating a positive momentum for change. She generated interest by speculating on which western province would be first to adopt a dower law.[192] She let her correspondents know that they were not alone. She told them that the Mutual Benefit Association was a club of "as fine women as were ever banded together for any good reason."[193] The M.B.A. was becoming a pressure group through which public opinion favouring dower could make itself felt.

Beynon Thomas actively sought the support of other women's organizations in an effort to create a lobby that would press Conservative premier Rodmond Roblin's government to bring in dower legislation. To that end, three lobbying approaches were made, all unsuccessful. The first came in February 1910. During 1909, Beynon Thomas had worked hard to persuade the Winnipeg Branch of the National Council of Women to endorse the dower cause. [194] At various Council meetings, she read the original "Old Woman" dower letter as well as others that she had published. By mid-February 1910, after reading a paper that Beynon Thomas had written on dower, the Council struck a committee to arrange a meeting with representatives of the government. [195] By the end of that month, a member of the committee had met with the government and the government had promised to bring in a dower law during the legislative session then in progress. That promise was not kept. [196]

In addition to the local Council of Women, the University Women's Club, founded on Beynon Thomas's initiative; the Women's Labour League; the Women's Christian Temperance Union; and the Icelandic Women's Suffrage Association had all endorsed the dower agitation by early 1911. [197] The second lobbying effort came on February 20, 1911, when a deputation of nine women representing these organizations met with the Premier at the Legislature. [198] Roblin claimed that "if there were any attempt to introduce the full dower law here there would be 1,000 indignant men here in less than an hour to protest it." [199] After expressing concern about any law that would "militate against the material prosperity of the country," he stated that "he could not recommend a full dower law in a country where millions of dollars [sic] worth of property changed hands many times each year." [200] The Premier did acknowledge that the province's property laws could provide some better protection for women. To that end, he asked Harvey Simpson, a member of the Conservative caucus, to introduce a bill in the 1911 session. [201] Simpson did propose such a bill based on recently adopted Alberta legislation. However, the Law Amendments Committee, after hearing from a delegation of women in support of the bill, killed it.

The third unsuccessful request for dower came in 1912 when the Women's Canadian Club of Winnipeg petitioned for improved legislation for the better protection of married women. Again, Harvey Simpson introduced a bill, this one somewhat different than the one he had introduced in the previous legislative session. The bill did contain a dower provision requiring that a wife consent to any sale or mortgage of her husband's property. It also contained other provisions, including one that would have provided for a wife and her family should her husband die intestate. The dower clause was ultimately dropped when legislators raised the familiar objection that a dower right would impede the transfer of land and conflict with the Torrens Land Titles system that recognized only registered interests in land.[202] Most of the other substantive provisions were also excised from the bill until all that was left after passage was a clause having more to do with protecting estate administrators than with protecting farm widows whose husbands had left no will. In her newspaper column, Beynon Thomas described the passage as follows: "A simple bill entitled *The Widows' and Children's Relief Act* has had a rough time in the Manitoba Legislature. It lost its head at one full sweep [the dower clause]; its arms went next, then its body was gradually hacked away until when in emerged it could not be recognized as it hobbled out on one crippled foot [the wife's 'possession on intestacy' clause]."[203] By the spring of 1912, Lillian Laurie's dower campaign had come to naught.

A Lifelong Companion

The failure of the three-time effort to lobby the Manitoba government for dower reform finally convinced Beynon Thomas that the time had come for a different kind of campaign. By early 1913, she was ready to accept that only a fundamental change in the rules redefining who could vote in provincial elections would produce desired law reforms for women. Before that suffrage campaign started, however, she married Alfred Vernon Thomas on September 27, 1911, in Winnipeg.[204] He was gifted intellectually, had eclectic interests, and was by nature adventurous and reformist in his orientation. Throughout his career, he wrote for newspapers, including contributing articles for the *Manchester Guardian*, a paper which he regarded as "the best newspaper in the world."[205] In short, he was a perfect match for Lillian.

Vernon was born in Manchester, England on November 2, 1875.[206] Upon enrolling as a student at the University of London, he decided on a career in business. A job as a representative of a lace firm took him to St. Gail, Switzerland and Heidelberg, Germany. After several years, his

Alfred Vernon Thomas
SOURCE: ARCHIVES OF MANITOBA

wanderlust got the better of him and he departed on a round-the-world trip, moving from west to east with the ultimate goal of arriving in New Zealand and Australia. He worked in Montreal for a time, continuing to submit articles to the *Guardian*, and then left for Winnipeg where he joined the *Manitoba Free Press* as a staff reporter.

From May to September 1910, Vernon took a leave from the newspaper to become clerk to the four-member Indian Treaty Commission headed by John Semmens, who was employed by the Department of Indian Affairs. Thirty-five years earlier, the Government of Canada had signed Treaty Number 5 with the Indigenous bands around Lake Winnipeg. With the extension Manitoba's northern boundaries anticipated, Semmens signed up seven more bands further into the interior in 1908 and 1909. The job of the Commission was to sign up the final three northern bands, located at Deer's Lake, York Factory, and Churchill, and to distribute treaty benefits to the earlier signatories. The Commission covered 3,000 miles by canoe, steamer, and York boat, a type of Hudson Bay Company sailing boat. Its route followed the Berens, Nelson, Burntwood, and Hayes Rivers flowing north to Hudson Bay. Thomas described the Indigenous peoples and the northern land in a series of newspaper articles. His album of 174 black and white photographs of the trip is held by the Archives of Manitoba.

It was a year to the month after his return from his northern Manitoba trip with the Indian Treaty Commission that Vernon married his fellow *Free Press* journalist.[207] The marriage certificate listed the bride as "Lily Kate Beynon," in contrast to her birth certificate where Lily was spelled "Lilly," and in contrast to the name "Lillian," which she signed in her daily life and which formed the first part of her pen name, "Lillian Laurie."[208] The witnesses to her marriage were her older brother Manning and Mary Dafoe, John Dafoe's daughter. When Beynon Thomas first arrived in Winnipeg, she babysat Mary and her younger sister Elizabeth and became friends with them.[209] Rev. Chancellor Teeter, Methodist pastor of the Beynon family at Hartney, married the couple. Two decades later, Teeter wrote to Beynon Thomas to congratulate her on the upcoming opening of her play, *Among the Maples*. He expressed the hope that her deceased Methodist ancestors would have shed their prejudices against the "dramatic arts" since their arrival in the "heavenly world."[210]

Although her Home Loving Hearts column appeared on her wedding day,[211] she did not mention her marriage. When her readers eventually learned of the wedding, they found it strange that Beynon Thomas had not commented on it and indicated that they would like to join together to give her a gift. Several months later, Beynon Thomas responded by writing in her column that she, "fully intended to make a full confession of my failings in deserting the ranks of spinsters... But I found that so many others had mentioned the fact that I did not think it necessary." She declined the offer of a gift, explaining that the editorial department, of which Home Loving Hearts was a part, did not handle money and so could not be expected to undertake the book-keeping necessary for such a gift. She asked only that her "good friends" wish her well, "the greatest gift you can give me."[212]

Beynon Thomas left behind sufficient material to cover the column during her one-month honeymoon in England. On October 25, 1911, in her first Home Loving Hearts column after her return, she wrote that it would be some time before she would be taking another long trip. Anxious to get back on the job, she asked her readers to send in suggestions for an "old-timers" page, for a Christmas page, and for "our winter work." The old-timers to which she referred were women in the West "who have done pioneer work, who have struggled from a small beginning to success."[213] The "pioneer number," as the "old-timers" page came to be called, appeared on December 1, 1911.[214] Beynon Thomas also wrote a special article on Westminster Abbey that was published in the *Free Press* on January 21, 1912.[215]

From the time of his arrival as a reporter at the *Free Press*, Vernon proved to be a "companionable associate" for the woman who would become his wife.[216] In November 1908 when she formed the Quill Club—a club for the purpose of "talking shop"[217]—he was present as a founding member. At the March 1909 meeting of the Club, he was charged with the gathering's entertainment. He put on a skit imagining the heights to which club members would reach by 1939. In the skit, he created a mock parliament and cast his wife as the leader of the women's suffrage list. Although he might already have been playing to his future bride when he did this, he could not have imagined how prescient he was in the use of the mock parliament skit as a device in the suffragette cause.[218] In 1911–1912, Vernon was at the founding meetings of the Political Equality League, which were organized by his wife and at which she was elected president.[219] Throughout his wife's career, he encouraged her, "even when editors were cool and uninterested."[220] Beynon Thomas described her new husband to her readers shortly after her marriage: "He is a journalist, so we have many interests in common in that way. He is almost as deeply interested in this page [the Home Loving Hearts page] as I am, and would not like me to give it up, so that as before I will be Lillian Laurie to all who are interested in our work, with the difference that I may understand a bit better the life of the married woman…"[221] She wrote this at a time when women who married were often expected to give up outside employment to keep house and raise a family.

The affection that husband and wife shared continued through their nearly forty years of marriage. When Beynon Thomas's first and only full-length novel was published in 1946, a novel about the impact of the atomic bomb, she dedicated it: "TO MY HUSBAND—Whose interest in world affairs has been a constant inspiration to me."[222] The Winnipeg Branch of the Canadian Authors Association marked the occasion by holding a tribute dinner for Beynon Thomas. At the end of the evening, her husband gave a few humorous closing remarks in which he reminded his audience that he was not just the husband of the honoured author but said, as a journalist himself, "I've earned my own living and paid my own way." He told how he, "came here 40 years ago, a green Englishman, and got a job on the paper where Lily Beynon worked." She befriended him and he "was greatly taken." These remarks won him hearty applause.[223]

Unusual for the time, the couple did not have children, and the reason for this is unknown. Beynon Thomas was 37 years old when she married. Having a first child in 1912, at her age, would not have been without risk. She had made a career as a journalist, one which her husband strongly supported and encouraged. She was fully engaged as a social activist committed to dower reform and woman suffrage. It was possible that she was discouraged when she remembered her mother's trials and tribulations raising a family of seven children with limited means on the remote Prairie. Decades later, in a June 17, 1939, reply to a letter from an Ontario cousin requesting family information, Beynon Thomas showed some ambivalence when she wrote, "We have no children and I see now we've missed a lot. On the other hand, there are compensations."[224] E. Austin Weir was a journalist who Beynon Thomas had known during his time in Winnipeg from 1913 to 1924 and later as a pioneer radio broadcaster who aired at least one of Beynon Thomas's plays.[225] In a May 19, 1960 letter to him, Beynon Thomas wrote, "I haven't a family but get lots of fun out of the successes of my friends [sic] children."[226]

It is clear that Beynon Thomas enjoyed young people. She often spoke to student drama and writing classes and saw great promise in young people.[227] In 1932 she told an interviewer, "I like young people and think this generation is brave, and frank and grand."[228] In 1933, she told the Confederation of Women's Institutes of Canada 8th Bi-annual Convention, held in Winnipeg, that "It is the duty of the youth of Canada to pioneer in the arts..."[229] In her 1946 speech to the twenty-fifth anniversary dinner of the Canadian Authors Association, Winnipeg Branch, she told her audience that "the age belonged to the young and earnest writer; that the groundwork had been laid and much is expected of the new writers."[230] It is not surprising, therefore, that a journalist interviewing Beynon Thomas three years later concluded, "She has an abundant faith in young people and in the future of Canada."[231]

Upon her return to Winnipeg from her honeymoon, Beynon Thomas passed the editorship of the daily women's page in the *Free Press* to Kennethe Haig (Alison Craig). She continued to publish stories in the daily paper, however, while concentrating her main efforts on her page in the *Prairie Farmer* and on writing short stories for magazines.[232]

CHAPTER 3

Clubwoman

Networking

In the 1900s, Winnipeg boasted a host of clubs, with interlocking memberships, in which like-minded women could meet to discuss ideas and pursue issues.[233] When Beynon Thomas moved to the city, she founded clubs, served on their executives, gave them advice on their organization, spoke at their gatherings, reported on their activities, and advocated for the establishment of permanent meeting rooms.[234] At one level, these were social clubs where middle-class women sipped afternoon tea.[235] Beynon Thomas often found herself "presiding over the tea cups"[236] when clubs were entertaining visiting writers. Sometimes she organized club programs that featured local authors as speakers.[237] Frequently, she was invited as an honorary guest at club head-table dinners. However, it is doubtful that Beynon Thomas would have paid the clubs much attention except that they also provided an opportunity to engage women who wanted reforms but who found themselves excluded from the halls of political power. At club meetings, and through club activities, she was able to advance issues related to feminism, temperance, economic security, home life, suffrage, and, later on, issues related to Canadian cultural identity.

Historian Veronica Strong-Boag has underlined the connection between these clubs and the broadening consciousness of women at the beginning of the twentieth century. She observed, "The tremendous growth of the women's club movement before 1914, mixing socializing and social service about equally, was the product of their first tentative explorations outside the home."[238] Earlier, Beynon Thomas had made similar observations in the *Free Press*: "... How short a time it is since a club woman was regarded as traitor to the duties of the home! Now the women in small towns and country places are enjoying clubs, and in the western provinces, the governments are aiding the farmers' wives in this matter. It is surely a change and a good one."[239] And, in a different article: "Regardless of the sarcastic jeers that are constantly being hurled at her work, the clubwoman of today is proving herself a power in national life. She has started a vigorous campaign to ensure the sale of pure food, to prevent the licensing of hotels, where thousands of poor girls are lured to destruction, to help girls to get a college education, to provide comfortable homes for girls earning less than six dollars a week, and for many other worthy objects."[240]

Historian Marjory Lang has commented on how the symbiotic relationship that developed between presswomen, like Beynon Thomas, and clubwomen contributed to the "widening sphere" that beckoned women:

> In the era before women won the vote, their parliaments were the clubs they formed for intellectual, philanthropic, or social reform. ... In the safety of an all-female forum, women could practice the mechanics of politics—how to conduct meetings, how to command attention from large gatherings... The journalists who followed club activities for the newspaper-reading public were, in a sense, the women's press gallery.[241] ... From the outset, the relationship between clubwomen and presswomen was a mutually self-serving alliance. Newswomen owed their jobs partly to the club phenomenon. When newspaper owners acknowledged that

club news might be a way of drawing female readers, they hired female reporters to cover meetings. ... Presswomen... did more than join existing societies; they used their public role in the press to act as agents of organization and recruitment for women's clubs.[242]

Supporting Social Reformers

Beynon Thomas moved to a city full of self confidence, one that historian Ramsay Cook described as follows:

> During the first two decades of the twentieth century no Canadian city could challenge Winnipeg as a place where exciting, even momentous, developments were taking place. The city's population more than quadrupled in those years as newcomers arrived from most parts of Canada, and almost from the four corners of the earth, to participate in the great boom that was to make Winnipeg at least 'the Chicago of Canada'.[243]

Cook cited the Special Supplement to the 1912 *Canadian Annual Review of Public Affairs*, which labelled the city "the gateway of a West which must grow to splendid proportions in production, population, and wealth; it is the capital of a province where public prosperity and individual opportunity are manifest."[244] The *Review*, in turn, may have been relying on a 1910 story in the *New York Herald Tribune*, reprinted in the *Manitoba Free Press*, under a bold headline that referred to the city as the, "Grainspout of the World's Granary—The Magic City of the Great Northwest, which Expects to Wrest Supremacy from Buffalo and Duluth and Even Chicago Itself.[245]

In the first decade of the twentieth century, Winnipeg's manufacturing output grew by 600 percent, making the city the chief industrial and financial hub in the Canadian West.[246] Grain drove the economic miracle. In 1911, Manitoba recorded a record wheat production of 60,275,000 bushels from 2,979,734 acres.[247] That wheat was sold on the Winnipeg

Grain Exchange and shipped to ports from that city. The Canadian Pacific Railway yards in Winnipeg were the largest owned by any single corporation in the world with 135 miles of sidings accommodating 12,000 cars and employing 4,000 men. At the other end of Main Street, the Canadian National Railway was opening new yards.[248] The *New York Herald Tribune* summed up the economic boom in a single sentence:

> Though Winnipeg's past growth and future expansion rest primarily on the fact that it is the focal point of Western Canada, at which centres the three great transcontinental railroad systems of the Dominion, that it is the mouth of the gigantic funnel into which and through which must pass the boundless Canadian harvests on their journey down to the tidewater and the great lakes, there has been material progress made here also in industrial manufactures, a progress which is likely to be appreciably stimulated by the new power plant.[249]

This boom created sharp class, linguistic, and ethnic divisions. The railway tracks in the center of Winnipeg divided the city. The south end, populated for the most part by the British-Canadian elite, comprised the business districts and the stately homes of the new suburbs along the Assiniboine River. The north end was inhabited by three groups: the impoverished, poorly educated immigrants who spoke limited English; the heavily unionized, low-paid wage earners who laboured in unsafe sweatshops; and the destitute humans who lived in cramped housing where poor sanitation spread tuberculosis, typhoid, and smallpox. At the time, these groups were seen as the "Strangers Within Our Gates," so-called by J.S. Woodsworth who borrowed that biblical phrase for the title to his 1909 book on immigration.[250]

A broadly based reform movement grew out of the social ferment created by these conditions.[251] Cook put it this way: "It would be surprising if a city, in the midst of a pulsating economic boom and experiencing social and economic frictions of growing intensity, should not produce an intellectual and political life of at least modest substance."[252] Heady reform movements made up of interconnecting memberships emerged: suffragists; socialists; labourites; social gospellers; prohibitionists; and reform movements advocating fair wages, safe working conditions, direct legislation, recall referenda, and public utility ownership. Leaders like J.S. Woodworth; Salem Bland; A.E. Smith and William Ivens, all Methodist ministers and professors at Wesley College; W.F. Osborne, college registrar and professor; and Charles W. Gordon (who wrote under the name Ralph Connor), Winnipeg Presbyterian minister and author, preached the "social gospel."[253] They believed in building Christ's Kingdom on earth, in the present, through service to the poor, the oppressed, the ill, and the marginalized.[254] Their followers ran charitable and recreation programs aimed at helping newcomers adapt, offered civics classes and intellectual debates aimed at stimulating the creation of a more equitable social order, and advocated for progressive law reform aimed at improving the living and working conditions of the most vulnerable.

Beynon Thomas belonged to or had close contact with organizations that promoted these causes, including such organizations as the Methodists,[255] the Women's Christian Temperance Union, the Direct Legislation League, the Women's Labour League, the Political Equality League, and the University Women's Club. Salem Bland was a lecturer in theology at Wesley College and a well-known social gospel advocate during her university days.[256] She counted as a friend J.S. Woodsworth,[257] perhaps the most prominent social gospel adherent, who, from 1907 to 1913, served as superintendent of the All Peoples' Mission, sometimes referred to as the Stella Mission after its street address. The mission provided charitable services, gymnasium activities, and instruction in areas such as language, cooking, health, hygiene, and childcare to the impoverished Central and Eastern European immigrants who settled in North Winnipeg. On many Sunday evenings, music, educational movies, and social events were offered.

In 1910, the All Peoples' Mission established the Peoples' Forum, often referred to as the Peoples' University. The unabashed goal of the Forum was to assimilate immigrants[258] through instruction that would enable them to become "intelligent Canadian citizens."[259] Beynon Thomas was a director of the Forum.[260] In a 1912 article in the *Christian Guardian* entitled "Building on Canadian Pre-Emptions," Beynon Thomas described how, on wintery Sunday afternoons, speakers at the Forum took up such subjects as 'Government by the People', 'Science and Religion', 'The Church and Socialism', 'Food and Food Inspection', 'Astronomical Discoveries', 'Shakespeare and his View of Life', 'The Dream of Labour', 'The Bible and the Land Question', 'The Battle of the Ages', 'The Religion for the People', 'Canadian Ideals', The Contribution of the Jews to Civilization', and 'God in History.'[261] Lectures held in Winnipeg's Grand Theatre attracted large, diverse crowds numbering over a thousand for popular speakers.[262] By 1914, the Forum had separated from the All Peoples' Mission and had incorporated in its own right. J.S. Woodsworth served as its first president. On one Sunday each year it sponsored a panel devoted to "The Woman Movement." On Sunday, March 1, 1914, Beynon Thomas spoke on "The Case for Woman." She argued that "Men cannot legislate for women. Men run riot in their respect for property and in their disregard for human life. Women would legislate in terms of the home and the child."[263] In 1915, she chaired a Forum panel.[264]

In a lengthy article appearing in the July 1914 edition of *Canada Monthly*, Beynon Thomas praised the work of J.S. Woodsworth.[265] The article was titled, "Practical Idealists: How One Man with a Dream and a Card Indexful of Facts Founded the Canadian Welfare League and What it Might Mean to Canadian Men, Women and Municipalities." It described how the Canadian Welfare League was founded in September 1913 to create a sort of "College of Community Building." Woodsworth, trained as a social service worker, was its first secretary.[266] Beynon Thomas was a member of its council.[267] The League set up its offices in the Winnipeg Industrial Bureau, the same building where the Winnipeg Branch of the Canadian Women's Press Club, of which Beynon Thomas was an active member, had the previous year established its clubroom.[268] In her article, Beynon Thomas described how Woodsworth, no mere theoretician, focused the work of the Canadian Welfare League on the search for concrete, scientific solutions that could be applied to pressing municipal problems. He undertook data collection on such issues as child welfare, care of immigrants, public health, housing, playgrounds, city planning, municipal sanitation and pure water, philanthropic institutions, and industrial organizations. Once collected, this data was available to be shared with other communities so that they could learn urban planning from the experience of successful towns and cities. Beynon Thomas deplored the fact that "municipal activities were placed in the hands of untrained men, elected haphazard," rather than in the hands of social work experts.[269] She decried the lack of a chair of sociology in any Canadian university in contrast to the many that existed in America.

Recruiting Professional Women

In October 1907, one month after the recently organized Canadian Women's Press Club (CWPC) had held its third meeting in Winnipeg, women journalists in that city decided to organize a local branch.[270] Beynon Thomas, still relatively new at the *Free Press*, became one of seven founding members of the Winnipeg branch and the branch secretary for its first year.[271] E. Cora Hind was the first branch president. Harriet Walker, co-proprietor with her husband of the Walker Theatre and a strong supporter of the suffrage campaign, was another member.[272] It was the beginning of Beynon Thomas's lifelong commitment to CWPC. She served on the national executive as auditor in 1908–1909 and as recording secretary from 1910–1913.[273] The Winnipeg Branch minute book noted that she addressed members on December 28, 1910, about her experiences organizing women's institutes in Saskatchewan several months earlier. She stressed the "extreme importance" of the institutes for combating the "maddening monotony of prairie life."[274]

She was elected Winnipeg branch's first vice president in 1915–1916,[275] and president in 1931–1932 and again in 1937–38. During both of her presidential terms, events with special significance for her took place. On April 29, 1932, during her first presidency, the branch honoured her with a reception in the *Free Press* boardroom following the opening night of her three-act play, *Among the Maples*, the first locally written three-act play to be staged in Winnipeg.[276] During her second presidency, Beynon Thomas

Winnipeg Women's Press Club clubroom, circa 1912 SOURCE: ARCHIVES
OF MANITOBA, WINNIPEG WOMEN'S PRESS CLUB COLLECTION

and the Winnipeg branch played host to the national CWPC Triennial
Convention held from June 20–24, 1938. Representatives from across the
country, including Nellie McClung, as well as delegates from England
and the United States, came to Winnipeg.

Beynon Thomas also took an active part in less serious branch birthday and Christmas dinners. In 1912, she gave a witty talk on receiving
rejection slips from editors.[277] At a 1930 New Year's Eve dinner held to
celebrate the anniversary of the club, Beynon Thomas represented "the
modern woman" in a procession that brought in the birthday cake.[278]
For the 1935 annual banquet of the Winnipeg branch, Beynon Thomas
authored a skit entitled "Front Page Stuff." In that production, four
women analyzed the reasons why they wanted to get on the front page
of a newspaper.[279]

Membership in the CWPC mattered to Beynon Thomas. She was a member in good standing until the end, or nearly the end, of her life. She maintained her membership until 1955 when she asked to be put on the associate member list because, as she said, she had "stopped writing for a few years." However, she regretted this change in status. In the early fall of 1959, she advised the CWPC that she had found associate membership "uninteresting as I had been a member in good standing almost fifty years. I guess my pride was hurt."[280] In order to correct the situation, she filled in the "Annual Work Form" required of all members and paid her fee. Where the form asked members to mention their "Outstanding Achievement of the Year," she noted that *Five Cents for Luck* was being aired on the radio and cited several other writing projects. She had received a membership card valid until May 31, 1960. Beynon Thomas's colleagues clearly thought that membership in CWPC was something that defined her and that she would want to be remembered by it.

Beynon Thomas became very active with a number of other writing clubs after she took up a full-time career as an author and short story teacher. In June 1932 she presided over a joint banquet of the Writers' Club and the Short Story Club, the latter made up of graduates of her short story courses. She was made an honorary president of the Winnipeg Branch of the Writers' Club on May 23, 1936, and acted as president of the Winnipeg Branch of the Canadian Authors Association.[281]

Beynon Thomas worked to organize the growing number of female university students. On April 14, 1909, she called together twenty graduates from Wesley College for the purpose of founding the University Women's Club (UWC).[282] A few days later, she was elected to the UWC's executive committee. The UWC strongly supported Beynon Thomas's campaign to have a dower law adopted in Manitoba and subsequently sponsored the 1911 visit to Winnipeg of British suffragette Emmaline Pankhurst as Beynon Thomas was starting her push for votes for women. On February 5, 1934, she served on the arrangements committee when the UWC marked its quarter century.[283] On January 26, 1937, together with the students of her writing classes, she put together a program for the club, "An Evening with some Winnipeg Women Authors."[284] That evening, the UWC president introduced Beynon Thomas by describing what she had done as an author, dramatist, and teacher. Beynon Thomas then introduced nine of her former writing students who told of how hard it was to write, of how Beynon Thomas had helped them choose topics ("what you know best"), of how sentences must be worked over and polished until they flow smoothly, and of how they had won prizes in story competitions.

Beynon Thomas also maintained her university connections through the Wesley Alumnae Association. In September 1916, along with J.S. Woodsworth, she was elected to the Wesley College Board as an alumni association representative.[285] This was the first time that the association was permitted alumni representation. On November 18, 1936, she spoke to the association of the joys and sorrows faced by early settlers in the West and of the courage of pioneering women in particular.[286] There is an alumni association membership card amongst her papers indicating that she was a member in good standing until March 31, 1961, just months before her death.[287]

Mobilizing Rural Women

Throughout this time, Beynon Thomas remained deeply involved in club activity that promoted the interests of rural women. Early in 1910, Hedley Auld, Superintendent of Fairs and Institutes with the Saskatchewan Department of Agriculture, attended the annual Agricultural Societies Convention in Regina. A man at the convention suggested to him that it would be helpful if a women's program could be arranged for the farm wives accompanying their husbands to future conventions.[288] In order to explore this suggestion, Auld met with Beynon Thomas in her Winnipeg office that June.[289] He was aware that she had been writing in her Home Loving Hearts pages about Ontario women's institutes that were organizing clubs to enable women to share homemaking ideas and attend domestic science courses. Auld discussed with Beynon Thomas how these institutes might provide a model for organizing similar clubs for rural Saskatchewan women.[290]

On June 28, 1910, Auld followed up this discussion by inviting Beynon Thomas to speak at the meetings held in conjunction with the annual farmers' excursion to the Dominion Experimental Farm at Indian Head, Saskatchewan. These meetings were to take place from July 26–28, 1910. He suggested that with her "intimate knowledge of Western conditions," Beynon Thomas would be an ideal person to discuss some of the problems faced by farm wives. He proposed the topic "Womens' [*sic*] opportunity in the rural home." In an oblique reference to the isolation faced by Prairie women, he indicated that farm women's chances for enjoyment were "found largely within the four walls of home." He was careful to suggest that should questions of homesteads and votes for women arise at the meetings, Beynon Thomas's, "usual tact would enable [her] to defer discussion of them until a more convenient season."[291] Beynon Thomas wrote promptly accepting the invitation but cautioning that she was, "not by any means a public speaker."[292] She mentioned her amusement that discussion of suffrage and homesteads was "so absolutely shut out" and indicated that, "while tempted to touch those topics I will refrain and deal with something quite harmless and non-political." She did, however, indicate that she wanted to make her address more comprehensive than life inside the four walls of the home and noted that women might be interested in women's institutes and the possibilities of outside work for women in rural districts. Auld responded that these were good ideas and further suggested that he hoped that by the time of the Indian Head visit he would be able to tell her "something of our plans for women's clubs or institutes."[293]

In September 1910, after the Indian Head meetings, agricultural extension work was transferred from the provincial Department of Agriculture to the University of Saskatchewan. Auld was named the University's first director of extension. The University was dedicated to community service, emphasizing in particular the provision of educational programs to rural areas. The University was also expressly committed to non-partisanship with respect to political issues and party affiliations. In his new job, Auld continued to help farm women develop homemaking skills that would make rural family life easier. He asked Beynon Thomas to speak at agricultural society seed fairs and, in her speeches, encourage rural women to organize clubs.[294] Starting in mid-November 1910, in her capacity as the first provincial organizer of what was to become the homemakers' clubs, she attended twelve seed fairs in the eastern and southern parts of Saskatchewan[295] and organized seven new clubs following Ontario's women's institute model.[296] She was paid $6 per day, the going rate for university extension personnel.[297] The first club was formed in the Saskatchewan municipality of Broadview on November 23, 1910.[298] Other clubs were started in Whitewood, Moosomin, Wolseley, Windthorst, Sintaluta, and South Qu'Appelle.[299]

Auld sponsored Beynon Thomas's tour as a prelude to setting up a province-wide organization of rural women's clubs. He invited forty-two women from eighteen communities to attend a special program for women to be held under the auspices of the Saskatchewan College of Agriculture in conjunction with the Agricultural Societies Convention planned for January 31–February 3, 1911 in Regina.[300] Auld was honouring the request made by male delegates at the previous year's convention that a women's program be prepared for the next convention so that wives could come along.[301] Despite biting cold, wind, and snow, delegates from eight of the clubs organized the previous fall accepted Auld's invitation.[302]

Beynon Thomas presided over the opening session. The *Regina Leader* described her as "a fluent speaker and one who is eminently fitted to gracefully fill such a position."[303] Her address was titled, "Women's Clubs, Their Nature and Purpose." She delivered it, "in a simple, straightforward, logical manner." In it she discussed, "the study of scientific home-making; of sanitation, ventilation, the composition of foods, hygiene, the care of children, the improvement of environment, etc., and to promote social intercourse."[304] She went on to say that housekeeping was as much a profession as farming and, like farming, it was a profession that required training. She maintained that "Women are not natural born housekeepers. They must make a study of it. If we require to learn how to feed stock it is much more important that women should learn how to feed children."[305] Specialization was needed because the farmer did not have time to learn how to be a housekeeper and his wife did not have time to master farming.

Initially, there had been some objection to separating men and women as many of the agricultural societies had women among their most active members. Beynon Thomas addressed this issue. Separate women's clubs were needed because the role of the farm wife was different than that of her husband and, like her husband's role, hers required specialized training.[306] Sessions later in the convention included a talk by E. Cora Hind on "The Model Kitchen"[307] and a presentation by Nellie McClung on, "The Importance of Social Life in Country Homes."[308] Though McClung and Beynon Thomas moved in similar circles, they would not work together until McClung moved from Manitou to Winnipeg in 1912. Beynon Thomas took the podium once again at the last session. In a speech entitled, "What Women's Clubs Can Do For Our Public Schools," she pointed out that clubs could provide practical benefits by seeing to it that the school was cleaned regularly, that reproductions of the old masters hung on the walls, that sewing and cooking be taught, that exercise drills be given, and that women be elected to local school boards."[309] The local press noted that, "Miss Beynon has had experience as a teacher, understands conditions in rural districts and keeps closely in touch with educational interests." On this basis, the press concluded that her opinion carried much weight.[310]

At one session, a delegate submitted a resolution asking that homemakers' clubs adopt the slogan, "Votes for Women." Beynon Thomas ruled the resolution out of order. When questioned by the press, she stated, "You can say emphatically that the convention has not touched these subjects [dower and suffrage] in any way, nor do we intend to now or at any future time."[311] Beynon Thomas was well aware that the clubs were being organized through the Extension Division of the Department of Agriculture of the University of Saskatchewan. The Department's dean opposed discussion of suffrage for fear that it would involve the University in party politics in violation of the University's stated desire to remain non-partisan in political matters. Still, a headline next day in a Regina paper read, "Woman refuses to let Homemakers [sic] pass resolution in favour of suffrage."[312] This caused Beynon Thomas some discomfort as she was already organizing for votes for women in Manitoba. However, upon her return to Winnipeg, she was able to explain the situation to her supporters.[313] Florence Lediard (aka Dame Durden), the Women's Page editor of the *Farmers' Advocate*, rose to Beynon Thomas's defence in her February column: "Two papers with a tendency towards yellow journalism... put sensational and untrue headings on their reports and were not careful as to facts. In case you have seen these, I will merely say that in no session was women's suffrage even mentioned, and the dower question was NOT shelved by Miss Beynon, who has done more to interest people in the question than any other dozen women in the prairie provinces. Enough said."[314]

At the close of the convention, the press noted that the programs were carried out in a business-like way and mentioned the parliamentary methods that Beynon Thomas had employed.[315] It reported her closing words to the gathering: "If you go home to organize Homemakers' Clubs in the spirit of this convention, they cannot fail to be a great success."[316] Forty-two years later, Beynon Thomas reminisced warmly about that first convention of the Association of Homemakers' Clubs of Saskatchewan: "To outsiders we, no doubt, looked to be just an ordinary group of women. But we knew that we were not just 'ordinary'. As we listened to the lectures, heard the discussions and learned of what must be done, we knew that we were helping to build a nation. Money was scarce—terribly scarce in those days—but every woman there was wealthy. Her wealth consisted of dreams. And what is money compared with even the pale shadow of a dream?"[317] As the meetings adjourned, Florence Lediard reported: "I was proud of the women who spoke... There was no affectation or putting on airs of wisdom or superiority—just a woman talking to women about things that women have close to their hearts."[318] The name "homemakers' club" was adopted as best reflecting the club ideal of promoting the interests of home and community.[319] The clubs went on to provide adult education, homemaking courses, social outlets, community rest rooms, travelling libraries, and rural nursing for women and children.

Auld's next step was to send Beynon Thomas, along with several professors, to the early summer fairs in 1911 to talk about the short agricultural courses that the University of Saskatchewan offered, to distribute bulletins on farming, and to promote the homemakers' club movement. University tents were set up at five fairs, including North Battleford, Saskatoon, Prince Albert, Moose Jaw, and Regina. The fairs ran between June 26 and July 7, 1911.[320] The tents, tables, folding chairs and supplies cost the University approximately $325, a sum equivalent to approximately $10,600 today.[321] The tents provided spaces where women could wait with their children while their husbands ran errands, served as rest rooms for women, and provided an area for Homemaker Club meetings and a place for giving talks. In her "Report of the Work in the University Tent" that Beynon Thomas submitted to Auld at the end of her tour, she commented on how "well patronized" the tents at the fairs were, their only rival being the poultry exhibits. She noted that many rural visitors had never even heard of the University of Saskatchewan. She recommended that more literature, more short courses for farmers' wives, and more travelling libraries be made available. She concluded that the University tent was "decidedly worthwhile" and that as a result of its educational efforts women would "for the first time realize that house-keeping and homemaking is [sic] not mere drudgery but a science ..."[322] Three years later, Beynon Thomas wrote an article for *Canada Monthly* magazine about her observations of people attending country fairs. She titled the article, "To the Visitor, the Exhibits Make the Show... But to the Exhibitor, the People Present an Ever Entertaining Spectacle" and concluded that, "It takes all kinds of people to make a world, and you find them all at a fair."[323]

Immediately following the fairs, Beynon Thomas and several other speakers were sent out at the University's expense to visit homemakers' clubs already in existence and to organize new clubs.[324] She reported that it was with feelings of doubt that she started her rounds because of the lack of familiarity of the clubs with the work that they were undertaking and the lack of literature available to them. She changed her mind, however, when she found that all but two of the existing nine clubs in the towns that she visited were increasing their memberships, setting up rest and reading rooms, encouraging sewing classes in schools, and enjoying the chance for town and country women to socialize. Beynon Thomas organized ten new clubs on this trip. In a letter to Auld, she suggested that the University publish bulletins to help the clubs. She further recommended that a permanent organizer position be created, to be filled by a Saskatchewan woman. She had in mind Abigail DeLury, a domestic science teacher from Moose Jaw, and the assistant that the University had provided to Beynon Thomas to help her with the tour. Beynon Thomas praised DeLury's efforts. The recommendation bore fruit in 1913 when DeLury was appointed director of women's work for the University extension department, reporting directly to the president of the University, a position that she held until 1930.[325]

Beynon Thomas attended the next provincial homemakers' club convention held at the invitation of President Murray of the University of Saskatchewan in Saskatoon from February 6–9, 1912.[326] Eight clubs had existed when the 1911 Regina organizational meeting was held; by the time of the 1912 convention, there were twenty-eight. Beynon Thomas presided at most of the sessions. That summer she did another provincial tour, this time visiting clubs at Briarcliffe, Pense, Cottonwood, Grand Coulee, Bladworth, Kenaston, Genrose, and Nolin.[327] The movement continued to grow. At the annual provincial convention held from May 26 to 29, 1914, at the University of Saskatchewan, over one hundred homemakers' delegates, representing over eighty clubs and several thousand women, gathered. Some had driven fifty miles in a lumber wagon to get to the train station that would take them to Saskatoon.[328] Beynon Thomas "spoke to the convention feelingly from the depths of a long country experience on the problem of, 'Learning to live together in neighbourhoods, clubs and homes'."[329] In her Home Loving Hearts column, she pointed out that the convention was managed by women: "something quite new… from the first to the last it was a woman's convention, one of the first of the kind I ever attended."[330] She also pointed out that practical solutions were discussed for providing nurses for country districts. In the same Home Loving Hearts column, she described a discussion at the convention on why women's suffrage was not being taken up by the homemakers' clubs: "It was pointed out that the people give the university a charter on condition that it keeps away from party politics and taking sides in religious controversies. The Homemakers' clubs are a branch of the university, woman's suffrage is a question in party politics, so if they take it up to push it they must go into politics and thus go against the charter that they decided on for the university."[331]

At the 1915 convention, the topic of Beynon Thomas's address was "Living 24 Hours a Day." The *Grain Growers' Guide* covered the event:

> She spoke of several classes of country people whose way of using this twenty-four hours was to be deplored. First there was the farmer and his wife (for she did not hold the wife blameless) who owned a beautiful big sanitary barn and a mean insanitary house, showing thereby that they valued the health of their stock above that of their children. Equally reprehensible were the folk who had both a poor house and barn, but who were the possessors of three quarters of a section of land and were saving up to buy more. And then there were the farmer folk who worked themselves and their children day in and day out without intermission or relaxation. [332]

Years later, Violet McNaughton, organizer of the Women's Section of the Saskatchewan Grain Growers' Association and editor of the Women's Page of *The Western Producer*, credited Beynon Thomas as the lead player in founding the homemakers' clubs: "It was mainly Lillian Laurie's persistent efforts that brought the Homemakers' Clubs into existence in 1911."[333] Two decades later, in 1933, Beynon Thomas was invited to address the Federated Women's Institute convention being held that year in Winnipeg. Her talk was mainly about the development of the arts in Canada but, after congratulating the members of the Women's Institute, she said that it was "coming home to her to attend, for she founded the 'homemakers' clubs' of Saskatchewan."[334]

During the years in which Beynon Thomas led the formation of the Homemakers' Clubs of Saskatchewan,[335] she was also active as one of the founders of the Manitoba home economics societies.[336] The impetus for forming these rural support organizations came in August 1910 when

a local group approached Premier Roblin who agreed to have two organizers go on a twenty-three-community lecture tour to encourage the
formation of societies. Just as the Saskatchewan homemakers' clubs were
parented under the auspices of the Saskatchewan College of Agriculture,
the Manitoba home economic societies were created under the direction of the Manitoba Agricultural College. Miss Juniper, dean of the
Household Science Department of the Manitoba Agricultural College,
was one of the society organizers who went on the tour. As was the case
with the homemakers' clubs in Saskatchewan, the home economics societies in Manitoba held annual provincial conventions. These conventions
took place in February each year in conjunction with conventions of the
Manitoba agricultural societies. Seventeen local organizations attended
the second Home Economics Society convention held February 14-16,
1911.[337] Beynon Thomas presided over the last day of the convention.[338]
In the summer of 1912, she wrote in the *Free Press* of her visit to one of
the largest Home Economics Society conventions. In her column, entitled "Women's Clubs in the West,"[339] she told how clubs were creating
a "sisterhood of woman" much as there already existed a "brotherhood
of man." In January 1913 she wrote another *Free Press* column, this one
praising the twenty Manitoba home economics societies for their work
encouraging the systematic study of the science of homemaking and
providing education for the betterment of conditions in rural areas.[340]

Like the homemakers' clubs, the home economics societies were restrict-
ed from discussing 'women's questions.' The societies' were affiliated with
the University of Manitoba which insisted that they remain politically
neutral.[341] E. Cora Hind reported in *The Western Home Monthly* that
when Nellie McClung was asked to speak at the women's meetings of
the February 1912 Manitoba convention she was told not to mention the
franchise, dower, homesteads, and other "kindred matters."[342] Also like
the homemakers' clubs, the home economic societies limited themselves,
with some exceptions, to domestic topics such as rest rooms, libraries,
childrearing, cooking and scientific homemaking, and efforts to reduce
the isolation felt by rural women.[343] In the fall of 1915, Beynon Thomas
was appointed to the Advisory Board of the Manitoba Agricultural

College, a position which she held until May 1917 when she moved to New York.[344] E. Cora Hind observed that Beynon Thomas was the first woman in Canada, and to her knowledge in North America, to receive such an appointment. She commented that Beynon Thomas had the extension work of the Manitoba Agricultural College "very much at heart," likely a reference to her work supporting Manitoba home economics societies. She also noted that Beynon Thomas's commitment to equality of educational opportunity for men and women would enable her to represent well the needs of women students on the Advisory Board.[345] Hind was probably hopeful that Beynon Thomas's presence would mean that Manitoba home economics societies would feel that they had a little more freedom to address political topics of interest to women.[346]

Shortly after the establishment of the Saskatchewan homemakers' clubs and the Manitoba home economics societies, Beynon Thomas played a leading role in the creation of two other farm women's organizations. In 1903, Manitoba farmers formed the Manitoba Grain Growers' Association (MGGA) and on January 27, 1906, four months after Saskatchewan entered confederation, farmers in that province established the Saskatchewan Grain Growers' Association (SGGA). Both associations were dedicated to fighting against the grain dealers, elevator companies, and railways that they felt were colluding to force farmers to accept low prices for their grain. Both lobbied governments for legislation that would ensure fair treatment of farmers and their families.

By early 1913 strong pressure developed to allow for the formation of separate women's sections in both associations. Two factors came together to provide the impetus for this. First, the grain growers' associations needed the support of farm wives in their battle against the powerfully entrenched interests that they felt opposed them. The men in the associations realized that it was difficult to argue for equality of the farm producer in the economic sphere while opposing equality for women in the political sphere. As a result, both associations endorsed women's suffrage early on. The SGGA endorsed woman's suffrage in 1912[347] and 1913.[348] The MGGA did so at their January 1912 convention.[349] A convention resolution in favour of votes for women was initially greeted with laughter. However, following speeches from J.W. Scallion, one of the originating members of the MGGA, and other influential leaders in the farm movement, the mood of the convention "changed to one of earnestness, and the motion was carried by a rising vote, the delegates cheering and clapping hands."[350] That support was renewed at their conventions in 1913[351] and 1914.[352] The endorsement at the 1913 convention was particularly significant because it not only reaffirmed "the attitude on woman suffrage that was taken by our last annual convention," but also added a direction to their central executive, "to cooperate with the Political Equality League to further the interests of woman's suffrage."[353] The 1913 endorsements by the two grain growers' associations came after Beynon Thomas addressed each of the association conventions in her capacity as first president of the Political Equality League, which she had been instrumental in forming in March 1912.

Second, since the homemakers' clubs and the home economics societies faced restrictions imposed by their university's financial sponsors on discussing political issues affecting rural women, another outlet had to be found where women could raise issues such as suffrage, dower, and homesteading. The possibility of forming women's sections of the grain growers' associations offered an avenue that women could use to make their views felt on politically charged matters. Many of the same farm women who were organizing to create a women's section within the SGGA were also active in organizing suffrage leagues to promote women's suffrage within their local communities. In response to a motion that passed in the fall 1912 session of the Legislature, Saskatchewan Premier Walter Scott indicated that his government would legislate suffrage provided that the province's women demonstrated that they wanted the vote. In early January 1913, Beynon Thomas in the *Free Press*, and in early February, Francis Beynon in the *GGG*, urged Saskatchewan women to write personal letters to the Premier and sign petitions in support of suffrage. In response, 170 personal letters were sent in, along with 100 petitions containing 2,500 signatures.[354]

In December 1912, Violet McNaughton, a Saskatchewan farm wife who would go on to become the first president of the Saskatchewan

Women Grain Growers' Association, wrote to F.W. Green, then secretary of the SGGA. She inquired if she was eligible to become a delegate from the local Hillview Grain Growers' Association to the upcoming SGGA convention to be held in Saskatoon from February 12-14, 1913.[355] Nothing in the SGGA constitution barred women from becoming delegates. This prompted Green to consider holding a "Woman's Congress" at the same time as the planned SGGA convention.[356]

In January 1913, Francis Marion Beynon, who in June 1912 had become editor of the Women's Page of the *GGG*, and who was in close contact with Violet McNaughton, had a long conversation with F.W. Green. Green indicated that the SGGA would like to have a meeting of farm women in conjunction with the upcoming convention.[357] He justified his decision to add separate women's meetings to his male membership by explaining, "You can't have a home without a woman," and "Home problems are farm problems."[358] Green asked Francis Beynon and Violet McNaughton to arrange the meeting. Understandably, Francis Beynon sought her sister's organizational assistance. Beynon Thomas had established the homemakers' clubs in 1910–1911 and had been writing columns in the *Prairie Farmer* on how rural women could organize clubs.[359] Francis Beynon then issued an invitation to Saskatchewan farm women in "The Country Homemakers," her column in the *GGG*, to attend the "convention of farm women" in Saskatoon, explaining that both Beynon Thomas and Nellie McClung were being asked to speak.[360] E. Cora Hind was also recruited for the event. In the end, approximately fifty women registered for the February 1913 meetings although up to one hundred attended.[361]

Beynon Thomas played an important behind-the-scenes role at the 1913 SGGA convention. She and Violet McNaughton held a "clandestine get together" to develop a scheme that would see the formation of a women's branch of the SGGA with a primary objective of promoting women's suffrage. The "clandestine get together" was described in a letter dated July 19, 1950 from McNaughton to "My dear Lillian Laurie": "You will remember our little secret meeting in your bedroom at the 1913 gathering of women who attend [*sic*] the Grain Growers Convention and how we felt that we must form our own organization in order... to be able to work for the Franchise."[362] The two women knew that the Saskatchewan homemakers' clubs, earlier organized by Beynon Thomas, could not become involved in political matters.[363] That bedroom meeting gave important momentum to the Saskatchewan suffrage campaign, led by McNaughton, coached by Beynon Thomas, and backed by the SGGA. The letter in which McNaughton described these events was written on the occasion of the 1950 publication of Catherine Cleverdon's seminal book, *The Woman Suffrage Movement in Canada*.[364] In the letter, McNaughton criticized Cleverdon's observation that the homemakers' clubs were "hives of suffrage activity." McNaughton's recollection, correct as it turned out, was that precisely the opposite was the case. It was the restrictions on the ability of homemakers' clubs to take up the suffrage cause that led to the formation of the Women's Section of the SGGA, a women's organization that would be able to engage in political activity such as advocating for the right to vote.

At the 1913 SGGA convention podium, Beynon Thomas addressed the social condition of farm women.[365] She spoke of the importance of women banding together in clubs. Some clubs had established rest rooms for country women, while others had established amenities such as lending libraries. She encouraged women to buy labour-saving devices, noting that waterworks could be installed in a house for the price of a decent coffin. She concluded with a theme to which she later returned in a May 1915 speech to the Homemakers' Convention.[366] It was important for women to leave time in their busy lives for play: "Each day has only twenty-four hours—they are your treasure... I beg of you not to put off living until tomorrow... Some people were old at twenty and others were young at seventy and it all depended upon their interest in human life."[367] Beynon Thomas may have had in mind how hard her mother had had to work to raise her family only to die young.

The *GGG* declared the 1913 SGGA convention an "unparalleled success." It noted: "The most extraordinary feature of the convention this year was the fact that the women delegates formed themselves into a congress and held their sessions in the University buildings. This action was heartily approved of by the Grain Growers' convention."[368] The women decided to seek full membership in the SGGA with the right to participate equally with the men. They also decided to establish a permanent Women's Grain Growers' Association that would meet yearly at the time of the SGGA meetings, with branches set up at the local level.[369] At their meetings, women would be free to discuss whatever matters of interest that they wanted, including political questions.[370] The women at the 1913 convention acknowledged that they were inexperienced in this kind of club work but they felt that they would be able to organize strongly enough to fight effectively for such causes as adequate medical aid for Prairie women and for suffrage.[371] Beynon Thomas took a leading part in encouraging them.

These changes required amendments to the SGGA constitution, amendments which could not be put in place before the next year's annual convention. As an interim measure until this could be done, and in order to organize the women's meetings for the 1914 SGGA convention, a women's section organizing committee was appointed with Beynon Thomas as its convenor. Saskatchewan farm women were chosen from each of the SGGA's fifteen districts to be on the committee.[372] McNaughton was chosen to represent the Hillview Grain Growers, her home district. The 1914 SGGA convention was slated to be held in Moose Jaw from February 11-13. As that date approached, SGGA Secretary Fred Green asked Francis Beynon for suggestions for the 1914 women's section program. She replied that while she, a presswoman, was prepared to help, Saskatchewan farm women should "take the matter in hand" and run, including chair, the convention.[373] Although Beynon Thomas had, at the 1913 convention, been appointed convenor of the 1914 organizing committee, both she and Nellie McClung declined in favour of having Saskatchewan farm women, led by Violet McNaughton, take charge of the 1914 event themselves.[374] Beynon Thomas and McClung felt that it would be an injustice to the committee of Saskatchewan women appointed at the 1913 convention not to give them a fair chance to organize the 1914 gathering.[375]

Beynon Thomas was to return to this theme of "developing leaders" amongst rural farm women, rather than importing outside leadership, in a March 1917 article in *The Canadian Thresherman and Farmer*. She wrote:

The women of the prairie are no longer looking away east or to the cities for their help, but already they have realized that the only help that can really help, is the help that comes from within. Truth is never like butter that can be put on from outside... The women who live on the prairie are the only women who fully understand the feelings and needs of the women on the prairie, no matter how beautifully other women may theorize about it. The truth about conditions, and the needs of rural life must be expressed by the country women, and they are learning to express all these things.[376]

Beynon Thomas became McNaughton's teacher. Years later, McNaughton told the story of how, in her capacity as a member of the committee to prepare for the organization of the Saskatchewan Women Grain Growers Association, she was required to address "an important gathering." Having never made a speech and "panic-stricken," she said that she was writing "in desperation" for advice to Beynon Thomas. The "important gathering" to which McNaughton referred was in all probability the 1914 SGGA convention that ultimately went on to formalize by constitutional amendment the existence of the Women's Section. Violet McNaughton was made the first president of the new section. The reply to McNaughton's request for advice on public speaking reflected Beynon Thomas's wisdom, experience, and commitment to the cause of women:

Whenever you are asked to speak, think carefully over what you wish to say and if you are afraid to trust your memory, put down a few notes. ... state your case clearly and simply... do not make the mistake of talking on and on... I would also advise you not to memorize your address... if you have difficulty in being heard in a large hall, try to learn to speak from the throat and not from the lips. You could practise on the prairie, speaking to your husband at a distance without perceptibly raising the voice. ... then trust yourself. You have a message, and give it with all the power that God has given you.[377]

This sound advice came from someone who seven years earlier had accepted John Dafoe's invitation to become a journalist because she no longer wanted to be a teacher "where one is constantly trying to be an example,"[378] and from someone who three years earlier had written to Hedley Auld that she was, "not by any means a public speaker."[379] In 1954, on the occasion of the Canadian Women's Press Club's Golden Jubilee, McNaughton expressed her appreciation for the advice that she had received decades earlier. She acknowledged Beynon Thomas's contribution, and that of the other presswomen, referring to them as "our own special friends" and "our godmothers" who professionally and personally inspired the Saskatchewan Women Grain Growers Women's Section of the SGGA throughout their formative years.[380]

Beynon Thomas continued her active support for the women's suffrage movement in Saskatchewan even after the formation of the Women's Section of the SGGA. On February 13, 1915, she was invited to be the lead speaker at a Provincial Equal Franchise Board open meeting in Regina. The *Regina Evening Province and Standard* reported that she "shredded" the argument against votes for women before outlining the efforts of the various Manitoba equality leagues to achieve the franchise. She made her point with a question: "What is the use of saying women's place is in the home in this age when so many women have gone outside the home into the business world and so many women are without homes?"[381] Saskatchewan became the second Canadian province to adopt suffrage legislation when Royal Assent was given to it on May 14, 1916.

Like her journalism, Beynon Thomas's club work was fueled by the aspirations of both rural women and their urban sisters for domestic security and equal economic opportunity. And, like her journalism, her club work would provide her with the army of women whose support and labour she would need in the upcoming suffrage campaign.

CHAPTER 4

A Grassroots Campaign

Committing to Suffrage

Lillian Beynon Thomas's campaign for women's suffrage in Manitoba began in earnest in early 1912 with the organization of the Political Equality League (PEL) and culminated in victory on January 28, 1916, when Royal Assent was given to a Bill that had passed third reading in the Manitoba Legislature the previous day. The Bill made Manitoba the first provincial or federal jurisdiction in Canada to extend the franchise to women on the same terms as those enjoyed by men.

The earliest antecedents of this campaign stretched back into the nineteenth century.[382] All efforts had come to naught.[383] From 1870, women in the Icelandic settler community north of Winnipeg had pressed for the vote. In 1893, the still young Women's Christian Temperance Union (WCTU), at its provincial convention, endorsed suffrage as a means for eventually achieving prohibition. In February of that year, the WCTU staged a mock parliament featuring a premier and five speakers arguing both sides of the suffrage question in earnest. Within days, the WCTU circulated a petition that was signed by an estimated five thousand men and women. In April 1893, the petition was presented to the Legislature, but a resolution based on it was defeated. In 1894, an additional two thousand names were collected, all from women, and the first actual women's suffrage bill was presented to the Legislature, but it was then withdrawn. At that point, E. Cora Hind founded an Equal Suffrage Club, the first English-speaking equal franchise association in Western Canada.[384] Dr. Amelia Yeomans was elected its president. The association petered out, although the Icelandic women presented several additional suffrage petitions to the Legislature in the first decade of the twentieth century.

In early 1910, Beynon Thomas still felt that women could have dower reform and any other law they really wished, "if only they would stand together and make their wants known."[385] At that time, she did not yet feel that the right to vote was a necessary precondition for the attainment of other reforms. Many women felt that suffrage was "mannish,"[386] that their place was, "in the home bringing up children right."[387] Beynon Thomas described this in her column:

> An ardent suffragette asked me a short time ago if I belonged to a suffrage association. I confessed that I did not and also that I had never been asked to join one. She was astonished and asked why women of the west were not more active in this matter? ... I gave it as my opinion that the women of western Canada, as a whole, did not wish the vote. I based my opinion on the fact, that, in a very large correspondence from the country districts I find that but a small proportion of the women are interested in getting the vote for women, and some bitterly oppose it, saying they hope the women of England fail in their agitation.[388]

Beynon Thomas qualified her opinion by stating that it applied only to her perception of the attitude that country women had on suffrage. She indicated that as editor of the women's page of the country version of the *Free Press* she had no means of judging the position of city women, who were reached only by the daily newspaper. She further maintained that more education was needed before there would be sufficient support for women's suffrage.

Nonetheless, Beynon Thomas's journalistic colleagues and friends began to discuss women's suffrage more frequently. On November 14, 1908, she gathered together ten people, mostly journalists, "interested in the formation of a society for the purpose of 'talking shop'."[389] They called themselves the Quill Club. Among those present were E. Cora Hind, George Chipman, Francis Beynon, and Vernon Thomas. At Quill Club meetings, members read and critiqued each other's compositions. They discussed, "how to get into print and be paid for being there." Nellie McClung visited in March 1909 and spoke on, "How to Write a Book." In September 1909, the club held its first meeting of its second season. Some members arrived late; three others did not return after the summer. The minutes recorded that, "the earliest arrivals spent the hour most profitably in a discussion on woman suffrage."[390] That was to be the last meeting of the club. The final minute book entry consisted of a brief, Delphic note: "Died and was buried, Nov. 13/1909. Who killed Cock Robin?"[391] The Quill Club would prove to be the forerunner of the Political Equality League (PEL) that Beynon Thomas organized two and a half years later. Quill Club members E. Cora Hind, Beynon Thomas, Francis Beynon, and George Chipman became charter members of the PEL.

By May 1910, Beynon Thomas had come to accept suffrage as a pre-condition for achieving other reforms. Perhaps it was the failure of the spring 1910 lobby for dower that convinced her. Perhaps the views of her friend and fellow *Free Press* journalist E. Cora Hind had an influence. In March 1910, and then again in October of that year, Hind editorialized in her column in the *Western Home Monthly* that women had "begun at the wrong end."[392] If women were to win the vote, other reforms that they sought would follow, "without the slightest trouble."[393] The columnist 'Philistia' confirmed this: "Miss Beynon [Beynon Thomas] came to the conclusion that the longest way round [working within the existing political system] was not in this instance the shortest way home [obtaining dower reform], so she became an advocate for votes for women as a definite means to a definite end."[394]

In any event, on May 9, 1910, Beynon Thomas told her *Free Press* readership that "the time had come" to organize a suffrage campaign: "The more study and thought I give to the subject of 'laws for women' and the progress women are making all over the world, the more strongly I feel that there is no use in any half way measures, and that instead of asking for a dower law, an alimony law or any other kind of law, women should come out clearly and ask for their full right: 'the franchise.'"[395] In her M.B.A. column, she told how a woman had recently asked what would be changed if women had the right to vote. Beynon Thomas replied, "I am not one of those who believe for a minute that all wrongs will be righted when women have the vote. But there are some better laws regarding women and children that will, I am sure, be passed when women have the right to express their views at the polls." She went on to give examples including a "death blow" to the liquor traffic and a dower law "or some other law just as good."[396]

Years later, in a letter to historian Catherine Cleverdon, Beynon Thomas described what motivated her to start a suffrage campaign:

> Our Political Equality League was organized by me because the laws regarding women were so terrible. No woman had any claim on the property not even her own clothes. I was editor of a woman's page in a weekly paper, the Free Press and Prairie Farmer. I started a correspondence column and the stories coming to me were so heartbreaking that I called a number of women together and after we had tried to interest our government in the matter and failed, we organized the Political Equality League.[397]

In 1959, near the end of her life, Beynon Thomas wrote a brief sketch for the Manitoba Historical Society entitled "Reminiscences of a Manitoba Suffragette." In it she confirmed that the 'Old Woman' letter to the Home Loving Hearts page on the need for a dower law, "was the final straw which made women in Manitoba rise up and organize the Political Equality League, with a determination to change such conditions."[398]

Beynon Thomas added a practical reason favouring enfranchisement. For this she was much indebted to South African intellectual and feminist Olive Schreiner, whose 1911 book, *Woman and Labour*,[399] was being widely read at the time. Schreiner maintained that household mechanization was freeing women from the drudgery of the traditional domestic tasks that bound them to the home and made them economically dependent on men. While this was happening, paid labour opportunities outside of the home were enabling women to become more economically self-sufficient. Beynon Thomas and her sister Francis both highly recommended Schreiner's book to their newspaper readers. Under the heading, "Olive Schreiner's Brilliant Book," Beynon Thomas cited critics who suggested that the book was destined to be ranked as one of the classics of the women's movement.[400] Francis described Olive Schreiner as, "one of the greatest women of this, or any other age," and enthused, "I would rather be the author of Olive Schreiner's book than accomplish any other conceivable feat."[401]

Borrowing Schreiner's argument, Beynon Thomas ascribed the "immediate cause of the present strenuous nature of the women's movement" to the need for women to adapt to their changing circumstances. In a 1914 pamphlet, she put it this way:

> The introduction of machinery has been a big factor forcing women out of their homes. In the older days a woman was her own spinner, weaver, dressmaker, shoemaker and baker. With the introduction of machinery those things could be done better and cheaper in the factory and so they were taken out of the home. ... Women went into business, not to take man's work, but to get back a little that had been taken from them. But when they got there, they found that they must take less wages for the same work as men. They found that the laws that had been made by men for men were all against them and in favor of the man.... The women found, as the men had found years before, that they could not get justice without the franchise. They must have some say in

the government before they could hope to be heard in their own behalf. Thus began the woman's Suffrage Movement… The real cause of the women's suffrage movement is the fact that women have begun to use their brains, and they have come to realize the fundamental truth at the bottom of all progress, that 'we all have an equal right to live and to say how we will live'. The immediate cause is the fact that women have had to leave their homes and go into business.[402]

Historians have suggested that one reason for the 1916 grant of suffrage related to the pioneering spirit shared by both men and women in settling the West. Catherine Cleverdon was an early proponent of this idea. She wrote: "On both sides of the [Canadian] border the feeling generally prevailed that women as well as men had opened up the country, had shared the experiences of settling a new land, and were therefore entitled to a voice in making the laws."[403] Ramsay Cook, in his introduction to the 1974 edition of Cleverdon's book, argued that farm suffragettes in the West had an advantage, "since they had to play the role of equal partner in pioneering conditions [loneliness, isolation, heavy work], their husbands could hardly fall back on the argument of different spheres [i.e., inside the home was the woman's sphere, outside the home, including politics, was the man's]."[404] Other theories exist: in 1918 the Lieutenant Governor of Manitoba stated that women's enfranchisement was adopted in recognition of the great service that women had rendered during wartime.[405] Beynon Thomas never disputed the reward theory of the Prairie suffrage movement—be it rooted in 'pioneering spirit', 'highly valued farm labour', notions of equal partnership, or wartime contribution—but none of this altered her primary focus, beginning with her dower campaign and then extending to other 'kindred' causes, on the need for suffrage in order to achieve social justice reforms that would protect vulnerable women.[406] However, her thinking evolved so that by 1914 she spoke in broader philosophic terms of democracy and the equality of women with men, but she never lost sight of her more immediate practical objectives.[407]

The suffrage campaign was formally launched almost two years after Beynon Thomas concluded that such a campaign was necessary. During those two years, while two other dower lobbies were being rebuffed by the Roblin government, proponents of women's suffrage concentrated on building a base of support amongst reform-minded individuals and groups. Endorsements came from the interlocking women's organizations to which Beynon Thomas belonged. By January 1911, the Winnipeg branch of the National Council of Women, which had long been reluctant to endorse suffrage for fear of offending those with political power;[408] the Local Council of Women, which had originally feared that their husbands' jobs would be threatened if it took a stance;[409] the WCTU; and the Women's Labour League had all declared themselves in favour of suffrage. Although he was referring to the Council of Women, the reason that historian Ramsay Cook gave for its shift in attitude towards suffrage applied equally to other women's groups and their goals. Cook observed: "… the range of the council's interests—hours of work, conditions of labour, the liquor trade, patriotism, the arts, public playgrounds, international arbitration, health laws, the white slave trade, and so on— had gradually helped women to understand that politics was the only effective route to reform, and only voters counted in politics."[410]

Organizing the PEL

By the spring of 1912, Beynon Thomas was ready to initiate and lead a grassroots suffrage campaign. On the occasion of the one-hundredth anniversary of that campaign, Linda McDowell, an expert on women's suffrage in Manitoba, observed, "I've always said that if [Beynon Thomas] had been running things today, she would have been running a strategy group that planned elections, because she was the plotter of the whole thing."[411] What had started slowly steadily picked up momentum until, after a frenetic three years, the goal was reached. By 1916, a province-wide organization had been put in place, two petitions (one massive) had been gathered, the provincial government had been lobbied for three consecutive years, pamphlets had been produced and distributed, doors had been knocked and canvassed, letters had been written to newspaper editors and MLAs, speakers had been trained and sent out across the province to meetings and country fairs, provincial election campaigns had been fought in 1914 and in 1915, a tent had been sponsored during the August 1913 Winnipeg Stampede, a mock parliament that became the turning point in the campaign had been staged in April 1914, and a last-minute intervention had been made in January 1916 to force the government to modify the proposed suffrage bill to permit women not just to vote in, but also to contest, provincial elections. There were all the trappings of a campaign including buttons on women's sashes and banners on city buses,[412] suffrage colours of purple and yellow,[413] and even a campaign motto, "Let Manitoba Be First," coined from a speech that Beynon Thomas had given to the provincial Liberal convention in 1914.[414] Throughout, Beynon Thomas was front and center, more often than not as the initiator of these activities. This was true despite the fact that campaigning did not come naturally to her. She felt very self-conscious in the limelight.[415] However, her passion for the cause motivated her, and her skills as an organizer, journalist, and speaker equipped her to take the leadership role.

As an organizer, Beynon Thomas brought a wealth of experience to the suffrage campaign. Through the Home Loving Hearts page in the *Prairie Farmer*, she had already united a group of far-flung, rural women into a "band,"[416] the term that she used to describe her readers that supported the dower cause. To champion that cause she had coordinated a letter-writing campaign to bring the pressure of public opinion to bear directly on local members of the Legislature. She had organized delegations to meet with MLAs and the Premier on three different occasions. She had spent summers travelling the rail lines to fairs in rural Saskatchewan communities, organizing farm women into homemakers' clubs to combat loneliness and to share self-help ideas. Through her newspaper columns in the fall of 1910, she had authored what amounted to a detailed manual on how to start a homemakers' club, how to put together an agenda for a meeting, and how to run a meeting in a procedurally correct manner.[417] She was to repeat a very similar set of instructions in February 1914, this time in connection with organizing suffrage societies: call a meeting in your home, appoint officers, decide what you are going to do and a plan for doing it, obtain literature, call another meeting to "talk about what has been done... point out the great need for the sake of the children, that women should help form the laws," and visit every woman in the community to get her to join the society. Women were encouraged to raise funds by holding public debates, to write the members of Legislature, to canvass, and above all to "Work! Work! Work!"[418]

As a journalist, Beynon Thomas published, with commentary, 442 letters on dower written to her Home Loving Hearts column from 1908–1910.[419] During her three-year suffrage campaign, from 1912–1915, she published 258 letters about votes for women.[420] Of these, 194 supported the vote.[421] She wrote forty-two editorials on women's suffrage, editorials which one historian has accurately described as didactic, authoritarian, and evangelical in their approach.[422] She used her newspaper columns to discuss why the changing role of women in society required that they be enfranchised; to motivate and educate supporters on how to campaign; and to provide detailed progress reports on suffrage activities.[423]

As a speaker, Beynon Thomas had come a long way from her shy early days when she had advocated for dower reform. She had developed her own distinctive, rational, and intellectual style.[424] In September 1913, after she gave a suffrage speech in the small northwestern Manitoba community of Minitonas, the local paper commented: "Her remarks were enthusiastically received. A notable feature of her address... was the total elimination of all mudslinging, although the subject dealt with was so highly controversial in character."[425] Reporting on a speech that she made on February 15, 1915, to suffrage supporters in Saskatchewan, the Regina *Evening Province & Standard* stated: "Mrs. Thomas is a convincing speaker, quietly empathetic and forceful. She took useful arguments against the votes for women and shredded them before outlining the effort to date of the various political equality leagues of Manitoba."[426] Nellie McClung recalled how, in the fall of 1915, Lillian disarmed a bitter, vituperative, anti-suffragist heckler at a dinner following a suffrage rally put on by the Brandon Board of Trade. The heckler was clearly motivated by unhappiness in his marriage. "Lillian's voice was always soothing," reported McClung, "but now it had a therapeutic quality, as she said, 'This case calls for a psychiatrist, and as this is not even a court of domestic relations, I think we will have to pass on.'"[427]

The first year of the suffrage campaign was devoted to organization. Beynon Thomas took the initiative. Sometime in 1911, and continuing into early 1912, at the suggestion of her husband Vernon, she held small preparatory gatherings of friends at her home to discuss the formation of an organization with the sole purpose of winning the vote for Manitoba women.[428] This was no informal get-together. A "Committee for Framing a Constitution" for a suffrage association was established and a draft was developed.[429] Lillian then called a formal meeting of what was to become the Political Equality League (PEL), which was on March 29, 1912 at the home of Jane Hample, a prominent businesswoman and philanthropist who would soon become the first woman elected to the Winnipeg School Board.[430] At a subsequent meeting, it was decided that the PEL, "was to be a Provincial Organization of which anyone in the Province may be eligible for membership, by paying a fee, and at any point where there are enough active members, they may organize a local branch, which must accept the constitution of the provincial organization."[431] On the motion of her husband, Beynon Thomas was elected the first PEL president.

Prominent members of the PEL included Vernon Thomas; Francis Marion Beynon; E. Cora Hind; George Chipman; Jane Hample; Kennethe Haig (Alison Craig), soon to become women's page editor of the *Free Press*; May Clendenan (Dame Dibbins), journalist; Anne Perry, journalist at the *Winnipeg Saturday Post*; Fred Dixon, reform politician and Independent MLA; Winona Flett, stenographer; and, from 1914 onwards, Dixon's wife, Harriet Walker (Matinee Girl), co-manager and publicity agent for the Walker Theatre and drama critic for *Town Topics*;[432] and Dr. Mary Crawford. When Dr. Crawford started practising medicine there was only one other woman doctor in Winnipeg, early suffrage leader Dr. Amelia Yeomans. Crawford became Chief Medical Inspector of Winnipeg Public Schools. In May 1911, several years after Beynon Thomas started her dower agitation, and a month after the founding of the PEL, Nellie McClung moved from Manitou, a small central Manitoban town located near the US border, to Winnipeg. She was immediately made president of the Winnipeg Branch of the Canadian Women's Press Club.[433] Although McClung was not a charter member of the PEL, she soon became the campaign's most charismatic speaker.[434]

Beynon Thomas's initial duty as president was to organize and chair the PEL's first public meeting. On May 14, 1912, eight hundred people packed the hall.[435] One of the main goals of the meeting was to increase membership. The ranks of the original thirty members swelled when one hundred new supporters signed up. Beynon Thomas opened the meeting with a discussion of the purposes and the organizational structure of the PEL. Nellie McClung and Rev. Dr. Charles William Gordon (Ralph Connor) gave the keynote addresses.[436] On June 27, 1912, a second meeting of the PEL, open to members and friends, was held "to consider methods of organization and propaganda."[437] The meeting was advertised by streamers placed on street cars.[438] Beynon Thomas opened the meeting by reaffirming that the best results could be obtained by educational methods rather than by a more aggressive policy.

Beynon Thomas believed that education was the key to changing people's minds.[439] Consistent with this, the aim of the PEL was defined as, "the education of public opinion along the line of demanding political equality for women."[440] From the outset, the League decided, "not to fight men and women who were opposed to votes for women but to explain to them what it meant to women and children who were in the power of the weak, coarse, unfair, sick or brutal men."[441] It was possible for the PEL to adopt an "education strategy" because of the many gifted journalists and speakers in its ranks.[442] Education meant that violent means were not being contemplated. In a 1944 letter to historian Catherine Cleverdon, Beynon Thomas observed: "No doubt the work done by the American and the English Suffragists helped us. We resented very keenly the fact that some English women came out and tried to stampede us into taking violent methods. We had not yet used peaceful methods and we refused to do anything violent until we had."[443]

The meeting then heard from representatives of four prominent lobby groups which had been invited to come and explain their techniques for persuading government to adopt law reform. The representative of the WCTU was called upon to describe the use of leaflets and pamphlets. George F. Chipman spoke on the value of forming strong local clubs in rural areas. A member of the Direct Legislation League dealt with lobbying government and a Royal Templar supporter focused on how the unfairness of the dower and inheritance laws could be used as a message to build support for women's suffrage.[444]

The structure of the PEL evolved from this point.[445] On April 1, 1913, Beynon Thomas yielded the presidency to Dr. Mary Crawford, who held the position until the league disbanded in 1917. This freed her to head up the Membership and Speakers Committees.[446] By the spring of 1914, the PEL growth in membership had become so rapid that the original organizational structure was proving inadequate.[447] The PEL's annual meeting, held on April 2, 1914, ratified a new constitution with provisions for stronger branch components.[448] The work of the PEL, including recruiting new members and training volunteers, was to be carried on through branch leagues to be organized in different locations. Each branch was to have its own executive committee along with four standing committees: Literature and Petition, Publicity, Membership, and Program and Social. Any provincial municipality with more than one branch league could form a district executive consisting of the presidents of the affiliated branches together with one representative for every twenty-five branch members over the first twenty-five branch members. The name of the League was changed to "The Political Equality League of Manitoba," followed by the local branch name, a reflection of the fact that the organization was growing beyond Winnipeg and into the rest of the province.[449] Significantly, one of the objects set out in the new 1914 constitution was, "To stimulate public opinion, by all lawful means, to the point of demanding political equality for women."[450] This was an explicit rejection of the violent means that were being employed by leading British suffragettes in their efforts at enfranchisement.

N.B.—The following Articles from I to X inclusive concern branch leagues.

ARTICLE I
NAME
The name of this League shall be " The Political Equality League of Manitoba." (...........branch).

ARTICLE II
OBJECTS
CLAUSE A—To unite all those in sympathy with the movement to gain political equality for the women of Manitoba.

CLAUSE B—To disseminate knowledge with regard to the legal status of women under present conditions.

CLAUSE C—To stimulate public opinion, by all lawful means, to the point of demanding political equality for women.

CLAUSE D—To promote the organization of affiliated Leagues.

ARTICLE III
OFFICERS
CLAUSE A—The officers shall be as follows :   President, two Vice-Presidents, Recording Secretary, Corresponding Secretary and Treasurer.

These shall compose the Executive Committee, with the addition of the conveners of standing committees and the retiring President.

CLAUSE B—The term of office shall be one year, dating from the annual meeting.

CLAUSE C—No officer shall hold the same office for more than two consecutive years.

CLAUSE D—Should vacancies occur during the term of office, new officers may be elected by a majority of voting members present at a business meeting, after due notification of each member previous to such meeting.

CLAUSE E—Any officer or convener who cannot be present at a business meeting must provide a substitute pro tem. from the membership, who shall fulfil the duties and present the written report of such officer. The absence of any officer, without adequate excuse

3

Constitution of the Political Equality League of Manitoba, 1914, p. 3 SOURCE: ARCHIVES OF MANITOBA FONDS, P192/3.

During this period, Beynon Thomas was actively organizing new branches. She spoke at meetings, usually held in local schools, that led to the formation of the Elmwood Branch in east Winnipeg, the Weston Branch in the west end of the city and the Laura Secord Branch in the south end. By mid 1914, the League had six city branches. As permitted by the new constitution, these emerging city branches were affiliated under a district executive that was called Political Equality League (Winnipeg Executive), sometimes known simply as the City or Winnipeg Executive. Beynon Thomas secured a position on the Winnipeg Executive by virtue of her election as President of the local Laura Secord branch.[451] She reported that by mid-July, "societies were springing up all over the province," and mentioned Balmoral, Baldur, Harding, Gimli, Swan River, Roaring River as well as others.[452]

The League completed its organizational evolution at its first annual Woman's Suffrage Convention held in Winnipeg from February 18–20, 1915.[453] The purpose of the convention was to establish a Provincial Suffrage Society that would "extend the organization of the PEL to the whole Province of Manitoba and to elect an executive to carry on the provincial work of the association."[454] Eight Winnipeg branches, together with a number of rural branches, had been established by the time that suffrage was granted in January 1916.[455]

Engaging the Public

By mid-1913, the PEL was able to concentrate on taking its message to the general public. The focus of activity during 1913 and early 1914 was the production and distribution of pamphlets, the training and dispatch of speakers, and the solicitation of signatures for, and the presentation of, the first suffrage petition. From the outset, the PEL regarded pamphleteering as an important means of educating the broader public and winning its support for suffrage. On April 26, 1913, the PEL passed a motion calling for the production of two pamphlets, one on the "Legal Status of Women in Manitoba," and the other on "The Homeless and Childless Women of Manitoba."[456] Dr. Mary Crawford prepared the former pamphlet; Beynon Thomas prepared the latter. Beynon Thomas had frequently addressed the justifications for extension of the franchise in editorials going back to 1910.[457] Her new pamphlet argued for the vote so that dower laws could be passed that would prevent a wife and family from having their home sold out from underneath them by an absconding husband and so that guardianship laws could be adopted that would give a mother entitlement rights to her children equal to those of her husband.[458] Nellie McClung prepared a pamphlet on citizenship. When it approved publication of the pamphlets, the PEL adopted a resolution that the pamphlets, "be mailed at intervals of three weeks to school teachers in all towns in Manitoba and others..."[459] Pamphlets were distributed at summer picnics, country fairs, public meetings, to candidates seeking election to public offices, to ministers of churches, to organizations such as the WCTU. Sixty thousand pamphlets were also mailed to Manitoba women and voters during the 1914 provincial election campaign.[460]

Every July since 1891, the Winnipeg Industrial Exhibition had put on an annual week-long event which it advertised as "Manitoba's Greatest Fair." By 1913, the fair attracted crowds in the order of 600,000 people including between 3,500 and 7,000 Americans from the northern United States.[461] It featured recent inventions such as cars and aeroplanes as well as the usual fair attractions such as amusements, sports, and horticulture and livestock shows.[462] The 1913 Exhibition refused the PEL's request for a booth at the fair from which pamphlets could be distributed even after the mayor of Winnipeg had interceded on the PEL's behalf. However, a different summer attraction, the Stampede,[463] which had originated in Calgary in 1912, moved to Winnipeg for its second year from August 9–14, 1913. The Stampede agreed to allow the League to put up a suffrage tent for free and accorded the League every courtesy.[464] The Stampede attracted upwards of 50,000 people a day but was not a financial success. This, and the outbreak of war in 1914, meant that the 1913 Stampede was the last held in Winnipeg. It moved to New York City in 1916 and then returned to Calgary in 1919 where it continues as the famous Calgary Stampede each July.[465]

Beynon Thomas described how the League had a "little tent on the Stampede grounds." She continued, "It is decorated with banners and cards and pennants. A big sign across the entrance shows that it is the tent of 'The Political Equality League of Manitoba.' Other signs are 'Votes for Women,' and small cards stating the present laws, as they relate to women and children in Manitoba."[466] Banners and cards were sold to pay for the cost of advertising and distributing the literature. Beynon Thomas also told her readers that her experience at the Stampede was "decidedly unpleasant."[467] She explained how embarrassing she found campaigning: "You may think it an easy thing to put a great yellow sash with 'Votes for Women' on it across your shoulders, and take banners with 'Votes for Women' in big letters, and distribute literature to great indifferent crowds of men and women and children, but it isn't easy. It was one of the hardest things I ever did and only a sense of duty to women made me do it."[468] Much of that literature that was distributed at the Stampede was tossed back with an insult such as "Those women!"[469] "Of course we were laughed at, pointed out as freaks," Beynon Thomas recalled, "but we remembered the woman in Alberta,"[470] referring to the "old woman" whose 1908 letter to *Prairie Farmer* had galvanized readers behind the dower campaign. Beynon Thomas's sister Francis wrote in her column in the *GGG*, that despite the "endless jests and insults" hurled at those distributing literature, the Stampede tent was the event that marked "the changing of woman suffrage from a mere academic question to a live issue in Manitoba."[471]

At a time before radio and television, getting the message out to the public meant sending out speakers. In March 1913, Beynon Thomas became convenor of the PEL Speakers Committee.[472] The Committee's mandate was to train speakers "in the art of public presentation of suffrage arguments" who could be sent "to any point in city or country from whence had come a demand."[473] The League had trouble keeping up with the demand.[474] Calls came from groups staging conventions and various city associations holding annual meetings. Further appeals came from organizers of church basement gatherings, adult education sessions, public debate, rural farm meeting hosts, and the coordinators of the Grain

Growers' annual meetings and the Brandon Winter Fair.[475] The demand only intensified during the 1914 provincial election campaign when suffrage speakers held forth at Liberal, Labour, and Independent candidate rallies.[476] Two years later, after the vote was won, Beynon Thomas described the contribution that her itinerant female orators made during the 1914 election: "Women have gone through the province speaking, going in all weather, and driving long distances, just for the love of the cause. No woman has ever received a cent of pay for her work …"[477] The results were described as "immediate and far reaching."[478]

Beynon Thomas constantly found herself addressing a variety of women's groups. On February 16, 1914, she spoke to one hundred women taking the home nursing course at the Agricultural College: "When you go back to your country homes, start something. I do not care whether it is a sewing class or a literary society. All roads lead to suffrage."[479] On May 7, 1914, she reminded the Southwest WCTU city women that they were directly responsible to their country sisters who found it more difficult to organize suffrage campaigns.[480] On September 3, 1915, she opened the Brandon suffrage campaign by arguing that women must be engaged in politics in order to understand the system, and take part in planning the system, under which their children were being educated.[481]

During the first three months of 1913, Beynon Thomas spoke at the annual gatherings of three large, politically influential farm organizations. In each speech she set out why women should be given the vote. She delivered the first of her three speeches on January 10, 1913, at the annual Manitoba Grain Growers' Association's (MGGA) convention.[482] A year earlier, the MGGA had strongly endorsed women's suffrage. Beynon Thomas began by noting that four years ago, "she would have been asked to speak on food values, child culture or home economics," but this year she had been asked to speak directly… on the woman's movement for the suffrage." In an obvious reference to unruly suffrage demonstrations taking place in Britain, events brought to mind by the Emmeline Pankhurst visit to Winnipeg on December 16, 1911,[483] Beynon Thomas stated that, "Western Canadian women did not associate militant methods with political equality. That happened in another country and under other conditions. Women here did not feel the need for such methods. That would be like knocking a man down before asking what was wanted. ...women asked for things ..."[484] When women did that, however, legislators, "their feet on the table... spoke of the personal appearance of the women."[485]

Beynon Thomas continued by giving a direct answer to those who, like Premier Rodmond Roblin, would deny women the vote by claiming that "a woman's place is in the home."[486] She argued that the traditional role of women in caring for the family meant that they now had to concern themselves with conditions not only in the home but in the schools, in the factories, and in the community. After a brief overview of the role of women through time, she concluded:

> Next machinery was invented to make cloth, shoes, etc. Children were taken out into the world to be educated and women were left in the home. They sat down to the menial tasks assigned to her, scrubbing, washing, etc. But another problem arose. Mothers and girls were in the home with little to do. Women were expected to stay in the home till some man came to marry them. ... But women looked out over the economic world and chafed. They broke out into the economic world at the typewriter keyboard.[487] The movement began, nothing could stem it and the full-orbed agitation for political equality for women was launched upon the world.[488]

These were changes that could not be dealt with in a political world reserved to men alone: "Women wanted the ballot because they were not like men." On some matters, such as trade reciprocity or resource conservation, men and women would probably vote the same way. However, on other matters, such as morality and compulsory education, there would be a very great difference in the way in which men and women would vote: "Men vote in terms of business and property, but we [women] vote in terms of humanity, in terms of social betterment."[489]

Beynon Thomas delivered this cogent manifesto powerfully. The *Winnipeg Tribune* reported that "loud and long applause greeted the address."[490] The MGGA reaffirmed its previous year's support for women's suffrage and its president promised that the MGGA "would do its utmost to accomplish the end of, 'votes for women,' as it would do for all worthy reform movements."[491] In her monthly column, E. Cora Hind reported that the men gave Beynon Thomas, "an attentive and appreciative hearing." She wrote: "Following the meeting Mrs. Thomas had quite a levee of those who wished to express their appreciation and tell her she had converted them to the necessity of making women their political equals if they hoped to greatly improve their own condition."[492]

A month later, this time at the Saskatchewan Grain Growers' Association's twelfth annual convention, held in Saskatoon from February 12–14, 1913, Beynon Thomas gave her second speech. The themes were the same as those of a month earlier:

> If there were no tired men, broken-hearted women and suffering children, I would not be here tonight, but because these do exist, I, in common with many others, have felt that the cause of woman's suffrage exerts a force it is my duty to follow. So often have I realized the sad condition of life; so often have I seen delegations of women return from our legislatures and parliaments in despair. We go there bearing a tale of life and death and are received politely and kindly, yet come away with the knowledge that what was vital to a human life has had to give place to something desirable to a property holder. Woman's place is the home, I hear, but do you think it is part of a mother's mission to sit quietly by and see her sons and daughters growing up under conditions which she knows are bad, but, through lack of power, is unable to remedy? I hope that this convention will declare in favor of woman's suffrage.[493]

The convention voted for a resolution declaring itself in favour of extending the vote to women on the same terms as were enjoyed by men.[494]

Beynon Thomas delivered her third speech of 1913 at the Brandon Winter Fair, a major agricultural exhibition held annually in mid-March.

That year, the fair included a women's section with a program largely put together by E. Cora Hind.[495] Not surprisingly, given her closeness to Hind, Beynon Thomas was invited as a speaker. Her talk was entitled "The Old New Woman," old because primary responsibility for family, childrearing, morals, and manners still rested with mothers, and new because mechanization and commercial production were replacing traditional housework and women increasingly found it necessary to take an interest in public questions outside of the home to defend their families. After rejecting the popular conception of the new woman as "harsh, aggressive and unmotherly," Beynon Thomas continued:

> ... The new woman is the old woman plus the added virtues of her environment and advantages. She will insist on work and the training that fits for work: she will claim financial independence: she will insist on preserving her own individuality: she will demand 'more living and less land'. She will be equal with man in every walk of life, and will take a keen interest in public affairs, schools, factories and so on. The mother has no right to limit her influence to the four walls of her home. Her responsibility reaches out into the world where her young sons and daughters must go.[496]

In addition to organizing, pamphleteering, and speaking, reaching out to the general public meant gathering names on petitions. Beynon Thomas was skeptical about the value of petitions signed by women.[497] In February 1909 she told the readers of her Home Loving Hearts page that she did not think petitioning would do much to help the dower cause.[498] She was not alone in her view. In 1912, Nellie McClung told one of the first suffrage rallies of the campaign that "[p]etitions signed by women are usually treated as a joke by the electors."[499] Nevertheless, in March 1913 the PEL resolved to circulate a suffrage petition. Perhaps because of the view that petitions signed only by women would have little impact, two petitions were prepared, one for voters (i.e., men) and one for non-voters (i.e., women).[500] In April, the PEL executive appointed Beynon Thomas's husband to be the convenor of the Committee to Prepare the Petition

Blanks. In May, Beynon Thomas was made a member of the committee. That month she encouraged her Home Loving Hearts newspaper readers to request petition blanks. She instructed them on how the blanks were to be filled in and where completed petitions were to be sent.[501] Approximately fifteen blanks were filled in with signatures at the Winnipeg Stampede.[502] Blanks were supplied to various organizations such as the grain growers' associations and the labour councils for the collection of signatures. Finally, in 1913, the petition, containing over 20,000 men's signatures, was presented to T.C. Norris, leader of the opposition Liberal Party, following which he agreed to support women's suffrage.[503]

CHAPTER 5

The Political Arena

The Mock Parliament

Having reached out to the public with literature, speeches, and petitions in 1913, the PEL turned to the politicians in 1914. This was the year in which the PEL decided "that the present political situation made it imperative that they step into the arena of practical politics."[504] The first step was taken by staging a suffrage play that attracted a great deal of attention in Winnipeg with its humorous satire aimed directly at the PEL's political opponents. Beynon Thomas originated the idea for the Manitoba parody. On a 1911 visit to Vancouver, she had attended a performance of a mock parliament entitled "A Session of the Provincial Legislature in 2014 AD" staged by the city's University Women's Club.[505] This inspired her, on January 12, 1914, to suggest that the PEL form a committee to organize a play along the following lines:[506] "Why not reverse the whole thing? Why not have a whole parliament and show the people just what it means to be in our place?"[507] It took the committee just two weeks to plan the play, *A Women's Parliament*. All members of the legislature were to be women; men were not allowed to vote in elections or sit in the

Walker Theatre program, April 16, 1914, cover (TOP) and interior (BELOW)
SOURCE: ARCHIVES OF MANITOBA, NATHAN ARKIN COLLECTION, P7543/1.

House. It was to be a "one-eyed Parliament"—a government of half the people [i.e., women], by half the people [i.e., women], for all the people [i.e., both women and men].[508] The female government, opposed to male enfranchisement, was to hear submissions from the female opposition pleading for 'votes for men.' Harriet Walker, part owner with her husband of the Walker Theatre, advertised as "Canada's Finest Theatre," arranged for the donation of that venue for the event.[509] At 1,800 seats, it was Winnipeg's preeminent theatre. In her autobiography, Nellie McClung wrote that she knew nothing about these plans until she arrived back in Winnipeg, after a two-week absence, to find all of the details in place.[510] She was generous in giving credit: "To Lillian belongs the honor of bringing in the idea, which really swept us into victory."[511] Beynon Thomas's inspiration foreshadowed her career, two decades later, as a playwright.[512]

The play took place on the evening of Wednesday, January 28, 1914.[513] Although it must not have felt like it at the time, the previous day's fortune had smiled on the actors. On the afternoon of January 27, a delegation of women from such leading organizations as the PEL, the MGGA, the YWCA, the Trades and Labor Council, the Icelandic Women's Suffrage Association, the CWPC, and the WCTU met with Premier Roblin.[514] Anticipation going into the meeting ran high. The day before, *The Winnipeg Tribune* described the excitement: "Like a thunderbolt from a cloudless sky, a body of local suffragists and sympathisers will descend upon Premier Roblin tomorrow morning with a demand for the extension of the franchise to women, or to hear a good reason why they shouldn't have it." The *Winnipeg Tribune* added, "Women's suffrage was the burning subject of speeches and debates in clubs and lodges of every order last week. It was even discussed from the pulpit," and concluded by reporting that the cause, "had been given renewed impetus by the mayor's recent declaration that he 'could see no reason why women should not be given the vote on the same terms as men'."[515]

One hundred and sixty women filled the legislative chamber and its galleries for the meeting with the Premier. McClung, speaking for the delegation, made their demand for suffrage plainly, pointing out that men had made laws for women that had failed because the male legislators had not had the benefit of women's viewpoints.[516] Beynon Thomas was seated in the front row of the delegation as Premier Roblin rejected the demand out of hand.[517] He pointed out the "hysteria of women in English public life." He maintained that in Colorado, where women had the vote, they shrank from the polls as from a pestilence.[518] He concluded that: "Women's place was in the home; her duty was the development of the child's character and the performance of wifely duties. To project her into the sphere of party politics would cause her to desert the true sphere, to the grave danger of society. I believe that woman suffrage would be a retrograde movement, that it will break up the home, that it will throw the children into the arms of the servant girls."[519] The *Free Press* editorialized the next day on the "whiskered poppycock talked by Premier Roblin," and noted that, "The Premier simply revealed himself once more an autocrat with the wraiths of feudalism still about him."[520] In her reply, McClung told the Premier, "We believe we'll get you yet, Sir Rodmond!"[521] This proved to be no idle threat. The next evening, playing the part of Premier in the Mock Parliament, McClung imitated Roblin to great effect as she denied men the franchise. McClung told of how in preparation for her role she, "could hardly wait to get home [following the delegation's meeting with Roblin] and practise it all before a mirror," and before her husband and eldest son.[522]

On January 28, the theatre was packed. Lawyers and doctors, rushing in late, were sent to the Gods, the cheap seats on the balcony.[523] The evening's entertainment started with the Assiniboine male quartet singing suffrage songs based on parodies drawn from popular music of the day. Then followed a short playlet originally set in London, England but adapted for Winnipeg.[524] In the playlet, *How the Vote Was Won*, women went on strike by leaving their homes until men gave up the platitude that "a woman's place was in the home," abandoned the fiction that women did not need the vote because they were looked after by men, and accepted women's suffrage.[525] The main event of the evening, the staging of *A Women's Parliament*, followed. The speeches were improvised by those playing the various roles.[526] At the end of the campaign, Beynon Thomas wrote, "Many people have asked for a copy of the play,

A Women's Parliament. No one has ever received a copy for the very good reason that there never was one written."[527]

The play featured, on one side of the Legislature, the governing party, led by Premier Nellie McClung. On the other side sat the opposition party which included Beynon Thomas as the Member for North Winnipeg.[528] The opposition requested "votes for men;" the government, of course, opposed it. Exact parliamentary procedure was followed with the session including petitions presented, motions offered, questions asked, and bills read. Beynon Thomas, speaking for the opposition, addressed the second reading of Bill 17, a Bill that would have conferred upon fathers the same rights of guardianship of their children as were enjoyed by mothers.[529] With tears in her eyes, Lillian asked, "Why not in the name of common sense let them have two parents?"[530] Then male actors, representing unenfranchised citizens, rolled onto the stage with wheelbarrows containing petitions asking for voting rights and equal laws. McClung rejected all requests perfectly mimicking the words, tone and actions used by Premier Roblin in his pompous rejection of the demands of the delegation of women whom he had met the day before. At one point, McClung sarcastically told the male supplicants that, "[p]olitics unsettles men, and unsettled men mean unsettled bills, broken furniture, broken vows and divorce... Man's place is on the farm."[531] Press coverage was extensive and enthusiastic. Reporters noted that two opposition members from the Manitoba Legislature "escaped from a stuffy civic dinner" to enjoy the performance.[532] One newspaper concluded that "Smiles of anticipation, ripples of merriment, gales of laughter and storms of applause punctuated every point and paragraph of what was unanimously conceded to be the best burlesque ever staged in Winnipeg..."[533] Beynon Thomas later wrote that the audience "almost rolled off their seats" with laughter.[534]

The mock parliament was repeated in Brandon on April 2, 1914[535] and again at Winnipeg's Walker Theatre on April 16, 1914.[536] On both occasions, attendance broke all records despite the fact that ticket prices for the April performance in Winnipeg had doubled from fifty cents to one dollar.[537] Both evenings opened with an additional skit. As the curtain rose a group of ladies in evening dress were playing cards. The

hostess announced to the others that she was the leader of the movement opposed to giving women the vote. The other women agreed that
they, too, did not want the vote. A group of gentlemen arrived with a
large bouquet of roses, which they presented to the ladies with thanks
for their opposition to women's suffrage. When the ladies noticed that
one of the men was the leader of "The Liquor Interest," and the others,
in order, "The Child Labor Exploiter," the "White Slave Dealer," the
"Political Boss," and finally, "Graft," they threw the flowers at them
with the hostess declaring, "If these are the interests I have been serving,
henceforth, Votes for Women!"[538]

The three performances of *A Women's Parliament* earned a total of
$1,000 for the PEL, sufficient to fund the rest of the suffrage campaign.[539]
Reviewing the campaign four years later, Anne Anderson Perry, journalist for the *Saturday Post* and member of the PEL, wrote: "The Mock
Parliament... was the climax of the propaganda and may be said to have
finally converted Winnipeg to the cause of woman suffrage."[540] Nellie
McClung thought that "it was a great factor in turning public sentiment
in favor of the enfranchisement of women,"[541] Beynon Thomas thought
that "it was the parliament that made the movement popular,"[542] and
her sister Francis concluded that "it added immeasurably to the prestige
of the movement."[543] Both sisters later noted the "strange coincidence"
that it was two years to the day from the first performance of *A Women's
Parliament* that Manitoba women won the right to vote.[544] Perry thought
that the play was a "powerful element in the downfall of the Roblin government the following year."[545]

Two Provincial Elections

While relations between the PEL and the Roblin Government continued
to be strained, relations with the Liberal Opposition continued to warm.
Opposition Leader Tobias Norris had pledged his support for suffrage
when he had received the PEL's petition a few months before the suffrage
play. He followed this up a month after the play with an invitation to
Beynon Thomas and to Nellie McClung to give keynote addresses at the

upcoming Liberal annual convention on March 27, 1914. The two invitees adopted very different speaking styles. As was their wont, Beynon Thomas was rational and cool; McClung intuitive and dynamic. Their message, however, was the same. Beynon Thomas started her speech by pointing out that she was the first woman in the history of Canada to be invited to address a political convention.[546] She went on to say that there were many reasons why women should be given the right to vote but one would suffice: "democracy." She reasoned that enfranchisement would encourage women to become better educated so as to be able to cast ballots favouring reform. She affirmed that the PEL's platform rejected violent methods in favour of education. Her final words, "Let Manitoba be First," became from that moment the slogan of the provincial suffrage movement. The press reported that she resumed her seat "amid a storm of applause."[547] The Convention went on to adopt the following resolution: "The Liberal party, believing that there are no just grounds for debarring women from the right to vote, will enact a measure providing for equal suffrage, upon it being established by petition that this is desired by adult women to a number equivalent to 15 per cent of the vote cast at the preceding general election in this province."[548] Beynon Thomas's and McClung's speeches cemented the alliance between the Liberal Opposition and the PEL.

By this time, the breach between the Conservative Government and the PEL had become irrevocable. During the fall 1913 sitting of the Legislature, Harvey Simpson, Conservative MLA from Virden, introduced a pro-suffrage resolution. Procedure was manipulated so that it never came to a vote.[549] Again, in the spring 1914 session of the Legislature, a similar pro-suffrage resolution was introduced, this time by G.H.J. Malcolm, an opposition Liberal member from Birtle. The Premier told government members of the Legislative Assembly that he would regard passage of the resolution as a vote of non-confidence. Simpson absented himself from the House rather than vote against his party. Other Conservative members voted to defeat the resolution on February 13, 1914, as instructed by the Premier.[550]

Rodmond Roblin had become Premier of Manitoba in 1900. His government had been re-elected with large majorities in 1903, 1907, and again on July 11, 1910, when it won one-half of the popular vote and twenty-eight seats to the Liberal opposition's thirteen. Roblin confidently sought a renewed mandate on July 10, 1914. The Conservative campaign booklet, entitled *The Record of the Roblin Government*, maintained that enfranchisement would "denigrate true womanhood" and would "emotionalize balloting." On the suffrage question, it concluded that, "Wifehood, motherhood and politics cannot be associated together with satisfactory results.[551] Beynon Thomas, McClung, and the PEL chose this moment to become fully engaged in electoral politics. They campaigned with fervour on behalf of Liberal, Labour, and Independent candidates who supported votes for women.[552] Beynon Thomas endorsed Fred Dixon, a pro-suffrage Independent candidate with deep Labour roots.[553] In an early campaign speech, she complimented "labour men" for their "proper grasp of their fundamentals of democracy."[554] She praised them for knowing that women's suffrage was necessary in order to safeguard the home and to protect workers' interest as wage earners.[555] Speakers, notably Beynon Thomas and McClung, took to the podium at election meetings; 120,000 pieces of literature, including Beynon Thomas's pamphlet, were distributed; and ministers of the cloth were encouraged to preach on women's suffrage. The WCTU was called upon to assist. The Laura Secord branch, presided over by Beynon Thomas, sent out workers on a thorough door-to-door canvass.[556] A final push was put on from June 28 to July 4, a week before the 1914 election. The PEL declared that week 'Suffrage Week in Manitoba' and urged its supporters to make a "special effort" to ensure that, "there shall not be any other topic of conversation that shall so fill the minds of the people of Manitoba that week as woman suffrage."[557] In her newspaper column, Beynon Thomas cited an observer who commented that, "the woman movement is the greatest religious movement of the day."[558] Francis Beynon called on readers of the Country Homemakers page in the *GGG*, "to spread the gospel ... of woman's enfranchisement."[559]

On Election Day, the Conservatives won twenty-eight seats, the opposition Liberals twenty, and an Independent, Fred Dixon, one, in Winnipeg Centre. McClung, who had spoken frequently to large crowds throughout the campaign, and who had addressed 5,000 people in Winnipeg the day before the election, was widely credited for the strong Liberal showing.[560] The Conservative stranglehold on government had been broken; the Liberals became the 'government-in-waiting.' Several months later, in November 1914, McClung moved to Edmonton so that her husband could take up a promotion but only after she had been honoured for her contribution to the suffrage cause at a reception by members of the Laura Secord branch of the PEL and their friends.[561]

Beynon Thomas continued to campaign for woman suffrage after the 1914 election. On January 10, 1915, she addressed the Young Men's Club of Grace Church on the subject of "The Progress of the Women's Movement."[562] A week and a half later, she told the North End Women's Council, "with optimistic fervor," that she looked forward to the time when women would regain equality with men in education, religion, and politics and thus make potent their voice in the affairs of the world. She concluded, against the backdrop of World War I then raging, that when this happened, "brute force would wane in its glory, and permanent peace would draw the race to the highest design for which it was created."[563] The implication was that if women had been involved in politics, World War I would never have happened.

The PEL held its "first annual" Woman Suffrage Convention at the Industrial Bureau in Winnipeg from February 18 to 20, 1915. Francis Beynon reported that Winnipeggers were excited "by the sudden appearance in the street cars of little yellow badges announcing that the wearers were delegates to the convention."[564] Nellie McClung wrote an "optimistic and inspiring letter" of encouragement to the delegates from her new home in Edmonton. She rallied the troops: "We are surely marching on—do you notice that we are called women now very often, not 'ladies,' and I haven't heard anything about the fair sex for a long time, so let us rejoice again." She alluded to the "jarring conditions" brought on by the war and looked forward to the day when women had a share in the legislation of the world.[565]

The highlight of the convention came on the morning of the second day, February 19, 1915, when a delegation of women met with Premier

Roblin. As was the case a year earlier when women had met with the Premier just several days prior to staging *A Women's Parliament*, the delegation was large, numbering 150 to 160 women from a variety of organizations.[566] This time, however, the meeting was held in the Premier's private office. The office normally held twenty to thirty people and so was cramped. Speakers in favour of suffrage included the PEL President, Dr. Mary Crawford, PEL First Vice President, Gertrude Richardson of the Roaring River Association representing rural women, and representatives from the WCTU, the Royal Templars of Temperance, the First Icelandic Suffrage Society, the MGGA, the Single Tax League, the Direct Legislation League, the Trades and Labour Council, and the Polish Club.[567] At one point, the Premier claimed that men were chivalrous in their treatment of ladies noting that he would always give a woman his place in a streetcar. Beynon Thomas pointed out that such an argument was "entirely irrelevant" to the case at hand.[568]

There was one other important difference between the 1915 meeting with the Premier and the one that had taken place a year earlier. This time, perhaps humbled by the mockery directed his way during the suffrage play, and by his close call with the electorate in the summer of 1914, a less bombastic Rodmond Roblin presented a "decidedly changed front."[569] He still refused to commit himself to any definite suffrage policy, but his refusal was couched in "much more courteous and gentle language."[570] He conceded that women had the "capacity for deciding on questions with regard to the public morals and welfare of the people... [and] that women would eventually accomplish their purpose."[571] However, he added that it would be necessary for women to struggle for an indefinite time longer[572] in order that the public might be educated and schooled in such a great reform.[573] On these matters, the Premier explained that he looked to Westminster for inspiration, noting its refusal to grant the franchise to the women of Great Britain.[574] Just as had happened a year earlier, shortly after the suffrage delegation met with Roblin, the Liberals brought forward a resolution in the 1915 spring sitting of the Legislature that would have extended the vote to women. This time the resolution was offered by T.C. Norris, the Leader of the Opposition. Again, the resolution was defeated by the governing Conservatives, this time narrowly, acting on orders from the Premier.

On the third day of the Woman Suffrage Convention, the final Saturday, recognizing the previous year's commitment by the Liberals to grant women the vote upon the presentation of a petition, a suffrage school was held. The steps that needed to be taken to collect names for the petition were discussed including, organization, literature, social events, advertising, programs and speakers.[575]

On May 12, 1915, Premier Roblin's government resigned when an inquiry found it guilty of corruption in tendering contracts for the construction of the new Manitoba legislative building. Tobias Norris and the Liberals took over. Within several weeks, the new premier received a deputation of women from the PEL who sought confirmation that the new government would honour the Liberal Party platform promise to grant woman suffrage provided that it was presented with a petition signed by women numbering 15% of voters who cast ballots in the preceding provincial election. In the August 6, 1915, election, 116,766 men had cast their vote.[576] The 15% formula meant that a petition containing 17,520 female signatures would be required. Norris gave his assurance that the pledge would be honoured. The PEL set a goal of collecting 20,000 signatures.[577] On June 5, 1915, Beynon Thomas wrote in her column, "Now, the women are getting ready to start on a signature campaign."[578] She advised that the chief societies collecting signatures would be the PEL, the WCTU and the Grain Growers and gave instructions on how petition forms could be obtained.

In the first week of July, Premier Norris called a new provincial election for August 6, 1915. The petition campaign, and the election campaign, ran simultaneously. For Beynon Thomas, and other suffrage leaders, the two campaigns were one and the same. As she had done in the 1914 election, Beynon Thomas supported F.J. Dixon's candidacy. In a speech delivered to his supporters on July 6, 1915, she emphasized that women wished the vote in order that they might stand with men in opposing political corruption and the fight against the liquor traffic.[579] McClung travelled back to Manitoba from her new home in Edmonton to give a major boost to the Liberals.[580] On election day, Premier Norris achieved a resounding majority, winning forty seats. The Conservatives won five. F.J. Dixon was re-elected as an Independent, and one Social Democrat was elected. On election night, McClung stood with Dixon, and three soon-to-be Liberal cabinet ministers, on the balcony of the *Free Press* building where they were cheered by the crowd.[581] Immediately after, McClung returned to Edmonton.

The Premier-elect, Tobias C. Norris, was returned from the rural constituency of Lansdowne in southwestern Manitoba. On August 10, 1915, he travelled to nearby Brandon and then on to Winnipeg where he was met at noon at the CPR station by every newly elected Liberal member. They were escorted to the legislative building in a victory parade of 600 automobiles. Members of the PEL occupied 285 cars, all decorated with purple and yellow flowers, the suffrage colours. Their cars were lined up in a special section of the parade. Beynon Thomas rode in the lead suffrage car along with several of the main suffrage volunteers.[582] The suffrage workers were in high spirits. One suffrage decorated car was lined up far from the suffrage section of the parade. When this was pointed out to the male driver of the car, he replied, "'To h... with suffrage, what the f... made you think this was a suffrage car?' at which point half a dozen women in the car, aware of the way in which the car was decorated with suffrage colours, doubled up laughing."[583] Reporting in the *Free Press* on the day's events and the reception that Norris received, Beynon Thomas wrote, "Manitoba women are proud that Manitoba will be the first province to enfranchise its women, and they are proud of the men who are going to do them that honor."[584]

Passing the Bill

After the election, in early September, Beynon Thomas formally launched the suffrage petition campaign in Brandon.[585] That same week she also spoke in nearby Virden.[586] A few days later, she took part as a canvass captain in central Winnipeg with her Laura Secord Branch of the PEL.[587] On September 23 she spoke to a rally of suffrage canvassers from the Fort Rouge branch before they headed out in Winnipeg to knock door-to-door in search of petition signatures.[588] On November 14, 1915, McClung, visiting Winnipeg from Edmonton for the second time in three months, addressed a packed auditorium at an event sponsored by the Laura Secord branch and chaired by Beynon Thomas. Before returning home to Edmonton that evening, McClung told her audience that suffrage would increase their self-respect and make them think better of themselves as citizens.[589] At the end of November, Beynon Thomas led a Ladies' Night discussion at the Industrial Bureau on the topic of, "Will Woman Suffrage Advance Economic Reforms?"[590]

Apart from her organizational and speaking skills, Beynon Thomas's major contribution to the petition campaign was as chief motivator and cheerleader. For this, she used her newspaper columns. On September 11, she wrote: "All over this province there are women on distant homesteads who have sent for petitions, and they are taking these petitions around getting women to sign. It grips the imagination to think of the women who are walking miles over our prairie roads these burning hot days just to get one signature."[591] By October 1, the required 17,520 signatures had been obtained. The goal was raised to 30,000.[592] On October 9, after giving the statistics on the number of leaflets distributed by canvassers, she wrote: "Never in the history of this province of Manitoba has there been such a great educational campaign as the women have carried on during the last few months."[593] Looking back in 1944, she said simply, "There was something heroic about it."[594] Years later she recalled: "Women went from farm to farm in country districts getting signatures to the petition. Some walked, some rode on horseback, some drove in a buggy or a buck board or in a lumber wagon, and I heard of one even riding on a stone-boat."[595]

Nowhere was her leadership more evident than in the defiant exhortation that she penned at the midpoint of the campaign in her column under the headline "New Dreams:"

> The women of Manitoba who are working to get the petition are dreaming new and greater dreams than ever before. They are dreaming of the great work the women of this

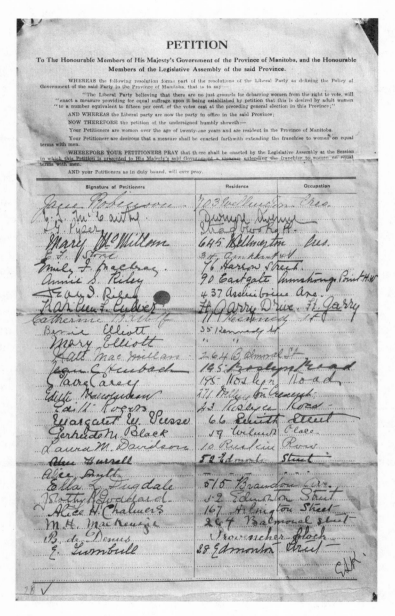

Political Equality League final petition for women's suffrage,
December 23, 1915 SOURCE: ARCHIVES OF MANITOBA, EVENTS

province, now they are stirred up, can do to better conditions. They are dreaming of the day when the liquor traffic will be banished, when every child will be compelled to get an education, when our mentally defective will have a home where they will be cared for and society will be protected from them. They are dreaming of the time when our treatment of criminals will be more humane, when our idea of university education will be an education for the many, not the few, when—but who can tell all the dreams that lighten the long walks and drives of our canvassers; dreams that may make of Manitoba, when dreamed by men and women together, a province to which other provinces will look for inspiration to make better conditions of life, not for the few, but for all.[596]

By early October, 55,000 suffrage leaflets had been distributed and over 6,000 petition blanks, with instructions for completing them, had been sent out. Each petition blank contained spaces for women over the age of 21 to sign. The last call for signed petitions went out on December 18, 1915.[597] An iconic photograph was taken on December 23, 1915, of four women with a stack of completed petition forms between them. Moving from left to right were Dr. Mary Crawford, PEL Chair; Lillian Beynon Thomas, PEL Second Vice Chair; Winona Flett Dixon, PEL provincial secretary in charge of gathering signatures; and 93-year-old Amelia Burritt. The main petition in the center of the photograph contained 39,584 signatures or 33.9% of the number of men who had voted in the August 6, 1915, provincial election. The PEL had gathered more than double the number of signatures required.[598] The petition was the largest ever presented to any legislature in Canada up until that time.[599] Amelia Burritt's separate petition, resting in her lap, contained 4,250 additional signatures that she had collected herself.

A delegation of sixty PEL members, headed by Beynon Thomas, presented the petitions to Premier Norris and his cabinet.[600] In her brief remarks, Beynon Thomas acknowledged the work of the very early suffrage

Presentation of final petition for woman's suffrage by the Political Equality
League to Tobias Norris, Premier of Manitoba, December 23, 1915.
Clockwise from back left: Lillian Beynon Thomas, Winona Dixon, Amelia
Burritt (age 94), and Dr. Mary Crawford. SOURCE: ARCHIVES OF MANITOBA

workers and of the farm women who, despite their onerous daily duties,
travelled long distances to get signatures during this final campaign.[601]
In a clear response to the delegation, the Premier announced that a bill
granting woman suffrage was nearly ready for the printers and would
be introduced early in the first session of the Legislature upcoming in
the New Year.[602]

Several days before the Bill was to be presented to the Legislature, a
member of the House who was sympathetic to the suffrage cause told
Beynon Thomas that he had seen the draft suffrage legislation and that
while it gave women the right to vote, it did not give them the right to
sit in the Legislature.[603] On January 5, 1916, the day before the new

Legislative session was to begin, Beynon Thomas asked the Attorney General to see the draft bill. The Attorney-General's lawyer agreed on condition that she not disclose the bill's contents, which were confidential, until the Bill had been tabled in the Legislature. She agreed. Upon reviewing the draft, however, she was horrified to learn that the bill in fact did not make provision for women to sit in the Legislature. She told the Attorney-General's lawyer: "I can't tell about [the absence of] that clause, but we can and will fight the principle of it."[604] That day, Beynon Thomas telephoned members of the PEL and, without disclosing what was actually in the Bill, asked them to contact their member of the legislature and inquire whether women were going to get the right to run for a seat. This resulted in a flurry of phone calls. Beynon Thomas also advised her sister, Francis, who was covering the MGGA annual convention in Brandon from January 5 to 7, 1916, of the situation. The Attorney-General was then told that if the bill was not changed Francis would arrange for a motion of censure of the Liberal government to be adopted by the women's meeting of the convention and that this motion, once passed, would be placed before the closing evening session of the main convention. When Attorney General Hudson heard of this plan, he quickly agreed that the bill would be changed to allow women to sit in the Legislature.[605]

The suffrage bill was introduced on January 10, 1916 by Premier Norris, given second reading four days later, and passed third reading with unanimous consent of the Legislature on January 27, 1916.[606] In an unprecedented move, members of the executive of the PEL, including Beynon Thomas, were invited to sit on the floor of the Legislative chamber during third reading.[607] When the Bill passed third reading, over a hundred women and men in the galleries, and the members on the floor of the House, stood to sing "O Canada." That completed, the members of the House sat down while the folks in the gallery sang "For They Are Jolly Good Fellows," at which point the elected members stood and responded in kind.[608] It was an historic display of enthusiasm.[609] Royal Assent was granted on January 28, 1916, two years to the day from the first staging the mock suffrage play, *A Women's Parliament*.[610]

Manitoba was the first among the Canadian federal or provincial jurisdictions to grant women suffrage. On that day, several prominent leaders from the PEL, including Beynon Thomas, met for tea at the Fort Garry Hotel in Winnipeg to celebrate and to send telegrams of thanks to Nellie McClung, at home in Edmonton, and Premier Norris, who had not been in the House for the final passage of the Bill. The *Free Press* reported that he was, "on government business,"[611] but the *Tribune* reported that he was "rumored" to have "purposely" taken the train for Chicago in order to miss the celebratory banquet that the city equality leagues were planning for members of the Legislature.[612] In her *Free Press* column published on the day that the suffrage bill received Royal Assent, Beynon Thomas told of how the women of the province, "are dreaming big dreams, dreams of having a province that will lead the world in social legislation."[613] She described how Political Equality Leagues across the province were arranging celebrations in their districts.

Several days later, on February 1, 1916, the city equality leagues held a grand celebration banquet at the Royal Alexandra Hotel.[614] At first Premier Norris, still annoyed at Beynon Thomas's manoeuvring to have the suffrage bill redrafted to include the right of women to sit in the provincial Legislature, declined the invitation. He changed his mind after being advised that politically it would be strategic to attend.[615] Years later, Beynon Thomas wrote that the Premier refused to speak to her. "However," she noted, "we made it up before he died."[616] Five hundred people attended the banquet.[617] The *Free Press* headlined the occasion on the next day's front page:

> To mark the consummation of hopes long cherished and worked for by the women of Manitoba, as exemplified in the extension of the franchise to women, and as an expression of their deep joy at their glorious victory as readily achieved, a banquet was given at the Royal Alexandra Hotel last night under the auspices of the Political League of Manitoba. The gathering was a representative one including nearly all the members of the government, the opposition, and the heads of many important organizations in the province.[618]

Many congratulatory telegrams were read at the banquet. Nineteen speeches, in the form of appreciative toasts, were made. Beynon Thomas, along with other prominent leaders in the suffrage movement, and the Premier, were seated at the head table. Beynon Thomas's toast to "the government," in which she mentioned each member of the cabinet in turn, was described in the press the next day as, "delightfully witty."[619] Despite the fact that Premier Norris was not speaking to her, she commented on his promise to bring in suffrage once the requisite petition had been received. She affirmed that through many years it was said of him, "You can trust Norris. He's a man of his word."[620] She concluded her toast to the government by underlining that democracy was about trusting the "home folks: …The government of Manitoba has carried through the most progressive and democratic legislation carried out in Canada, and will go down in history as being the first government to fully trust the people."[621]

Beynon Thomas reflected on the entire suffrage campaign a few days after the banquet in a column entitled, 'Trusting all the Home Folks.' She wrote, "It is all over, even the shouting. The women of Manitoba are now citizens, persons, human beings, who have stepped politically out of the class of criminals, children, idiots and lunatics." She warmly credited McClung as, "the outstanding personality in the suffrage campaign in Manitoba … [who] made woman's suffrage an issue in this province much sooner than would have been possible without her help."[622] At the conclusion of her article, Beynon Thomas referenced her campaign slogan to make Manitoba the first jurisdiction to enfranchise women: "Democracy is enthroned. Manitoba has led the way in the greatest step ever taken by a government in Canada. Manitoba has been first to trust all the people."[623]

Two years before her death in 1961, the Manitoba Historical Society asked Beynon Thomas to describe how it happened that Manitoba women were the first in Canada to win the vote. She began with the words, "There is a tide in the affairs of women."[624] Her reference was an adaptation of the words spoken by Brutus in Shakespeare's *Julius Caesar*.[625] Perhaps the idea to use the quote came from her recollection of Nellie McClung's 1946 autobiography, *The Stream Runs Fast*.[626] There, McClung quotes herself from the 1914 meeting that the PEL delegation had with Premier Roblin immediately preceding the play, *A Women's Parliament*. At that meeting, McClung said to Roblin: "But I wish to tell you again, Sir Rodmond, as clearly as I can make it, that we are going to create public sentiment in this province, which will work against you at the next election. Did you ever hear that quotation about there being a tide in the affairs of men, which taken at the flood leads on to fortune?"

The Forgotten Women

When the province of Manitoba was formed in 1870, ss. 17 of the *Manitoba Act* enfranchised all males, including Indigenous and Métis men, who met the age, citizenship, and householder qualifications. However, in 1875, provincial legislation reversed course and disenfranchised "Indians or persons of Indian blood receiving an annuity from the crown." Why were the voting rights of Métis men not removed? At the time Manitoba joined Confederation, the Métis were far more numerous and far more politically powerful than the Indigenous population. This is evident from their resistance in 1869–1870 led by Louis Riel, from the degree of inter-marriage between the Indigenous and settler populations stretching back to the arrival of fur traders, and from the political involvement of men such John Norquay, himself Métis and Manitoba premier from 1878 to 1887. Women were not given the vote when Manitoba was formed in 1870. Settler and Métis women first acquired that right when suffrage legislation was passed in 1916. However, Indigenous women were ignored in the suffrage campaign by their sisters and continued to be deprived of the vote as a result.[627]

It may be that suffrage activists found it inconceivable that Indigenous women would be enfranchised given that Indigenous men did not have the vote. That aside, one wonders why Beynon Thomas, given her empathy for marginalized peoples, especially for women immigrants, would not have included Indigenous women in the suffrage cause. Some suffrage leaders, including for a brief time Nellie McClung, opted for a selective franchise that excluded non-Anglo-Saxon women in the 1917 debate over the federal enfranchisement. Beynon Thomas took the opposite position. She argued strongly that federal enfranchisement of women should be universal, that it should include "foreign" women settlers, and not just those from English-speaking countries. However, "universal" for Beynon Thomas did not include Indigenous women.

Beynon Thomas, like other suffragist activists, was blind to the idea that Indigenous women, like all women, should have the vote. Historian Sarah Carter has described these activists as wearing "Suffragist Blinkers."[628] She pointed out that "most prairie suffragists were keenly aware of the marginalization of Indigenous peoples and that they were colonizers who had replaced them and profited from their land and resources."[629] She continued, "[Settler colonialism's] underlying impulse is ... to elevate settler families as legitimate and therefore entitled to land."[630] Carter includes in a list of "major players" who "personally knew Indigenous people and sometimes wrote about them" Beynon Thomas and her sister.[631]

From 1874 to 1882, just prior to her family's move west in 1889, Beynon Thomas's maternal uncle had served as a missionary to Indigenous peoples in the North-West Territories. When she moved to Winnipeg in 1906, Beynon Thomas started working closely with inner-city organizations that sought to aid those, including Indigenous people, who were in need of assistance. In one of her earliest short stories, published in 1907, Beynon Thomas described the funeral of an Indigenous man whose corpse was burned on a pyre. The participants were described as "cruel barbarous savages" who chanted a "blood-curdling" dirge.[632]

In a 1910 article, Beynon Thomas mentioned sailing past St. Peter's Reserve and seeing Indigenous people in Selkirk. St. Peter's was located on the Red River north of Winnipeg near Selkirk, Manitoba. Some of the Cree and Saulteaux band members on the reserve had earlier been persuaded by missionaries to reduce their dependence on hunting and trapping in favour of taking up agriculture. When they became prosperous, the government started a campaign, using questionable and fraudulent tactics, which resulted in band members being dispossessed of their land and, in 1907, the reserve being dissolved altogether. Beynon Thomas would have known of these events which were notorious at the time. On this trip, she may have been accompanied by her husband, Vernon, who in 1910 was working as a clerk for the Department of Indian Affairs distributing annuities to Manitoba First Nations.[633]

The letters written by farm women settlers to Beynon Thomas's Home Loving Hearts page do not appear to have come from Indigenous women, although even their limited participation, if there was such, could have been hidden by the fact that correspondents used pseudonyms. The homemakers' clubs in Saskatchewan, a movement founded by Beynon Thomas, was meant for settler women only. There is no evidence that Beynon Thomas asked Indigenous women to play any role in the PEL or in the suffrage campaign, or even that she or her campaigners asked them to sign suffrage petitions.

Beynon Thomas campaigned in the provincial elections of 1914 and 1915 for independent candidate Fred Dixon. She must have been familiar with his article "Let the Women Vote," published in the *GGG* just before the 1915 provincial election. In that article, he stated, "There are certain members of society who are very properly barred from voting, namely: idiots, criminals, insane persons, and treaty Indians; ..."[634] Similarly, in 1934, chronicling her road trip with her husband through the Red River Valley in Manitoba, Beynon Thomas observed that, "Neither the Indians nor the fur traders wanted the settlers."[635] She then commented on the "courage" of the settlers in triumphing over these obstacles and the forces of nature.

With respect to Indigenous peoples, including Indigenous women, Beynon Thomas shared the prejudices of her time, a bias which she may have taken for granted. What caused Beynon Thomas to exhibit this bias especially given her tolerance, indeed her kindness, for disadvantaged people in general? First, Beynon Thomas, who came with her family to Manitoba in 1889, was part of the first wave of Anglo-Saxon settlers, mostly from Ontario. This wave of newcomers was intent on taking land by displacing the Indigenous population and on imposing political and social structures that would ensure settler dominance. Second, granting Indigneous people the vote would have given them political power,

power that was inconsistent with the settler colonialist objective of dominance. This would have precluded Beynon Thomas from considering that
Indigenous women should have the vote. Third, Beynon Thomas's campaigns for suffrage, dower, and other land law reforms,[636] reforms that
were limited to benefitting settler women, implicated her in the colonial
settler enterprise of dispossessing Indigenous peoples. Carter provides
the following persuasive explanation for this: "Dower and homestead
rights were causes unique to the suffrage campaigns on the Prairies. Both
essentially involved land and the desire of settler women to have access
to land they believed should be theirs. Land recently wrested from its
Indigenous owners was at the heart of the settler colonial project, as well
as the suffrage cause. Settler women were complicit in the dispossession
of Indigenous land, and they sought the right to acquire more in a region
where land was the main source of income."[637]

CHAPTER 6

Transitions

Dower Realized

Tides come in and tides go out. World War I, which dominated all else in its time, ultimately caused the post-suffrage tide to go out on the women's movement in Manitoba. The War split the movement along diverse fault lines: imperialist suffragettes versus pacifist suffragettes; pro-conscription suffragettes versus anti-conscription suffragettes; selective federal franchise suffragettes versus universal federal franchise suffragettes. As if these divisions were not enough, women having won the vote lost the unifying focus that the suffrage cause had given their movement. Further, as historian Ramsay Cook observed, "[w]hen the promised utopia did not materialize, some women appear to have lost interest in politics. Others wondered if the struggle had really been worth the effort."[638]

The leadership of the women's movement struggled with resentment between those who had fought the suffrage fight and newcomers who only now emerged from the shadows to co-opt women's organizations, claim leadership positions, and promote political points of view in opposition to those of their pioneer sisters. Anne Perry, herself one of those pioneer crusaders, could barely conceal her bitterness when she looked back on the outcome of the suffrage campaign in an article entitled "Shoals Ahead" published in 1920 in the *GGG*:

> Already there is a floating to the surface, in the body politic, of the grasping, greedy, 'practical' woman, who lifted neither hand nor voice to gain the vote for their sex, because to be a feminist was to be unfeminine, but who, now the battle is won for them by their more courageous, honest sisters, are very willing to steal the spoils of conquest and climb with them to power. Of these cuckoos there are many and there is a corresponding submergence of those better, finer women who worked not for power or personal aggrandizement but for an idea and an ideal. … Not only are there plenty of rifflers in the nest the suffragists had builded [*sic*] for the future home of the sex, but the women's clubs are to day [*sic*] more and more tending to become areanas [*sic*] of political intrigue.[639]

Beynon Thomas did not share any doubt about the value of enfranchisement. Shortly after her move to the United States, she sent an M.B.A column back to Winnipeg. In it she declared that she had no idea of the benefits of suffrage until she observed the situation in New York City where women did not yet have the right to vote:

> The very fact that [Manitoba] women are recognized as voters has made a wonderful difference. The [provincial] government has recognized this fact in many ways. Very few boards have been appointed without some women, and in all public functions the right of women to some part has been recognized. It has all taken place without much fuss or blowing of trumpets, but it has taken place. Women have been appointed on the university council, on the board of studies, on the widows' pension board, and many others.[640]

Post suffrage, for the rest of 1916 and into early 1917, Beynon Thomas turned her attention and her considerable proselytizing energy to winning support for reforms to better protect the women and children whom she had championed throughout. She wrote columns on law reform in both the *Free Press*[641] and in *The Canadian Thresherman and Farmer*.[642] She addressed meetings,[643] including an address in June 1916, to the Saskatchewan Homemakers' Club, the organization that she had been instrumental in founding six years earlier and which was now holding its largest-ever convention. The *GGG* paraphrased her optimistic speech as follows:

> Politics, the supposedly evil and malign side of human life, was boldly introduced into the deliberations of the convention by Mrs. A.V. Thomas, who argued that politics touched every side of our lives, and that the sordidness of them was not a necessary attribute of politics, even of the party type, but a reproach to our own sense of honor and our ideals of citizenship. ... But the woman of today, having accomplished her political emancipation, has... set forth upon the high road. The new power combined with organization will enable women to accomplish almost anything they undertake, and the striving for things will develop and bring out all the latent powers in them. The three things which the speaker hoped those present would do something very definite about were the teaching of sex hygiene to children, medical aid for rural districts and the study of international relations.[644]

In a speech on January 11, 1917 to the Women's Auxiliary of the MGGA, which was meeting in Brandon in conjunction with the MGGA's annual convention, Beynon Thomas suggested that the need for rural hospitals, for medical inspection of rural schools, for home economics to be taught in those schools, and for the election of women to local school boards were all matters, "worthy of vigorous action."[645] Her views carried weight.

With suffrage attained, the PEL set about reinventing itself. At its annual convention on February 16, 1916, Francis Beynon, in her column in the *GGG*, reported that, "Like that legendary bird, the Phenix [*sic*], the Political Equality League of Manitoba has been transformed and taken on a new lease of life under the name, The Political Educational League of Manitoba [PEdL]."[646] The convention then set about determining "what women want."[647] Beynon Thomas reminded the gathering that under the existing guardianship laws, husbands were given exclusive guardianship rights to their legitimate children. She asked delegates, "How about seeing those mothers are given equal guardianship rights with fathers over the children?" She continued, "I would like, too, to see that the inheritance law is amended so that the father is not the sole heir of the child who dies without a will."[648]

The convention set up a Legislative Committee that systematically worked to develop proposals that would better the lot of women. During 1916, it "gathered material from the four corners of the earth, and... studied our laws and the laws of other countries and compared them and weighed their merits and defects."[649] On December 11, 1916 it brought forward to a meeting of the PEdL's district (city) executive, of which Beynon Thomas was now honourary president,[650] a law reform package consisting of draft legislative amendments to several acts.[651] The reform package included the following suggested amendments: a widow was to receive the first $2,500 from her late husband's estate regardless of his will or intestacy; a mother was to be given the right to inherit to the exclusion of the father should her illegitimate child for whom she had provided care died intestate; a mother was to have equal rights of guardianship as the father; women were to be given the same right to vote and to sit on municipal councils as men; and, in the absence of a dower law, the *Homestead Act* was to be amended to provide wives with protection should her husband attempt to sell or otherwise dispose of the family home.[652]

Following these discussions, the PEdL sent out 500 copies of the draft amendments to women's organizations throughout the province and invited comments.[653] The amendments were presented for input to the Winnipeg Branch of the Local Council of Women, representing nearly all organized women in Winnipeg. On January 11, 1917, Beynon Thomas presented them to the MGGA convention in Brandon.

Both organizations endorsed the amendments.[654] Armed with these endorsements, Beynon Thomas and the three other delegates from the PEdL met with Premier Norris and members of the government on January 23, 1917.[655] They presented their reform requests in the form of prepared amendments to the *Wills and Insolvency Act*, the *Infants' Act*, the *Homestead Act* and the *Municipal Act* in order that these amendments might be placed before the session of the Legislature then ongoing. At the end of the meeting, the Premier promised that the proposed amendments to laws to better protect women and children would be considered. He even intimated that some of the suggestions might be adopted. It all came to naught, however. The 1917 winter legislative session was nearing completion. It had been occupied almost entirely with reforms to education and with the conscription debate.

Given her earlier dower agitation, it is not surprising that Beynon Thomas's primary interest was in obtaining some kind of dower law. One option would have been to give a wife a one-third life interest in all lands possessed by her husband at any time during their marriage. This traditional approach would have created an unregistered interest in land, something that would have run counter to the Torrens land titles system in effect in Manitoba.[656] Another option would have been to prevent a husband from selling without his wife's written consent the home in which his wife and family lived. In rural areas the home was defined as the farmhouse in which the family lived together with a certain number of acres surrounding it. (In the city the home was defined as the house in which the family lived together with a certain number of the city lots upon which it sat.) This latter option was referred to as a 'homestead law', not to be confused with existing federal legislation that granted new settlers homesteading farms. It was the option adopted in Saskatchewan and Alberta because, being limited to the current home as opposed to all land possessed at any time during marriage, it did not interfere with land transfer as extensively as the more traditional approach.

Beynon Thomas ultimately came to favour this narrower homestead law approach. She offered her own justification for it, consistent with her views of women's equality. Partly as a result of urbanization, partly as a result of the war, she noted that, "[t]he tendency of the times appears to be toward economic independence for the married woman." She went on:

> The trend of modern life is more and more for women to be wage-earners and have their own property. ... To the modern business woman it appears too much to ask a man by the act of marriage to tie up all his property so that he may not sell, or mortgage, or trade without the consent of his wife. ... The modern business woman feels that way because she would not care to have her property tied up and subject to the whimsical consent of an inexperienced man. All the women want by the amendment to the present law is to protect the married woman and her children so that the home may not be taken from them...[657]

A dower act in the form of homestead legislation was passed the next year during the 1918 Session. Royal Assent was given on March 6, 1918. In his speech proroguing the 1918 Session, the Lieutenant-Governor stated that this act was, "in keeping with the recognition of the new status of womanhood of our province, and the great service they have rendered to the state in this time of war."[658] The new law came into effect on September 1, 1918. Beynon Thomas, however, had to witness all of this from afar, having left Manitoba in May 1917 to join her husband in voluntary exile in New York City. Their pacifist views had made Winnipeg too inhospitable for them to stay in the province, but her dower agitation had finally resulted in successful reform.

The Federal Franchise

During 1916 and early 1917, another matter apart from law reform preoccupied Beynon Thomas. The issue concerned the right of Manitoba women to vote in the Dominion election expected in late 1917.[659] The *Dominion Election Act*, as it applied to Manitoba, provided that "any person" who was eligible to vote in a provincial election was eligible to vote in a Dominion election.[660] The words "any person" were not gender qualified, possibly because at the time the legislation was put in place the probability of women obtaining the vote seemed remote. However, when Manitoba women obtained the provincial franchise in 1916, it appeared that they had also become eligible to vote in the next Dominion election. The situation was similar in British Columbia where women obtained the provincial franchise on April 5, 1917. There was a complication, however.[661] To be able to vote, one had to be registered on the voters list. The Dominion government generally used the provincial voters list for this. Where a provincial voters list was more than one year old, the Dominion government could, if it chose, draw up a new list. By the summer of 1915, the existing Manitoba provincial list was more than one year old and so did not, of course, contain the names of any women. The Dominion government decided to draw up a new list for use in Manitoba in the next Dominion election. After Manitoba women won the right to vote in 1916 and it became clear that women were intending to register in great numbers when the new Dominion list was being prepared, the federal government dropped its plans to draw up a new list. This manoeuvre left the old provincial list in place, thus throwing into doubt the ability of Manitoba women to vote in the 1917 Dominion election.

The situation was even more difficult for women in Saskatchewan and Alberta. The *Dominion Election Act*, as it was made to apply to these two new provinces when they joined confederation in 1905, stipulated that "any male person" entitled to vote in a provincial election would be entitled to vote federally. Francis Beynon, in her column in the *GGG*, referred to the "male" gender qualification as "a little joker which was slipped into the election act" so as to debar the women of Saskatchewan and Alberta, who had won the provincial franchise on March 14 and April 19, 1916, respectively, from voting federally.[662]

The right of women to vote in Dominion elections played out against the backdrop of World War I. Women who were pacifists and opposed to conscription held to the more traditional suffragette view favouring universal women's enfranchisement for Dominion elections. In the summer of 1916, the WCTU held a national conference in Winnipeg and passed a resolution calling on the federal government to grant all women the right to vote federally. Other women, anxious to support the war effort, were prepared to accept selective women's enfranchisement that would give the right to vote in the next Dominion election only to women born in Canada or Britain. They were prepared to see immigrant women born in foreign countries excluded from the Dominion franchise. They did not feel that they could count on the patriotic loyalty of these "alien" women whom they feared might cast anti-war votes.

During the last months of 1916, Beynon Thomas and Nellie McClung, by now the closest of suffragette allies and friends, found themselves on opposite sides of selective franchise/universal franchise debate. In early December 1916, Prime Minister Borden visited Winnipeg on a tour to recruit soldiers while Nellie McClung happened to be in the city. At a chance meeting, she suggested to Borden that she would, as a wartime expedient, be prepared to support the enfranchisement of Canadian- and British-born women even if the vote was not extended to other naturalized women who represented a significant portion of the female immigrant population. In other words, she was ready to support selective enfranchisement. McClung's rationale was that the votes of British and Canadian women were needed in constituencies where husbands and sons were absent at the front and where, as a result, the votes of male naturalized aliens risked the election of anti-war candidates. McClung also reasoned that suffragettes should take advantage of the opportunity that the War created to advance their cause. Partial enfranchisement was better than none at all and would help pave the way for full enfranchisement after the War. [663] Although she did not mention it, her support for the War effort may also have been influenced by the fact that her eldest son had volunteered and was serving on the front.[664]

McClung's position was immediately and strongly denounced by both Beynon Thomas and her sister Francis in their newspaper columns. Beynon Thomas editorialized that if a woman left her own country for Canada and was doing her part to make a decent home for her family and to raise her children as good citizens, then that woman's birthplace should be of no consequence in deciding her eligibility to vote.[665] She wrote:

It is opposed to the whole suffrage campaign (which has been based on democracy) to now ask for a federal franchise that will exclude some of the most prominent workers in the cause of suffrage. This week a letter from a Scandinavian woman, who had the vote before she left her home sixteen years ago, and from whose home town the bars [serving alcohol] had been banished, came protesting against any request for the franchise that would exclude such women as herself, who have made this country their home for sixteen years and worked to make it equal to the home they left.[666]

In a personal letter to her friend and Saskatchewan suffrage leader Violet McNaughton, Beynon Thomas wrote that the suffragists of Manitoba "would not hesitate to put up a fight" against the selective franchise, adding by way of reference to the ongoing War, "if democracy is of no use in a crisis, I am inclined to think it is no use anytime."[667] In her Country Homemakers column, Francis Beynon wrote: "I believe in democracy… and if a serious attempt is made to exclude these new women citizens from the franchise my tongue and pen will do their little part by way of protest."[668] Both women criticized McClung for voicing her opinion without consulting her suffragette colleagues.

By then, McClung, faced with the criticism of the Beynon sisters, retracted her position on selective enfranchisement in favour of giving all women a federal ballot. She wrote letters to both journalists, which they published.[669] The letters were similar. McClung made it clear that when she had earlier advanced the arguments in favour of selective enfranchisement that she was expressing her personal view only and not suffragette policy. "I quite realize that our forces must not divide," she wrote, "for the cause we stand for has in it the whole well-being of humanity and as such cannot be jeopardized by a difference of opinion over a method of procedure."[670] As a result, she agreed to change her position and support universal federal enfranchisement. Beynon Thomas praised McClung as someone who, "in her whole public life has stood for the principle of democracy."[671] In a similar vein, Francis Beynon referred to McClung as a "generous woman" and wrote that she was glad the two would, "still be able to work together as we have done in the past with so much pleasure and profit."[672]

Beynon Thomas's categorical rejection of McClung's selective enfranchisement position was not without contradiction. She had, herself, been strident in arguing that the federal franchise should only be extended to women in provinces where women had fought for and won the vote.[673] This was itself a kind of selective franchise, one based on provincial enfranchisement rather than country of birth.[674] In a letter to Violet McNaughton dated September 17, 1916, Beynon Thomas referred to women who had not fought for and won the provincial franchise but who now wished the Dominion franchise as "todies [sic]." She wrote, "When we have fought the fight we will be able to use it wisely. But the women who have not fought have no vision.[675]

In another letter to McNaughton, this one dated December 21, 1916, Beynon Thomas wrote that the Manitoba suffragette members of the PEdL, unlike suffragettes in other provinces, had not appointed two representatives to the Dominion Franchise Board, a women's lobby group established to pressure the federal government for female enfranchisement. According to Beynon Thomas, the Manitobans, contrary to "the majority of the [Dominion Franchise] Board," were not prepared to ask for a universal federal franchise that would benefit women who had not worked for and won the provincial franchise.[676] However, in mid-February 1917, Beynon Thomas did agree to serve as one of the two PEdL's representatives to the Dominion Franchise Board on the understanding that it would petition the federal government for universal rather than selective enfranchisement.[677] Perhaps she felt that she would have been able to convince "the great majority of the Board" that the Dominion franchise should not be granted to women who "consider it beneath them to work for the [provincial] franchise and be called suffragists."[678] Her agreement to serve as one of the PEdL's representatives on the Dominion Franchise Board was an indication that as of mid-February 1917 she had not yet decided to leave Winnipeg to join her husband in New York.

Beynon Thomas's columns during this period urged women to "keep on writing" in favour of reforming the *Dominion Election Act*: "It would be well for every woman in western Canada, to, as the children say when writing a letter, take their pen in hand and write a letter to Premier Borden and their Dominion member suggesting that at the coming session of the Dominion legislature, the Election act of the Dominion be changed to give the women who secure the provincial franchise, the federal franchise automatically, as it is given to the men."[679] She noted that it would be, "a sorry thing, for Canada to lag behind 'darkest Russia'."[680]

Beynon Thomas frequently addressed various audiences on the issue of the Dominion franchise. On January 11, 1917, she was invited to explain to the full body of the annual MGGA convention the federal voting rules as they affected women.[681] Following the talk, the MGGA approved a resolution supporting Beynon Thomas's position in favour of universal enfranchisement.[682] Two weeks later, Beynon Thomas addressed the WCTU on "Women and the Franchise."[683] On February 15, 1917, she spoke at the annual convention of the PEdL on the federal franchise.[684] Division within the ranks of the PEdL over the issues of conscription and the franchise immediately became evident. PEdL endorsed conscription by a standing vote of 15 to 6. The original leadership, including Dr. Mary Crawford, the outgoing president, and Beynon Thomas, the honourary president, voted against supporting conscription. Next, the PEdL sided with Beynon Thomas against any attempt to limit the franchise to British- and Canadian-born women.

McClung's initial declaration of support for selective enfranchisement may well have encouraged Prime Minister Borden to adopt selective enfranchisement as his government's policy. He may have felt that McClung's influential stature in the women's movement would result in the newly enfranchised women voters supporting his pro-war, pro-conscription Unionist party in the upcoming federal election.[685] In advance of that election, the Borden Government passed two pieces of electoral reform legislation, both of which came into force on September 20, 1917. On the one hand, women whom Borden considered more likely to support the war effort were enfranchised. The *Military Voters Act* gave the vote to British subjects, including women, who served in the Canadian forces. A companion piece of legislation, the *Wartime Elections Act*, gave the vote to women who were mothers, wives, sisters, or daughters of living or dead members of the Canadian or British military serving or who had served overseas during the War. On the other hand, women whom Borden considered less likely to support the war effort were denied the vote. The *Wartime Elections Act* disenfranchised "enemy-alien" citizens, including women naturalized after 1902.

Although McClung's flirtation with selective franchise lasted less than two months, it accentuated divisions in the PEdL that contributed to its demise[686] and provided Borden with an argument that was useful to him in his opposition to the universal enfranchisement of women at the federal level.[687] However, the damage that McClung's support for the selective franchise caused to her personal relationship with Beynon Thomas was more fleeting. The two were at the time, and continued to be, the closest of friends.

New York City

On the afternoon of January 17, 1917, and continuing into the session on January 18, Fred Dixon, "Independent Progressive" member for Winnipeg Center 'B', and a candidate for whom Beynon Thomas had actively campaigned during the 1914 and 1915 provincial elections, stood up in the Manitoba Legislature during the Debate in Reply to the Speech from the Throne, and denounced the War, blaming it on the military policy of all European nations, on the munitions makers, on economic repression, and on Germany's fear of unrest among its unemployed during the recession. He rejected conscription, arguing that the government should conscript wealth before men and stating that he would not sign a national registration card. He criticized Premier Norris for publicly suggesting that those who refused to sign cards should be jailed. At the adjournment on January 17, the press reported that the overflow crowd in the galleries and corridor, many of whom had relatives in the trenches, greeted Dixon's remarks with a "silence, pregnant with suppressed emotion."[688]

When the session adjourned for the day, Dixon asked for permission to conclude his speech the next day. His request was granted, and the

Evening Tribune described that "Two *Free Press* reporters hurried from the press gallery and congratulated Mr. Dixon on his 'great speech'."[689] One of those reporters was Vernon Thomas. Shortly thereafter, *Free Press* editor John Dafoe, who had two soldier sons at the front and not much patience with pacifists, fired Thomas.[690] Several weeks later, Thomas left permanently for New York City where he found work on the New York *Journal of Commerce*.[691] Thomas earned six dollars more a week than he had been getting at the *Free Press* in Winnipeg.[692] Still, there was bitterness about the way in which he had been treated by Dafoe. Francis Beynon wrote to Violet McNaughton with the news: "I didn't have an opportunity to tell you about the turn our affairs have taken. When I got home from Edmonton I found that Mr. Thomas had been dismissed from the *Free Press* editorial staff for shaking hands with Mr. Dixon on the floor of the house. That's how much freedom there is left in this country."[693]

Beynon Thomas carried on briefly with her planned activities, although she must have felt increasingly uncomfortable. On January 23, 1917, less than a week after her husband had walked onto the floor of the Legislature to publicly support Dixon's criticisms of Premier Norris's pro-conscription stance, she was part of the four-person delegation that met with the Premier to press for the law reforms, including homestead dower, advocated by the PEdL.[694] A year earlier, she had manoeuvred to force the Premier to allow women to stand for election to the provincial Legislature, something that had resulted in the Premier refusing to speak to her.[695] By early April 1917, she had made the decision to move to New York City.[696] Apart from being reunited with her husband, NYC had another attraction. Her sister had spent several weeks on holiday in August 1916 taking a creative writing course at Columbia University.[697] Francis must have enjoyed her time there because she later described it as "that Mecca of all writers on this continent."[698] This would have caught Beynon Thomas's attention for she had already had several of her own short stories accepted for publication by such Canadian mass-market magazines as *Maclean's*, *Chatelaine*, *Canadian Courier* and *Canada Monthly* and such American ones as *Saturday Evening Post*, *New Story Magazine*, *Red Book and Colliers*.[699]

Beynon Thomas left Winnipeg on good terms with her journalist and suffragist colleagues. The haste of her departure was evident from the speed with which the testimonials arrived. On April 21, 1917, Nellie McClung, then living in Edmonton, wrote to Beynon Thomas, "acknowledging her great devotion to the cause of women." She continued, "I am glad that your way and mine lay together for four good busy years, when it was my good fortune to work beside you and share your wise counsels and your delightful companionship." She pledged that "time or distance will never dim or fade the strong affection which knits our souls together."[700]

Beynon Thomas was much feted during the last week of April. At its regular weekly afternoon meeting, Harriet Walker presiding, the CWPC presented Beynon Thomas with a gold pin set with turquoise and pearls, "in recognition of her long standing connection with the club and in view of her early departure to live in New York."[701] Beynon Thomas signed the club's Minute Book with heartfelt and, as it turned out, prophetic words, "This is not good-bye."[702] The PEdL held a farewell reception and program of music at which the Winnipeg Branch presidents and Beynon Thomas received the guests.[703] On May 1, the Laura Secord Branch of the League PEdL, of which Beynon Thomas was the charter president, held an evening in her honour hosted in the home of Jane Hample.[704] Beynon Thomas was presented with "a purse of gold" and a scroll reading: "The history of our League shows that not only were you the original mover in the forming of our Society but that we owe to your good judgment and self sacrificing labours a large measure of the success which has attended us in obtaining the vote for the women of Manitoba. ... We realize that not only our League but others in this City owe their beginning to your efforts and that to the women of the rural districts of our Province you have given sympathising support in the solving of their problems."[705]

It was important to Beynon Thomas that organizations could flourish without her at the helm, but from the accolades bestowed upon her, it is clear that these organizations were well aware of her work in establishing them and maintaining them.

On May 2, the day of her departure, Beynon Thomas's last column appeared in the *Prairie Farmer*. It began with the poignant words,

"Everything comes to an end... it is 'good-bye'." She reminisced about the evolution of the Home Loving Hearts page over its decade of existence. Then, in two short sentences, she summarized the overarching goal of her journalistic efforts, and declared success. "Four walls no longer bind the minds of our women," she wrote. "They have reached out to the district, then to the nation, and now, it is with the great international problems they are wrestling," the latter referring to the ongoing war. She advised that she was "leaving letters on hand" for publication until the new editor could take over and that for the next month, she would send articles from the south so that her readers could "follow her wanderings." She used her last words to express the hope that "this page has made even one independent thinker more," and then she laid down her MBA pen.[706] And that was that. The day after her departure, the *Free Press* reported: "Scores of friends of Mrs. A.V. Thomas gathered at the C.P.R. station yesterday afternoon to bid her farewell. Mrs. Thomas is en route to join her husband, a former member of the *Free Press* staff ..."[707]

On May 16, 1917, Francis wrote in her Country Homemakers column in the *GGG*, about what it was like to travel with her sister from Winnipeg to the Manitoba border. "I had occasion the other day," she wrote, "to accompany a lady of excellent repute in this country to the immigration office to secure a passport. She entered jauntily feeling that, being a respectable wage-earning adult, the neighbours across the line would be very glad to have her as a citizen. As a beginning they fined her eight dollars for daring to cross the boundary into their territory and they held an inquisition." Francis went on to tell of how the immigration officer aggressively interrogated her sister, especially about the fact that her sister, and not her sister's husband, was paying for her travel ticket. Francis noted that this "scandalized" the immigration officer and drew the conclusion that, "Apparently a woman capable of supporting herself was not nearly so desirable a citizen as one who had to depend upon some man for support." After being queried over a number of insignificant details of a trip she once took to Britain, Beynon Thomas was then turned over to a male doctor who asked, "such intimate personal questions as one might expect from one's own family doctor."[708] With this final challenge to her independence from uncomprehending male officialdom behind her, Beynon Thomas was off to join her husband in New York City [NYC] to start of a new chapter in her life.[709]

Francis Beynon left her position as women's editor at the *GGG* and arrived in NYC on June 30, 1917, to join her sister and brother-in-law in voluntary exile.[710] She brought news of how difficult times had been for her in Winnipeg over the last few months. Latterly the total number of returning soldiers on Winnipeg streets had greatly increased, many of them severely injured. An anti-conscription meeting had to be cancelled even though legal. It could not be held for fear of bloodshed after the police refused to be responsible for order if the meeting went ahead.[711]

Beynon Thomas planned to take up short story writing in NYC.[712] Following her sister's earlier example, she enrolled in a post-graduate course in short story writing at Columbia University. She studied under Dr. Blanche Colton Williams and got to know the students in her class as they perfected their craft. Dr. Colton Williams was a noted American Professor of English, author, and writer of the leading 1917 text *A Handbook on Short Story Writing*, (1917) which emphasized the principles of short story structure. Beynon Thomas also became especially interested in drama, attending plays in the NYC theatre district almost daily and enrolling in a course in writing drama.[713]

In the first week of December 1917, Nellie McClung, who was on a speaking tour of the United States, wired from Boston that she would be arriving in NYC the next day to visit Beynon Thomas and her husband overnight before going on to Washington, D.C. where she was to address a convention of American suffragists. If there had been any lingering awkwardness arising out of the tension a year earlier owing to their difference over the enfranchisement of foreign women during the War, that was well behind them. Vernon's affection for McClung was evident in his report to J.S. Woodsworth on the visit: "I believe that she is a good person, earnestly anxious to do good. She has her oldest boy on the front, in the trenches, a mere boy, and so there you are. It is difficult for her to think that it is all wrong. Yet in her heart she hates war and well knows that it is wrong. We must remember that she has travelled a long way from the prejudices in which she was brought up."[714]

During this time, Beynon Thomas was sending Gertrude Richardson, her old suffrage comrade from Swan River, Manitoba, articles about opposition to the War in NYC. Gertrude had started a Peace Crusade and Beynon Thomas, an avowed pacifist, acted as one of her foreign correspondents.[715] Vernon carried on an active correspondence with his friend, J.S. Woodsworth, in which they shared their pacifist feelings about the War.

Early in her NYC stay, Beynon Thomas became interested the work that the Episcopal Church was doing aiding sailors through the Seaman's Church Institute of New York. Founded in 1834, the Institute provided temporary shelter for seamen from around the world who arrived at the Port of New York. In 1913, the Institute opened a twelve-storey building at 25 South Street in lower Manhattan, complete with a lighthouse structure on the top. By 1919, it was providing dormitory lodgings for seamen along with a lunch counter, a lost and found department, a library and reading room, a storage area for baggage, a Seaman's Bank for Savings, a Navigation and Marine Engineering School, an employment bureau, a post office, and a chapel. A distinctive, functioning lighthouse, paid for from public donations, and dedicated to the memory of the passengers and crew who perished with the *Titanic*, was erected on one corner of the building.

Sometime in 1918 Beynon Thomas began to write reports for the Institute's monthly magazine, *The Lookout*, on the need to create more humane conditions for sailors. By 1919 she was asked to edit the magazine.[716] It was a natural fit. Instead of editing a women's page dedicated to helping isolated rural Manitoba women, she found herself editing a magazine dedicated to helping lonely sailors far from home. Beynon Thomas wrote heroic stories of sailors often down on their luck, but she also used her pen to plea for donations from her readers to enable the Institute to continue its work:

The Seamen's Church Institute has had no small part in changing the conditions on the waterfront. It has provided a home for the nearly eight hundred men in wholesome surroundings. It has provided two doctors to care for their health and four Chaplains and a House Mother to care for their other needs. ... Unless we get more help from our friends there will have to be retrenchment, and it will have to be in the social and welfare work. We will have fewer concerts and religious services. We will have to stop visiting the sick and caring for those in trouble. ... In other words, we have built up a great institution, and led the men to expect help when they are in trouble. Now in their greatest need we will have to fail them, unless we are more generously supported. It is a matter of dollars and cents.[717]

The Seamen's Church Institute at 25 South Street, circa 1917. Note the lighthouse tower at the top of the building. SOURCE: CRONOBOOK

Beynon Thomas had a second task at *The Lookout*. She published a weekly bulletin, posted in sixty-four ports around the world, whose purpose was to reunite missing seamen with their families. Circumstances varied as Beynon Thomas explained: "A sailor is the easiest person in the world to lose! Often their families are poor and forced to move from place to place during the long absence of their men folk and so are lost. Often the sailor himself wishes to be lost. Sometimes a young man runs away to sea against his parents' wishes; sometimes domestic infelicity encourages a man to vanish, or a disgraced man wants to efface his memory."[718] In her tracing activity, Beynon Thomas enlisted worldwide contacts amongst sea captains and crews, seaport dwellers and sweethearts, and the police. In earlier times Beynon Thomas facilitated contact between isolated farm wives, seeking and giving advice by arranging for an exchange of letters between them through the Mutual Benefit Association columns in the *Prairie Farmer*. Now, in New York, she used the resources of *The Lookout* to help missing seamen and their relatives make contact by putting them in touch with each other through an exchange of addresses.

Beynon Thomas and Vernon were comfortable in NYC, but they missed Winnipeg and felt cut off from their friends.[719] Vernon, even though he was getting a very close view of American industrial and financial organization, and even though he had a higher salary than he had had in Winnipeg, felt uneasy about his employment. For one thing, he was not sure how long his job at the *Journal of Commerce* would last. For another, he chaffed at working for the "ordinary, daily newspaper press" with limits beyond which a journalist could not go. He hoped to find work either writing more in-depth articles unconstrained by conservative editors or working as an activist promoting his pacifist and social justice principles. He was anxious to "quit just earning a salary." He thought about searching for a less restrictive journalistic forum that would still provide him "with a modest living."[720] Conditions in Winnipeg were improving. With the arrival of peacetime, Vernon believed that "war mania was dying down a good deal…"[721] He was encouraged by the results of the 1920 provincial election in which Premier Norris's seat count was cut in half and his government was reduced to a minority. He was especially pleased with the election of eleven Labour/Socialist candidates led by

Fred Dixon.[722] In any event, he decided to leave NYC. The Canadian Immigration Service recorded that Vernon, occupation "newspaperman," returned to Canada in August 1921 to seek employment.[723] He found work with the *Winnipeg Tribune* where he soon rose to become the well-respected Municipal Editor, doing the kind of in-depth journalism that he yearned for, although not as a champion of pacifist causes. Instead, he made reporting of municipal ownership of utilities his journalistic specialty until his retirement in 1944.[724]

During this period, Beynon Thomas had a health scare. Though the nature of this health scare is unclear, it was evidently quite serious. On March 21, 1942, in a letter of condolence to Lucy Woodsworth on the death of her husband, J.S. Woodsworth, Beynon Thomas recounted how she had nearly died while being operated on in New York, "I was so close that in some strange way I looked over the edge."[725] In May 1922, her name appeared for the last time as editor on the masthead of *The Lookout*. She returned to Winnipeg to rejoin her husband, who was also having health difficulties. In an article in the June 1922 edition of *The Lookout*, Archibald Mansfield, Superintendent of the Seamen's Institute, remarked on Beynon Thomas's, "broad sympathy, her dry humor, her shrewd and tolerant insight into human frailties…" and described her going as, "an irreparable loss to the Institute."[726]

Francis, who had been doing publicity work in the Institute's Ways and Means Department, took over Beynon Thomas's job as editor of *The Lookout*. In the years that followed, Beynon Thomas's summertime vacations saw her returning often to NYC to visit her sister, to renew literary acquaintances, and to do occasional editorial work. Whatever her health scares had been in 1922, she evidently felt comfortable travelling again. In the decade following her departure from New York, she visited Vancouver, Victoria, Ottawa, Quebec, Fredericton, and Halifax. In August 1934, she toured Manitoba, including a visit to Churchill on Hudson Bay.[727] She wrote about her visit to the northern port in the *Winnipeg Tribune* in one of a series of articles "Abroad in Manitoba", published in the fall of 1934, that chronicled her travels by car throughout Manitoba that summer.[728] After decades of activism at home, she was finally getting a chance to see the broader world.

CHAPTER 7

The Urge to Write

Writing Classes

As a young person, Beynon Thomas harbored a "girlish urge to write."[729] She left the teaching profession, one of the few occupations open to her, for journalism, where she learned the power that words could exert while editing the Home Loving Hearts women's page. Taking refuge in NYC in order to escape the jingoism of World War I Winnipeg, she not only found work as the editor of the Seaman's Institute monthly, she also took the opportunity to study short story writing classes at Columbia University. In addition, she regularly attended theatre. Upon her return to Winnipeg, she eschewed journalism, possibly feeling alienated after her husband's experience with Dafoe and the *Free Press* and, as she indicated, "preferring to select her own themes and make her own working time" as an author and playwright.[730] In order to supplement her income, she started to offer adult short story writing courses in her home modeled on those she had taken at Columbia.

On September 18, 1922, she advertised in the *Winnipeg Tribune*: "SHORT STORY COURSE. Based on Columbia University methods.

Applications being received for class beginning Oct. 1st."[731] From that time until 1947,[732] when she was 73 years old, she advertised in both Winnipeg dailies for students for three-month courses starting most years at either the beginning of October or the beginning of January. Her course offerings ranged from those on technique and construction to English composition, and were designed for beginners, advanced students, and reporters. Some classes could be taken by correspondence. Sometimes the advertisements listed examples of Beynon Thomas's short story publishing successes; sometimes they mentioned that her students were selling their stories to leading Canadian and American fiction magazines.

Beynon Thomas's students, whose numbers included Gabrielle Roy,[733] appreciated her efforts. She was demanding and insisted on output.[734] Following advice that she had received at Columbia, she told students that if they got an idea, they should get it down on paper: "So many people talk about what they want to write, but never write it."[735] She recommended that students select their "type of story ... what [they] best knew to write about."[736] She encouraged them to keep on trying.[737] Students recalled how she was a master of the art of giving criticism and advice kindly, how they learned to take and give criticism of each other's work at their weekly classes,[738] and how she was able to smooth out any clash of opinion so that meetings ended happily.[739] Many of Beynon Thomas's students had their short stories accepted for publication.[740]

Over the twenty-five years that Beynon Thomas's classes ran, the alumnae formed three separate clubs. On May 31, 1924, a group of students from the first two years of short story classes got together at Beynon Thomas's home and formed the Short Story Club. Beynon Thomas was made the honourary president. In 1932, a second group of alumnae formed the Inkslingers Club. Beynon Thomas was invited to be the head table guest at their first annual dinner held on May 26, 1937. Although the focus of these two clubs was encouraging and critiquing members' writing, there was an important social aspect to their activities. Year-end banquets were a staple. Current short story class students were almost always invited to join. Frequently, events were organized jointly with other literary groups, most notably the Winnipeg Writers' Club and the

Winnipeg Branch of the Canadian Authors Association.[741] A third group of Beynon Thomas's alumnae organized the Pen-Handlers Club in 1940. This was a more studious affair. The membership, made up of professional Winnipeg women writers, originally consisted of ten graduates of Beynon Thomas's courses. Eventually membership was limited to sixteen writers and was by invitation only. Each member read and had her work critiqued at least twice a year. Rules were strict. "Girl-talk," recipes, and children were verboten as conversation topics.[742]

Not all of Beynon Thomas's teaching took place in her short story courses. After her return from NYC, she constantly found herself at the podium as a speaker invited to instruct on the craft of short story writing. These invitations must have been welcome, in part because they confirmed her growing reputation in Winnipeg as a leading author publishing in both Canadian and American mass-market fiction magazines, and in part because they gave her an occasion to advertise the availability of her courses. She lectured on topics ranging from "The Short Story" to "Fiction in Modern Education" with audiences including the Winnipeg Teachers' Club and the Winnipeg branches of the Canadian Authors Association and the Women's Press Club. She also took time to encourage the playwriting aspirations of high school students. In November 1939, she gave a talk at Gordon Bell High School to eighty-five students in the writers' club on the topic of writing radio plays.[743] From time to time she adjudicated writing competitions in which aspiring young authors participated.[744]

Writing Method

The mass-market, or pulp fiction magazine[745] industry, was thriving during the inter-war period. Demand for magazine advertising had been increasing since the late nineteenth-century industrial expansion in the United States. Magazines needed copy to carry their advertising. Stories that were light, exciting, and upbeat were in demand.[746] The same was true in Canada, although in 1913 E. Cora Hind regretted that the low prices paid by Canadian magazines meant that anyone who wished to make an income from their pen had to send their best efforts south of the border.[747] In 1936, at a lecture attended by Beynon Thomas's short-story class, Byrne Hope Sanders, editor of *Chatelaine* magazine, explained what women's magazines were looking for from a Canadian perspective: "What is needed for the woman's magazine today are 'escape' stories and topical articles of interest to women from coast to coast. Women love to imagine themselves in glamorous situations." Hope Sanders gave as examples stories of 'young love'. She went on to set out the three main requirements for a saleable manuscript: a good story, a knowledge of the technique of story writing, and submission to the proper magazine market to which the story would be of interest.[748]

Beynon Thomas was suited by disposition and life experience to be a writer. She was curious by nature. In October 1932, she told an interviewer, "I like folks. ... I think all new ideas have an impact on life, gradually changing people. I am extremely interested in everything."[749] Her curiosity extended to the past: "As a child I often liked to imagine what period of history I would have liked to live in."[750] It also extended to the future. In 1946, she published her first novel, *New Secret*, an exploration of what the development of the atomic bomb might mean for ordinary people. To do this, she abandoned an historical novel that she had been writing.[751] She felt that 'the bomb' was a topic that should concern everyone.[752] Seven years after the book was published, Beynon Thomas, then 76, told an interviewer, "I'm glad to be living in an age of such perplexing problems. They present a challenge to all thinking Canadians."[753]

Beynon Thomas's fictional characters reflected her empathy for folks who were down on their luck. One interviewer felt that her characters had, "the vitality of living people. ... They are the reflection of life itself seen through the keen mind of a tolerant observer. Love of humanity is the keynote of Beynon Thomas's personality."[754] The April 1932 issue of the Winnipeg Little Theatre publication, *The Bill*, featured a story on Beynon Thomas's three-act play, *Among the Maples*. The play took place on an Ontario farm in the early 1890s. It noted her creation of, "real characters who live revealed as they are by a sympathetic understanding of human nature."[755] This was particularly true of her women characters, who were often portrayed as hard working, struggling heroines who resolved crises that frequently required them to rescue their families from poverty or from weak men.

Beynon Thomas's men tended to be weak figures who were bullies, or were inconsiderate, or who drank too much, or were victims of unfortunate circumstances that they were unable to overcome. In her three-act play about the youthful development of Abraham Lincoln, *As the Twig is Bent*, young Abe's father constantly scolds Abe for his interest in education and urges his son to follow him instead into farming. Abe's stepmother, however, supports his reading and education despite his father's objections. Eventually, the father yields to his wife and son.[756] In Beynon Thomas's novel, *New Secret*, the main protagonist, a young husband returning from the Second World War, could see little reason to live in a world where the atomic bomb might destroy everything in an instant. However, his wife, "Little Dutch," short for "Little Duchess," was patient while he went off in search of himself. She ultimately preserved their home by giving birth to their son, which gave her husband "something meaningful to live for." One reviewer noted, "The characterization of 'Little Dutch' is excellently done, standing out in sharp contrast to the portrait of her husband."[757]

Beynon Thomas's stories and plays generally featured domestic scenes set in rural and small-town locales. When she was 71, she told a reviewer that, "There's something very fine about small-town life and the environment makes for a more individualistic type of person—the sort of person who makes an ideal character for a short story."[758] She drew upon her experience growing up, teaching, and travelling in rural Manitoba to create her plots and characters. Her understanding of rural life and its problems was also informed by her editorship of the women's pages. The setting for her play, *Among the Maples*, was captured in a description by one of the play's reviewers: "From the glimpse through the frosted windows of snow banks piled high, through which meander the old snake fences of pioneer Ontario, to the very last detail of the cozy farm kitchen with its cellar trap, its polished plates, and the old copies of 'Globe' in the paper holder on the wall, it brought back memories of many a home back east, and many a one transplanted west."[759] Another reviewer added even more detail: "the bootjack, the water pail, the trap door to the cellar, with its store of strawberry and rhubarb preserves, the woodshed and the spotless kitchen equipment, were all there."[760]

Beynon Thomas's technique of story writing had its origin in Dr. Colton Williams' short story writing courses at Columbia University.[761] The Columbia University method stressed the elements of composition. Beynon Thomas adopted this approach in her most successful short story, "Five Cents for Luck."[762] W.R. Kane, editor of *The Editor Magazine*, wrote to her in September 1927 asking if she would outline for his readers the genesis and development of the story. She replied:

> Five Cents for Luck... like most of my short stories, was comparatively easy to write after—and that after means a lot—I had written the introduction. The story was written in a week for a competition in a Canadian magazine. Four days of the week were spent on the introduction—three days sufficed for the body and conclusion. ... I wrote seven thousand words in order to get less than three hundred words of introduction. My greatest difficulty is getting the proper angle of narration. ... My second difficulty is mood. That difficulty is solved by the time the introduction is satisfactory. It is likely that the mood influences my choice of the angle of narration. ... My plots grow out of an incident that has intrigued my imagination and touched my emotions. ... After I have introduced my main character, the trait of character that is going to dominate the story, the mood, the atmosphere, the situation, a hint of the complication or the full complication, the necessary back history, and if possible started the action, I mentally picture my story in definite scenes as one does a play. Each scene has its beginning, middle and end, or climax, all leading just a step nearer the final climax.[763]

Plot, with its elements, dominant storyline, subplots, crisis, climax, happy resolution, and moral lesson, was integral to the short story.[764]

Her plotlines, reflecting her mass circulation magazine audience, were simple, often romantic. She used plot to carry themes that conveyed a strong moral message, much as a parable would. "Good," after much struggle and hardship, invariably won out. Endings were happy for decent folk. The mood was often humorous and there was frequently a strong romantic element.[765]

Short Stories and a Novel

While she was conducting her short story courses and emphasizing productivity to her students, Beynon Thomas was providing an example. Just as she had advised her students, she too wrote "what she best knew."[766] Except for the period when she was living in NYC and for several years after her return to Winnipeg while she was recovering her health, she was publishing.[767] Her lifetime literary output included eleven articles, one of which was published in a scholarly journal; twenty-seven short stories published in at least sixteen Canadian and American fiction magazines; ten plays, either one, two or three acts in length; and one novel. This catalogue does not even take into account her journalistic work.

Beynon Thomas's stories won prizes. "Life Demanded Too Much," was awarded $1,000, one of three prizes in the January–May 1935 *True Story Magazine* manuscript contest sponsored by Macfadden Publications, Inc. In his letter to Beynon Thomas advising her of the award, Bernarr Macfadden wrote, "It will interest you to know that your story stood out among the many submittals as a most vivid and compelling experience."[768] In June 1936 *True Story Magazine* published a second short story, "Sheltered Woman," which also was awarded a $1,000 prize.[769] Macfadden Publications awarded Beynon Thomas a third $1,000 prize, this time for "Love the Conqueror," which was successful in the September–November 1936 *True Story* manuscript competition.[770]

In September 1927, Beynon Thomas published "Five Cents for Luck," her most successful short story. It was the winning entry, out of 936 submissions,[771] in *Maclean's* magazine first-ever short story contest.[772] Beynon Thomas submitted her story under the pseudonym

"L.N. Soames."[773] Judging was blind.[774] Both members of the judging panel, Dr. George Locke, Chief Librarian of the City of Toronto and President of the American Library Association, and Professor M.W. Wallace, head of the Department of English in the University of Toronto, felt that Beynon Thomas's submission was the best. Mazo de la Roche, who entered the contest with her story, "Good Friday," placed third behind Beynon Thomas.[775]

"Five Cents for Luck" was a poignant story. It told of a destitute home-steading family whose crops had failed for three consecutive years owing to hail, drought, and frost. The family clung to the hope that better times were ahead with the coming of a railroad spur line. Jim, the husband, had to find work in Regina. The couple's son needed new boots, but when enough money was scraped together and the boots arrived, they were both for the same foot. The son became desperately sick from being chilled due to his leaky old boots. His ever-optimistic mother, Jean, realized that she was down to her last five cents. She was ready to use it to write to her husband and say that she was abandoning the farm and would come to Regina with the children to do odd jobs. She happened to hear that the long-awaited railroad line was coming nearby. She met the train with twenty dozen eggs that her chickens had laid. The superintendent on the train remembered the struggle that his grandmother had had when she had nothing to sell except butter. The superintendent bought the eggs, placed a regular order for the future, and offered Jim work on the line. Jean assured him that the country near her farm through which the rail line was being built was a "great country." The story ended with the superintendent muttering, "A great country! God, how could it be anything else, with such stuff going into its making." Beynon Thomas explained that the inspiration for her story came directly from her contact with Prairie women: "'Five Cents for Luck' grew out of a story told to me by a pioneer woman, about sending for boots for her son, and when they came, ninety miles across the prairie, they were both for one foot—such a little thing but so terribly important."[776]

"Five Cents for Luck" was a story of the triumph of the human spirit over harsh Prairie conditions. It was also a story of the strength of a simple

FROM TOP, CLOCKWISE

"She raised her hand and placed her lips where her husband's hand had rested." Sketch of husband leaving for work in the city and his wife returning to the farm for the winter. "Five Cents for Luck," winner of short story contest. SOURCE: *MACLEAN'S MAGAZINE*, SEPTEMBER 15, 1927, P. 3.

"'Give me back that letter and the nickel. I'm going to have one more try,' she said." Sketch of wife saying the she would not abandon the farm and join her husband in the city but would try once more, despite their poverty, to save the farm. "Five Cents for Luck." SOURCE: *MACLEAN'S MAGAZINE*, SEPTEMBER 15, 1927, P. 5.

Lillian Beynon Thomas. SOURCE: *MACLEAN'S MAGAZINE*, MAY 1, 1927, P. 10.

woman, a heroine facing insurmountable odds who would not give up. She fought to the end and saved her family and the farm. The story was developed almost entirely through dialogue. It could have been the script for a stage play. The characters were very human, very real; one empathized with them quickly. Beynon Thomas was possibly writing about her own mother who worked herself to the bone raising her family and about her father who moved from job to job, never enjoying real success in any endeavour. In the case of the Beynons, there was no happy ending, no five cents for luck. Beynon Thomas's mother died of cancer; her father became "physically ailing, his manner distracted and erratic and not simply contentious."[777] In the end, unlike the wife in the story who did not have to move from the farm to Regina, Beynon Thomas did have to make her way to the city, to Winnipeg, to build her career. The story was rooted in Western Canadian settler reality and in family values.

The announcement of the short story contest winners was carried in many Canadian newspapers, including in *The Globe*, at the end of April 1927.[778] First prize came with an offer of publication in *Maclean's* and $500, the equivalent of $4,300 in today's currency. When *The American Magazine* expressed an interest in publishing the story, the *Maclean's* editor agreed to withhold publication in his magazine until September 1927 so that the story could appear roughly simultaneously in Canada and the United States.[779] He negotiated a further $500 publication fee for Beynon Thomas for the American rights making her story a very profitable venture indeed.[780]

There is a pattern to many of Beynon Thomas's stories: rural settings, poor folk, hardship, a plot developed through dialogue, good ultimately triumphing over evil, and a moral lesson to be drawn. The main character in "Rubber Heels"[781] was a country doctor who valued "tough and hardy" folks over "pampered" folks, whom he called "rubber heels," because they always had a shock absorber between them and the "real" things of life. Some years earlier, the doctor had broken off his engagement with a city woman whom he loved, because he thought that she was too pampered to lead the difficult life on the remote prairie. Chance brought her to the rural community where the doctor was practising. She proved to him that she was as tough as he was when he was obliged to call on her assistance in dealing with an isolated, at-risk woman who was about to give birth. As a result, the doctor was forced to admit his error in ending their earlier romance. Beynon Thomas concluded that the doctor then did, "what any sensible man would do in the circumstances."

"Lights in the Window"[782] opened with a classic domestic farm scene: "Mother Carson was slicing potatoes into the frying pan, watching baby Marie to see that she did not fall off the couch...". Mother Carson, a farm wife, was close to her eighteen-year-old son and depended on him to run the farm while her husband searched in town for much needed work for the winter. She became jealous when her son started to show an interest in the nineteen-year-old rural schoolteacher who was boarding with the family. When her son saved the teacher's life during a fire at the farmhouse, the mother realized that he and the teacher were in love. After recalling her selfish parents' objection to her own marriage at a young age, she accepted that there was room in her son's life for both his girlfriend and his mother.

"Jimmy's Perfect Day"[783] followed the usual formula. The story began with Jimmy's parents, struggling Prairie farmers. Beth, Jimmy's mother, was seen busy wringing out the living-room curtains and holding them up to consider how she could turn them so that the necessary darning would not show. She was preparing a perfect day for Jimmy's tenth birthday tomorrow, a day when the doctor was expected to confirm that he had recovered his ability to walk and could abandon his crutches. On the day of the party, a hailstorm blew in and destroyed the crop on which Jimmy's parents were depending to meet their debt on their farm. Jimmy's parents went ahead with the party despite this. The neighbours, decent folk, having watched the parents persevere with the party in order to make their son's day perfect, were so impressed that they put up a loan that saved the farm and made the day truly perfect.

Beynon Thomas's last short story, "Hugh Dorion Comes Home," started with the usual scene of Prairie domesticity: "Hugh Dorion strolled into the farm house kitchen. ... He stopped beside the kitchen table where his sister Beth was putting chocolate icing on a cake."[784] Hugh was returning from World War II with a "bum arm and a game leg," which greatly affected his mobility. Before the War he had excelled at everything, especially sports. He looked forward to taking over the farm and had a high school sweetheart who he had known from childhood. However, he was in despair fearing that all of that was in the past given his physical condition. Shortly after returning, he went out into a field to recover a goose that had been injured by a hunter. The goose was struggling to get away. Ultimately, the bird found the strength to take flight. Hugh asked himself, "Could he do as the goose was doing, get so busy finding out what he could do he wouldn't have time to think about what he couldn't?... Could life again be an adventure?"[785] Hugh realized that he could still farm: "There was the earth and the sun and the rain and the wind and the seasons and he was there to work with them. Just to be alive was an adventure."[786] As with so many of Beynon Thomas's stories, a homespun piece of wisdom led to a happy ending. The story of how an injured veteran overcame his disability would have been welcomed by the author's immediate post-war readers.

In 1946, at age 72, Beynon Thomas wrote her first novel, something that years earlier she had hoped to do. In *New Secret*,[787] young Bob Harrow, former prisoner of war, returned to his rural farm home but was unable to pick up where he left off. He was despondent over the destructive power of the newly split atom: "I want manufacturers to stop making goods; I want farmers to stop sowing seed; I want men and women to refuse to bring children into the world until we face the fact that straight ahead suicide for the world..."[788] He became estranged from his wife and returned to college where he was recruited to do work on an atomic bomb project because of the specialized knowledge that he had gained in university science studies undertaken before the War. Bob ran across an ex-girlfriend from high school who was mixed up with a spy ring that was interested in any information about the bomb that Bob might possess. What followed were scenes in which drinks were spiked and sentries were overpowered. Bob ultimately had his faith in living restored by a minister who convinced him that the adoption of Christian principles would help humanity channel its God-given creative impulse in constructive ways. He was also helped by a scientist friend who suggested that nuclear fission offered good possibilities such as cancer research. Bob's wife gave birth to their son. "Ever since the night my son was born," Bob concluded, "I have realized there is some living force in this world—call it Life, God, whatever you like—that is worth living for and I'm going to live for it."[789]

New Secret dealt with the impact that splitting the atom would have on individual lives and on the human race. Strong emotion moved Beynon Thomas to find a philosophy for the atomic age: "I was working on an historical novel, but when I heard the first reports of the atomic bomb, I decided that here was something more important to write about."[790] She recounted the origins of her book in a speech that she made to the Winnipeg Branch of the Canadian Authors Association: "A group of scientists came to Winnipeg. They were entertained by the Astronomical Society. At dinner I sat beside a man who talked about splitting the atom. After that I read everything I saw. Why did I? I don't know. I felt desperate. I couldn't sleep. So I wrote *New Secret* from what was in my heart."[791] It is not surprising that Beynon Thomas found herself at a dinner hosted by the Astronomical Society. Her husband, Vernon, was a member of the Winnipeg Centre Royal Astronomical Society and contributed the monthly "Star Map" feature in *The Winnipeg Tribune*.[792] Nellie McClung suggested *New Secret* as the book's title.[793] The secret revealed in the book was that atomic fission could be used not only for destruction, as was the case with its well-known use in the bomb, but also for good, as was the case with its lesser known potential for treating cancer and for supplying energy for the production of comfortable homes and nutritious food.[794]

The book received mixed reviews. Those offering praise called the book, "definitely a book to read."[795] It was described as a "novel of today,"[796] the first to deal with an urgent issue, "the fictional possibilities of atomic energy as a book-length story."[797] Nellie McClung wrote: "It is constructive… It's swift moving and dramatic and reads like a Perry Mason thriller, but it makes its impression. I believe it will really help young people especially."[798] The *Globe and Mail* described *New Secret* as a "simple, well-constructed novel of novelette length."[799] One critic said, "The characters are crystal clear, doubtless due to Mrs. Thomas' experience in writing plays."[800]

Other critics were less positive. One reviewer stated bluntly that the book was not worth publishing.[801] An Edmonton critic commented that the novel was "a bit of night-club-gun-man sensationalism that doesn't ring quite true."[802] A Toronto columnist stated that the story was a "melodramatic yarn of the type which perhaps would have been most successful as a radio thriller, where staccato dialogue and crackling sound effects would cover up some of the thinness of character and implausibility of situation."[803] A *Montreal Gazette* critic noted the large extent to which Beynon Thomas's novel used conversational exchanges rather than more conventional descriptive passages to advance the plot's action. That caused him to ask, "How far can the technique of the stage be applied to novel-length fiction?" Though critics were not equally impressed with Lillian Beynon Thomas's writing style, it was clear that she enjoyed sharing fictional stories and used dialogue between characters as one of the primary ways to advance plot and character. It is no surprise, then, that she was already focusing on playwriting.

CHAPTER 8

"The Play's the Thing"

A Canadian Three-Act Play

In the opening decades of the twentieth century, the dramatic arts in Winnipeg were bookended by the first stage performance in the new Walker Theatre in December 1906 and by the last stage performance in the same theatre in 1933. Touring professional acting companies of high calibre and major cultural attractions arrived regularly in the city.[804] The Depression and competition from the emerging motion picture industry meant that these groups stopped coming. They were largely replaced by local Little Theatre companies that staged non-professional, non-commercial productions with a focus on original and experimental plays. These were grouped under the umbrella of the Manitoba Drama League, whose purpose was "to foster amateur drama and all of its energies bent on that one thing."[805] In an article in the *Free Press* on April 15, 1933, this amateur "revival" was described as "essentially Canadian... propelled by the enthusiasm of the common people.... People, young and old, are climbing out of the orchestra seats, over the floodlights, onto the stage—with all that this must mean in the way of greater community interest, cultural and artistic advancement in education and pleasure."[806] There was much talk that the staging of Canadian plays by these community theatre groups was encouraging the development of a uniquely Canadian theatre tradition. In April 1933, under the patronage of the Governor General, the Right Honourable the Earl of Bessborough, Canada resumed a pre-World War I practice with the re-instatement of a Dominion Drama Festival, "now being propelled by the enthusiasm of the common people."[807] Little Theatre groups competed in regional one-act play competitions. The winners then went to Ottawa to compete in the Dominion Drama Festival.[808] This development was seen as part of the country's cultural coming of age just as the 1931 Statute of Westminster was seen as a part of the country's political coming of age.

Beynon Thomas's shift to playwriting in the early 1930s was not surprising given her long-standing interest in the theatre and the development of her short stories around dialogue. She created the plotlines for those stories by envisioning entire scenes in her head.[809] A theatre critic who co-managed Winnipeg's leading theatre, Harriet Walker, had been Beynon Thomas's friend from the days in which they both played leadership roles in the Manitoba suffrage campaign. Beynon Thomas had the idea for, and acted in, the "One-Eyed Parliament," the mock parliament skit that became one of the turning points in the campaign. When Beynon Thomas moved to New York City, she became an avid patron of the theatre in that city.

In 1931 Beynon Thomas wrote a three-act play, *When Jack Canuck Was Young*.[810] Her theatrical breakthrough, however, came in 1932. In that year, her three-act play, *Among the Maples*,[811] was staged as the last major production of the season at the Winnipeg Little Theatre, an intimate playhouse at the corner of Main and Selkirk.[812] The play was set in a farm kitchen in southern Ontario in the early 1890s. The action took place between the feuding Tories and Grits at election time. Intertwined with much election skulduggery was a romantic plot that featured the daughter of a die-hard Tory. Her father insisted, in a somewhat bullying fashion, that she get on with marrying the rather arrogant Tory candidate to whom she was engaged. The difficulty was that she and the

World
Premiere
"AMONG
THE
MAPLES"

By Lillian Beynon Thomas
Winnipeg Playwright

TONIGHT at 8.30
LITTLE THEATRE

Friday, Saturday, Monday, Tuesday
and Wednesday

Tickets, 50c and $1. At Wpg. Piano
Co.; noon to 6 daily, or Little Theatre
box office.

CLOCKWISE FROM TOP LEFT

'"Wrote Canadian Play,' Lillian Beynon Thomas, local author, whose splendid play will be staged at the Little Theatre for five nights, commencing April 29. SOURCE: *WINNIPEG FREE PRESS*, APRIL 23, 1932, P. 27

"Among the Maples," advertisement.
SOURCE: *WINNIPEG FREE PRESS*, APRIL 29, 1932, P. 14.

'Canadian Play Opens at the Little Theatre. "Among the Maple (sic)," written by Lillian Beynon Thomas, of Winnipeg, had its premiere at the Little Theatre Friday night. The Canadian comedy is set in Ontario in the '90's. The scene shows three of the principal players William Phillips and Mrs. Robert Frost, (as Mr. and Mrs. Gordon, of Gordon Corners), and Tim Eaton as, "The General," water witcher.' SOURCE: UNIVERSITY OF MANITOBA ARCHIVES, *THE WINNIPEG TRIBUNE*, APRIL 30, 1932, P. 28.

Grit candidate had fallen in love. After a devious rescheduling of an all-candidates' meeting, the farcical kidnapping of the Tory candidate, a staged ghost sighting, a false murder allegation, and the disappearance of the critical ballot box, the romantic triangle was finally resolved when the Tory candidate won the election but then abandoned his fiancée for another woman who had just become fabulously rich upon the discovery of oil on her farm. The defeated Grit candidate was happy to trade his disappointment in politics for the opportunity to marry the love of his life. Taking centre stage was his fiancée's understanding Scottish mother who brought her controlling Tory husband around to accepting that the daughter knew what was best for own happiness. All the while, the mother peppered her advice with a series of bromides that she attributed to Robbie Burns. The play was very funny.

This was typical Beynon Thomas, the rural farm scene, taken from her Ontario childhood, the know-it-all Tory father, just like her own stubborn Grit father, and the Scottish mother who held the family together, just like her own mother. The play's male characters were preoccupied with party politics, in Beynon Thomas's opinion one of life's lower callings. Did she have in mind Premier Rodmond Roblin? The Scottish mother, who was scripted with a heavy brogue accent, reminded her Tory husband, who was anxious to have a son-in-law of his own political persuasion, that their daughter had a right to marry for love rather than politics: "Dinna forget father we're a' folks afore we're either Grit or Tory."[813] These words recall Beynon Thomas's 1913 speech to the MGGA convention when she observed that, "Women wanted the ballot because they are not like men."[814] Men, she believed, were obsessed with baser pursuits such as partisan political feuding; women aspired to nobler heights such as law reform, as was the case for the suffragettes, or love, as was the case for the Scottish mother.

Beynon Thomas conceived the idea for her play when, "the figures in the tales she had so often heard kept moving across her mind."[815] She was encouraged by Professor R.F. Jones, president of the Winnipeg Little Theatre, to write the script. She augmented the memories of her own Ontario childhood "among the maples" with stories that she had read in old newspapers of the 1880s and 1890s. The executive of the Winnipeg Little Theatre held a play reading in early January 1932[816] and was impressed by the script's "excellence of the character drawing" and by its "vigorous comic spirit."[817] They selected the play to close the 1931–1932 theatre season with a five-day run from April 29 to May 4. *Among the Maples* was staged by the Little Theatre's Community Players amateur troupe assisted by over seventy Winnipeggers who took part in its preparation for presentation.[818] The playbill announced that the play was a "world premiere… of a new three-act Canadian play, written by a Canadian, with a distinctively Canadian setting…"[819]

The play was received with great enthusiasm, at least locally.[820] Even after five days running, people still had to be turned away on the last evening.[821] The *Tribune's* theatre critique described the opening night audience as, "the happiest and most joyful that the writer has seen in nine seasons of faithful attendance."[822] The critic continued: "With a skill most unusual for a new dramatist, Mrs. Thomas gets her characters into action right from the start, and she keeps them moving right to the drop of the final curtain. With many authentic touches, she makes the rural community of 'Gordon's Corners' come to life with its domesticity, its red-blooded politics, its old-fashioned piety, its superstitions, and its love affairs. And all the while she keeps the audience on the verge of delightful laughter, as some well-recognized character passes in review."[823] "It is to be doubted," the *Free Press* reviewer agreed, "whether a more warmly enthusiastic and appreciative audience ever filled the Little Theatre …"[824] The *Ottawa Citizen* noted that the Winnipeg Little Theatre was living up to its reputation as a pioneer and a leader in the community drama movement in Canada and then qualified this by adding, "a position long occupied by the Ottawa Little Theatre."[825] Only then, and in a somewhat backhanded fashion, was the *Citizen* complimentary of *Among the Maples*. "It has received the praise of the local critics, which does not mean a great deal, but discounting enthusiasm and the joy of coming on a Canadian play that commands respect, it appears that what is left is something of substantial merit."[826] The University of Manitoba drama students brought back the play over two nights on August 7-8, 1970.[827]

The staging and reception of *Among the Maples* was seen as evidence of growing public interest in amateur drama productions sponsored by community theatres.[828] It was also seen as a sign that a uniquely Canadian tradition in the dramatic arts was emerging.[829] One of the most cherished dreams of the Winnipeg Little Theatre and its company of actors, the Community Players of Winnipeg, was to produce drama that was essentially Canadian.[830] Membership in the Little Theatre was open to any citizen and included admission to Members' Nights, which featured new Canadian plays.[831] By 1933, the Little Theatre had offered some twenty-two Canadian one-act plays. *Among the Maples* was its first full-length Canadian production.[832] The press called it a "Made in Winnipeg Play; in every aspect—play, production, costuming, acting, setting and sets—it was the product of Winnipeg artistic energy."[833] Something of this pride was evident in the telegram that Beynon Thomas received on May 6, 1932 from her sister, her sister-in-law, and the House Mother of the Seaman's Church Institute, all living in New York City. The telegram read: "Congratulations. Broadway has nothing on Winnipeg now."[834]

Drama Festivals Revived

After the success of *Among the Maples* in April 1932, Beynon Thomas returned the following November with a one-act play, *Jim Barber's Spite Fence*. Her new play was staged by the Community Players at the Little Theatre on the first Members' Night of the new season.[835] Beynon Thomas directed it herself.[836] The plot opened when two seniors, Jim and Jane, who lived next door to each other, began feuding after one of Jim's prize chickens scratched out one of Jane's prize rose bushes. Jane retaliated by killing the offending chicken. Jim struck back by building a spite fence, that is a fence constructed out of spite that serves little purpose other than to annoy the neighbour. The fence blocked the sunlight necessary for Jane's roses and made Jim's yard too hot for his chickens. Jim's daughter and Jane's son were embarrassed by their parents' quarrelling. In order to put an end to the bickering, Jim's daughter urged her father to move to her farm and, likewise, Jane's son urged his mother to move to his farm. Jim and Jane, neither of whom wanted to move, devised a plan whereby they would pretend to be getting married in order to foil any talk of their moving to their children's farms. The children caught on and decided to call their parents' bluff by pretending to go for the preacher. When the children left, Jim and Jane realized that their children were calling their bluff by bluffing themselves about going for the preacher. Jim said to Jane, "Callin' our bluff. Then mebbe we can call theirs, Jane." Jim proposed marriage and Jane accepted. The children returned. Jim and Jane asked where the preacher was. The children said he was waiting in his garden, at which point Jim and Jane, to the astonishment of their children, told them to fetch the preacher right away. At the very end, there was a 'twist' when a thought crossed Jim's mind. He asked, "Jane Hathaway, was it the way you planned this [our getting married] all the time?" And, of course, Jane's last word was, "Mebbe!" Very clever! Familiar elements of Beynon Thomas's writing style were evident throughout. The setting was a small rural village, the characters were simple, almost stereotypical, the dialogue between Jim and Jane set a humorous mood, and the plot twists and turns as the audience tries to guess who was bluffing and who was not. At the final curtain, there was a happy ending, the spite fence came down and there was a moral lesson: grown children do not always know what is best for their aging parents. As Jane said to Jim, "They [the children] mean to be good to us, Jim, but I'm thinking there's a bit of a bridge between youth and age and a span's missing in the middle."[837]

Spite Fence was one of nine plays, three of which were Canadian, entered in the Manitoba Regional Drama Festival held in Winnipeg from March 16–18, 1933.[838] It tied for first place with one other play, *A Man Born to be Hanged*, which was staged by a group of amateur actors, known as the Masquers' Club, all employees of the T. Eaton Co. Limited of Winnipeg.[839] The adjudicator praised Benyon Thomas for her "brisk and clean cut presentation." He recommended that both of the winning entries be invited to participate in the Dominion Drama Festival to be held in Ottawa on April 24, 1933. The Festival's Ottawa organizers agreed and both plays were invited to the nation's capital.[840] Before that invitation was accepted, the two plays were again staged in Winnipeg, once on March 31 and the next day on April 1, 1933. Grain magnate James A. Richardson donated the Dominion Theatre for the occasions. The programs were sponsored by the Winnipeg Branch of the Women's Canadian Club and were intended to be a kind of dress rehearsal for the Ottawa competition.[841] Ticket proceeds were to be used to defray the cost of sending the two Manitoba plays to the capital.[842] The *Free Press* drama critic thought that there had been considerable improvement in Beynon Thomas's play since its staging two weeks earlier in the Regional Drama Festival: "'Jim Barber's Spite Fence,' produced by the Winnipeg Little Theatre members' night committee, has been very considerably changed and improved since it was first presented at the Winnipeg Little Theatre. Amusing and sparkling with clever lines then, it has now added to its other virtues the very important one of a clear cut and well developed plot that is crisp and exceedingly 'good theatre,' where before it meandered far too much."[843] *Spite Fence* was the only unpublished, original play of the twenty-four plays coming from eleven regional drama festivals that competed at the Dominion Drama Festival.[844] It did not win, but the other play from Manitoba, *A Man Born to be Hanged*, did. A week later, on May 1, 1933, the two Manitoba plays were featured in a program at Margaret Eaton Hall in Toronto[845] and several days later on May 5, both were broadcast across Canada by the Canadian Radio Broadcasting Commission.[846]

Spite Fence had a long run of popularity with amateur theatre companies and audiences alike. Upon returning to Winnipeg from the Dominion Drama Festival, Beynon Thomas staged the play on June 7, 1933, as an entertainment at the 22nd annual convention of the Manitoba Women's Institutes. The provincial director of the Dominion Drama Festival, Lady Tupper, wife of Sir Charles Tupper, former prime minister of Canada, introduced Beynon Thomas and praised her play.[847] Beynon Thomas said that this occasion was like, "coming home to her ... for she founded the Homemakers Clubs of Saskatchewan."[848] She noted that, "Canadians have now reached the place in their national development where they can create their own arts as well as their own material products," and she added, "The time has passed when Canada felt dependent on foreign countries for music, plays, and all forms of art."[849] In 1935, Samuel French (Canada) Limited published the play.[850] *Spite Fence* was entered by the McCreary Women's Institute as one of the nine plays in competition at the June 1937 Manitoba Regional Drama Festival.[851]

Beynon Thomas penned several more plays during the 1930s including a one-act play, *Northern Lights*,[852] featuring the Aurora Borealis in a dramatic role probably for the first time,[853] and *Auld Lang Syne! A Play in Two Acts*.[854] In November 1935, she wrote *John Black: the Pioneer Minister*, an historical drama, in three acts, about western Canada's first Presbyterian minister. It attracted a large audience over three nights and was reviewed as a "remarkable production." Beynon Thomas researched records in the possession of the still existing pioneer Presbyterian Church of Kildonan to create dialogue for scenes in which neighbours brought their small differences to be adjudicated by the High Court of the Church. One striking scene recalled Minister Black defying the citizenry who wished to track down a fugitive Métis and take the law into their own hands. [855] The play was subsequently entered in the 1936 Manitoba Drama Festival.[856]

In October 1936, Beynon Thomas was among a group of nineteen Canadians, three of whom were Manitobans, to receive the Canadian Drama Award "in recognition of outstanding service in the development of Canadian Drama."[857] Like the growth of amateur Little Theatres across the country, and the revival of the Dominion Drama Festival, this award testified to the emphasis on creating a uniquely Canadian form of live theatre, a movement in which Beynon Thomas was an important early pioneer. In the summer of 1939, Beynon Thomas was one of six writers and the only Canadian to be awarded a scholarship to attend a six-week course in fiction and drama put on by the University of Colorado in Boulder, Colorado.[858] While there, she wrote a three-act play, *As the Twig is Bent*, which chronicled the life of Abraham Lincoln from ages eleven to seventeen. Beynon Thomas carefully researched her subject to find little known facts about his early life and to ensure historical accuracy.[859] The play tells of how young Lincoln, over the strong objection of his father, but with the encouragement of his stepmother, eschewed a farming career in favour of self-education in reading, writing and speaking. A Play Reading Council of fifteen local judges chose *As the Twig is Bent* from amongst two hundred plays for production in the summer of 1940 by the Coach House Theatre, Oconomowoc, Wisconsin.[860] They also submitted it as their first choice, along with ten other plays, to the final jury in the competition for the $300 Marjorie Montgomery Ward Baker Contest for the best original comedy in America.[861] The play was costly to stage and described as the most ambitious ever presented at the summer theatre. Pearl Roos, television director in the only experimental TV station in the mid-West, directed a very large group of eighteen actors drawn from the Chicago Radio and Laboratory Theatre. Two youthful Lincolns had to be cast to cover the age range of the leading character. The larger than usual opening night audience gave the play a "splendid reception." The local press next day described it as "splendid ... a four-star performance."[862]

In 1932, the year in which Beynon Thomas broke through as a playwright with *Among the Maples*, Canadian radio broke through with the passage of an *Act Creating the Canadian Radio Broadcasting Commission*. By 1936, when the successor Canadian Broadcasting Corporation (CBC) was created, over one million homes, spread across the country, had purchased radio licences. Beynon Thomas quickly became adept at using radio both as an interviewee and as an author. On July 15, 1933, the Western Regional Network of the Canadian Radio Broadcasting Commission broadcast *Spite Fence*.[863] In 1938, in her capacity as president of the Winnipeg Branch of the Canadian Women's Press Club, Beynon Thomas hosted the national triennial convention held in Winnipeg.[864] The convention was notable for holding its first ever 'radio day'.[865] On March 10, 1939, while visiting Winnipeg, Rupert Lucas, supervisor of drama and production for the CBC, stated that Winnipeg had more promising radio playwrights than any other city the same size in Canada. He announced that Beynon Thomas had been commissioned to write a radio serial entitled *Out on the Farm*.[866] She finished the radio special three months later on June 17.[867] In February 1941, Beynon Thomas gave a talk on CBC radio entitled "John Black of Old Kildonan." It was based on her 1935 play.[868] Around the same time, while she was Governor of the Committee of Arts and Letters for the Winnipeg Local Council of Women, Beynon Thomas gave another radio talk, this one entitled, "Mother Goose Rhymes for Every Age."[869] In April 1949, she was one of three judges who awarded prizes to two university students in a competition sponsored by the Winnipeg Branch of the Canadian Authors Association for the best radio short story script.[870]

Her plays would resonate with Prairie women for decades to come. In February 1960, a Winnipeg radio listener, Norma MacDougall, wrote to the CBC recalling that a great number of years ago the network had produced *Five Cents for Luck*. She wrote: "I remember that play with gratitude and it would be difficult to tell how big a part it became in our personal lives. Mine, and a gallant young husband who died very early in life." Norma went on to make a request: "Because the prairie farmers are again visited with the frustration of a good crop which cannot be harvested [likely due to an early frost], I think a repetition of that inspired little story would again carry the message of hope that the Author intended it should."[871] She added that many wished the play could be produced again and concluded: "It would please them and it would also give happiness to the lady who wrote it as she, in the twilight of her life, is showing all of us the gracious way of growing old." That same year, on August 15, 1960, between 8:30–9:00 p.m., the CBC rebroadcast an adaption by George Salverson of the 1933 version of *Spite Fence*.[872] After three decades, Beynon Thomas still had her fans!

Television arrived in Canada in 1952, in time to broadcast the Coronation of Queen Elizabeth II. During the 1950s, TV expanded across the country. Beynon Thomas had had some early contact with television in 1940 when Pearl Roos directed *As the Twig is Bent* at the Oconomowoc Coach House Summer Theatre in Wisconsin. At that time, Roos was the television director in Chicago at the only experimental television station in the midwestern United States.[873] At the time of Beynon Thomas's death, Miriam Green Ellis, a member of the Winnipeg Branch of the Canadian Women's Press Club, wrote to "Kay," likely Kay Dalton, a member of the Pen-Handlers writing club. The letter contained copies of Beynon Thomas's obituary and a newspaper article about Beynon Thomas's life. In the article, Miriam wrote: "... the last time I telephoned her she was trying to work out the technique of the T.V. play. Quite unlike most of us, she did not thrust the whole thing aside as not worthwhile, but deliberately dug in to find out what it was all about."[874] Beynon Thomas was an adventurous writer right up until the end of her life.

Canadian Cultural Nationalism

During the 1930s, Beynon Thomas resumed the public advocacy role that she had left behind at the end of her suffrage campaign. While that earlier campaign had been aimed at achieving legislative reform by targeting Manitoba's politicians, this later campaign was aimed at fostering Canadian cultural nationalism by targeting the country's cultural community. In particular, she sought to convince writers of the importance of developing a uniquely Canadian literature to go along with the nation's growing political and economic independence. The revival of the provincial and Dominion drama festivals, along with the development of national radio and later television audiences, were evidence that the creation of a unique Canadian cultural identity might be possible.

In April 1932, shortly after the success of *Among the Maples*, Beynon Thomas spoke to the annual meeting of the University Women's Club. Her topic was "The Makings of Canadian Drama." At that meeting, the Club charged its incoming executive with the task of promoting Canadian drama in whatever ways that it could devise. The club formed a special study group to support the Winnipeg Little Theatre.[875] A few years later, in May 1936, Beynon Thomas told the annual meeting of the Canadian Writers' Club of Winnipeg that she was optimistic about the prospects for Canada's Arts and Letters: "There is a renaissance in literature and the cultural things of life coming just as the revival of learning followed the dark ages."[876] The club elected her honourary vice president.[877] At the January 1940 central meeting of the Book Group Guild, Beynon Thomas, who was in charge of the program, was emphatic about the direction that writers should follow: "As Canadians we want to know ourselves. We want to know what we think and what we feel."[878]

In late 1946, a year after the end of World War II, Beynon Thomas made two major public speeches, both dealing with the arts. These were among the last of her career. Her message was delivered in the form of a challenge; her language was rich in imagery. She delivered the first of these speeches on November 16, 1946, to a general meeting of the University Women's Club, a club that she had founded in 1909. She called her talk "Only One North Star."[879] She began by stating that the progress of the future would be in the arts and sciences. She continued: "Would it not then be a worthy aim of the University Women's club, and for that matter, all women's clubs, to encourage if only by honoring them, those men and women who do possess rare talent? Encouraging these talented ones to cultivate their particular talents would serve to emphasize an individuality in Canadian arts. This in turn would emphasize the nationhood of Canada to other peoples. Help Canadian art to be guided by its own North Star, rather than to follow in the footsteps of others."[880]

She was even more emphatic a month later when, in her second speech, she spoke to one hundred fellow writers at the Christmas banquet of the Winnipeg Branch of the Canadian Authors Association. The Association was honouring her for her publication of *New Secret*. She began by saying that Canadian writers had no need to "cling to the skirts of Britain or the coat tails of Uncle Sam." They should, "insist upon writing about themselves and expressing themselves." She continued: "Yes, we've been good copyers. We've fallen for the fads. We could write what other places wanted. But we have a country of our own to write about." She went on to urge the establishment of a school of Canadian writers who would express their own ideas. She ended by rhetorically asking, "Have I made my point?"[881]

Beynon Thomas particularly addressed her plea to young Canadians who were starting careers in writing, drama, and the other arts. In June 1933, she outlined what she expected to several hundred delegates attending the eighth bi-annual convention of the Federated Women's Institutes of Canada and the annual meeting of the Women's Institute of Manitoba,

TOP Jacket Cover, *New Secret*, Toronto: T. Allen, 1946.

BOTTOM Lillian Beynon Thomas autographing her novel, *New Secret*, at Eaton's department store on November 1, 1946. SOURCE: ARCHIVES OF MANITOBA

both being held jointly in Winnipeg: "It is the duty of the youth of Canada to pioneer in the arts as the older people have in the development of the country. Brawn, not brains, has been eulogized in Canada, and in the past, we have looked to other countries for our art. We are past that stage and worthwhile work of Canadian artists in every branch should be appreciated and developed."[882] She delivered this same message seventeen years later when, on January 19, 1950, speaking to the twenty-fifth anniversary dinner of the Winnipeg Branch of the Canadian Authors Association, she referred to the period since World War II as "The Golden Age" for Canadian writers and continued, "We found that editors wanted articles and stories about Canada and only Canadians could write these. If you can express what you feel you will probably [find] some place for it because people want to know about Canada."[883] She went on to impress upon the association's members the fact that "this age belongs to the young and earnest writer, that the groundwork had been laid and much is now expected of the new writers."[884] Beynon Thomas was passing her literary torch.

CHAPTER 9

The Passage of Time

Looking Back

From the time that she was diagnosed with a tubercular hip when she was a child, Beynon Thomas had never enjoyed robust health.[885] She carried on, increasingly immobile as a result of arthritis.[886] Although she was slowing down, there were still teas, and dinners, and some writing. Her writing no longer consisted of short stories and plays. Rather, she looked to the past in order to document the lives of women who had made unique contributions to the province.

In 1936, speaking to the alumnae of Wesley College, her *alma mater*, Beynon Thomas described the joys and sorrows experienced by early settlers in the west. Beynon Thomas returned to this theme on November 25, 1947 when she delivered a lengthy and carefully researched paper, entitled "Some Manitoba Women Who Did First Things," before the Historical and Scientific Society of Manitoba.[887] The paper was subsequently published as an article in the Society's *Transactions* series.[888] It consisted of nearly two dozen short biographies of Manitoba women. "Confronted with an abundance of material," Beynon Thomas explained, "[I] decided to write only of women who [were] dead and who during their life in Manitoba did something that had never been done before."[889] Her article was divided into three sections: "the romantic period, the realistic period and the social [justice] activities of our very early days."[890] In some ways, that division reflected different aspects of Beynon Thomas's own life.

The first biography, from the romance period of Beynon Thomas's article, read like a romance from one of her short stories. After stating that "men are adventurers" and "women follow them or accompany them to strange lands because of their love for them," she told how a young woman disguised herself as a man in order that she might be recruited by the Hudson Bay Company agent in Stromness, Orkney Islands, Scotland to go to Rupert's Land in Canada's northwest. In that way, the woman hoped to follow her lover who was supposedly already there. Whether she left the Orkneys to follow her lover, or she left the Orkneys together with a suitor who had gotten her pregnant, is a matter of some speculation.[891] In any event, the woman found work in Rupert's Land for the Hudson Bay Company until her disguise as a man was exposed when she was about to have the baby. She is remembered as the first white woman employed by that fur trading company in Western Canada and the first white woman to give birth to a white child in what is now North Dakota. Beynon Thomas concluded that, "... someday, someone with an imagination and a strong pen, will make this story the basis of a romantic novel ..."[892] Perhaps Beynon Thomas saw herself as the possible author of that romantic novel.

Another of the biographies, included in the realistic period of the Beynon Thomas article, reflects Beynon Thomas's more pragmatic nature. The biography was of Margaret Scott, who moved west to Winnipeg from Colborne, Ontario in 1856. Margaret worked for a time as an expert stenographer but left that job to convince governments to provide nurses for the poor, aid for immigrants, and hygiene for schoolchildren. Noting that Scott had become known as "Saint Margaret of Winnipeg," Beynon Thomas wrote, "I was really impressed by her sound common sense accompanied by so much idealism."[893] This calls to mind Beynon Thomas's 1914 article in which she praised

J.S. Woodsworth as someone who sought concrete, scientific solutions for resolving municipal problems in the areas of sanitation, health, and urban planning.[894] Like Margaret Scott and J.S. Woodsworth, Beynon Thomas endeavoured to improve the condition of women not only through idealism but also through practical action in such areas as dower, suffrage, other law reforms that would benefit women, and the promotion of the arts.

In the third period of the article profiling women who had undertaken social justice activities, Beynon Thomas portrays the work of three of her contemporaries: E. Cora Hind, her colleague at the *Free Press* who became Winnipeg's first woman typist and the first woman agricultural editor in the West; Jane Hample, prominent Winnipeg businesswoman, a founder of the Knowles Home for Boys, the first woman to be elected to the Winnipeg School Board, and a financial backer of the successful suffrage campaign; and Harriet Walker, co-owner of the Walker Theatre, patron of the dramatic arts, and great supporter in helping Beynon Thomas stage *Among the Maples*.[895]

In her last pieces, Beynon Thomas glanced back at her personal history. In "I Remember," published in a souvenir booklet marking her hometown's seventy-fifth anniversary,[896] Beynon Thomas recalled her family's arrival in the West, the rented farm in Hartney, her mother's refusal to open the post office on Sundays, prayer meetings, and the excitement around the rumour of the coming railroad. In 1957, Beynon Thomas wrote an unpublished, six-page manuscript entitled, "A Little Town and District Looks Back: Hartney is Celebrating 75 Years of Greatness."[897] She tells the story of how pioneering homesteader James Hartney brought Red Fife wheat to the settlement subsequently named after him and how the early ripening qualities of that wheat enabled homesteaders to beat the frost. Finally, in September 1959, two years before her death, Beynon Thomas published "Reminiscences of a Manitoba Suffragette" in the Manitoba Historical Society's *Manitoba Pageant*.[898] She opened by asking, "How did it happen that Manitoba women were the first women in Canada to win the right to vote?" Then, speaking in the third person, she answered by placing herself at the beginning of the suffrage movement. "It did not

just happen," she wrote, "[t]he editor of a weekly newspaper in Manitoba…
started a women's page that was called 'Home Loving Hearts'."

Companions

In the space of thirteen months, from September 11, 1950, to October 5,
1951, Beynon Thomas lost her husband, Vernon, her close friend Nellie
McClung, and her sister, Francis. They were three of the most important people in her life. Now, at age 77, she must have felt that her world
had left her behind.

Upon his return to Winnipeg from New York City in 1921, Vernon
had joined the *Winnipeg Tribune* where he became that paper's highly
regarded municipal editor before retiring in March 1944. He was in
good health until the end. On Thursday September 7, 1950, after a dizzy
spell while playing golf, he suffered a heart attack that evening. He had
a second heart attack on Saturday, and a third fatal attack on the next
Monday as he was preparing to see the doctor.[899] Vernon was 74 and just
several weeks shy of their fortieth wedding anniversary. He was buried
in Winnipeg's Brookside Cemetery.[900] Vernon and his wife were particularly well matched through their interests in politics, writing, journalism,
and travel. Nellie McClung wrote a moving letter shortly after his death,
which Beynon Thomas saved in her papers: "… I know that it is a lonely
time for you. You will miss him at every turn. You were great compan-
ions all these years, and you will feel that you have lost your right arm."[901]

Nellie McClung was 77 when she passed away on September 1, 1951, a
month before Francis died. Beynon Thomas and McClung were born less
than a year apart and spent much of their youth in rural Manitoba. Both
were teachers, authors, committed feminists, and dedicated social activists. They agreed on the need for laws that would guarantee the political
independence of women and provide them with economic security. They
believed that a woman's place was not only inside the home but, equal with
men, outside of it as well. The two stood shoulder-to-shoulder at speaking
events during the suffrage campaign. McClung credited Beynon Thomas
with the idea for, and production of, *A Women's Parliament*, the critical

turning point in the campaign.[902] Immediately prior to the 1917 federal election, they had their only serious disagreement when McClung initially favoured a selective extension of the female enfranchisement but soon adopted her friend's position favouring universal enfranchisement. Time and distance did not dim their friendship. Although they saw each other less often, McClung went out of her way to pay Beynon Thomas a warm visit in NYC, and they made a point of meeting when McClung occasionally visited Winnipeg to address various authors' groups. They last met in person at Christmastime in 1938, when McClung stopped over on a return train trip from Ottawa to Calgary so that the two friends could have coffee in the Winnipeg CPR railway station restaurant.[903] In 1946, McClung suggested the title for Beynon Thomas's book, *New Secret*,[904] and recommended it to all adults and children.[905] In September, 1950, upon Vernon's death, McClung concluded her tender letter of condolence with the words, "I'll love you forever. You have always been my dearest friend."[906]

Throughout their lives, Beynon Thomas and Francis shared much in common. Both trained as teachers on their way to becoming journalists and women's page editors for Western Canadian farm newspapers. Both campaigned vigorously for women's suffrage. Both opposed Nellie McClung when McClung briefly supported the selective federal franchise proposal.[907] Both retreated to NYC in self-imposed exile after Winnipeg proved hostile to pacifist viewpoints. When Beynon Thomas returned to that city in 1922, Francis took over her sister's job as editor of *The Lookout*, and then subsequently spent the next three decades as a freelance author in NYC while Beynon Thomas was doing the same in Winnipeg.[908]

Perhaps Francis was a little further to the left of Beynon Thomas in her political views.[909] Beynon Thomas tended to be more pragmatic and measured in her outlook; Francis more theoretical and emotional. Early in 1951 Francis fell ill with cancer and was operated on.[910] Beynon Thomas was seriously concerned but not well enough to travel to New York to visit her sister. A short time later, Francis returned to Winnipeg and seemed to be improving in health.[911] However, four months later, she was struck with paralysis as she and her sister were going to an evening dinner party.[912]

She died in hospital on October 5, 1951, at age 67, and was buried in Brookside Cemetery, the same cemetery in which Beynon Thomas's husband had been buried a year earlier.[913]

An Enduring Legacy

Nellie McClung is generally credited with the success of the suffrage campaign in Manitoba.[914] Typical is a 1959 statement about McClung made by Irene Craig in the *Manitoba Pageant*: "It is said that her pen and her gift of oratory were probably the most effective weapons in the Manitoba crusade."[915] That view is understandable. McClung was an exuberant speaker with a charismatic personality and high public profile. However, she joined the campaign only when she arrived in Winnipeg in May 1911 and left after 1914 with two brief returns, one during the 1915 provincial election campaign, the other three months later during the final suffrage petition drive. Beynon Thomas, quiet and unassuming but intensely focused, was constantly present from June 1908, with the publication of the "Old Woman" letter that started the dower campaign, through mid-1910 when she realized that dower reform would not be possible without women's suffrage, to well after the vote had been won in January 1916. She founded the PEL, was the campaign's chief strategist, and was the architect of the campaign's grassroots political organization which was well ahead of its time. She was actively engaged in all aspects and major events of the campaign, including originating the idea of, and producing, the 'one-eyed' mock parliament skit, central to the campaign's success. She was the organizer of the Speakers' Bureau, was a prominent speaker herself, was a writer and distributor of suffrage pamphlets, was a participant in lobbying government, was active in both the 1913 and 1915 suffrage petition drives, was engaged in both the 1914 and 1915 provincial election campaigns against Premier Roblin, and was the main chronicler of campaign progress and chief motivator of campaign supporters through her numerous columns in the daily *Free Press* and the weekly *Prairie Farmer*. At the end of the campaign, she was instrumental in having the wording of the suffrage bill changed so that women could

stand as candidates in provincial elections. Beynon Thomas was generous in the credit that she gave the campaign's other leaders and workers
who were slogging it out on the ground.[916]

With her return to Winnipeg in the summer of 1922, Beynon Thomas's
journalistic career came to an end. She left it behind in favour of a career
as a short story writer and playwright, a career that would give her more
freedom and independence. As she transitioned, she could already count
two remarkable accomplishments. One was her success in winning homestead dower, a law that gave women and their families the right not to be
involuntarily dispossessed by their husbands of their family home. This
was all the more notable given that other social justice reforms had to
wait much longer. Her second accomplishment, the leadership role that
she played in winning suffrage, has been largely overlooked. This repre-
sents a significant gap in the history of the campaign to win the vote for
women. The *Free Press*, the newspaper in which she, as Lillian Laurie,
spoke to the hearts and minds of Prairie settler women, wrote nothing
of her achievements at the time of her death in 1961. Nearly six decades
later, that newspaper published an article in 2018 acknowledging, but
not explaining, the omission: "Despite Beynon Thomas's leading role in
securing the right for women to vote, when she died ... on Sept. 2, 1961,
it was noted only by the family's paid obituary on page 19 two days later.
... We'll never know why Beynon Thomas's death didn't generate a news
story in the *Free Press*."[917]

In a letter dated February 26, 1973, responding to a query from historian Ramsay Cook, Howard Beynon, Beynon Thomas's brother, addressed
this oversight: "I dont [*sic*] know what accounts of the suffrage movement
in Manitoba you [Cook] have read, but, in general, Nellie McClung did
not get all the credit, or nearly all the credit for the movement at the time.
She did not come to Winnipeg till the movement was well on the way to
success."[918] There has been one other attempt to complete the record. On
the occasion of the unveiling of a statue honouring Nellie McClung on
the grounds of the Manitoba Legislative Building in 2010, the *Free Press*
published the following commentary by Mary Ann Loewen:

> I was intrigued to read of the soon-to-be unveiling of a
> sculpture of Nellie McClung... However, I was disappointed
> to read that it was Nellie who 'in 1916... got the vote for
> Manitoba women.' Yes, McClung was hugely instrumental
> in this significant and necessary step toward gender equal-
> ity, but she was by no means the only one responsible for
> this feat.... But because Nellie had an outgoing personality
> and was thus given the role [of Premier] in the now-famous
> Mock Parliament, because she wrote popular novels, hers
> is the name that easily rolls off our tongues when we think
> of Manitoba and women's right to vote. In fact, people like
> Lillian Beynon Thomas... were also heavily involved. ... I
> think it behooves us to represent a more accurate history
> that remembers the quieter people, too.[919]

It is possible to misjudge the contribution that Beynon Thomas made in achieving suffrage. Some may consider the contribution of others more important. Some may point out, rightly, that the continuing exclusion of Indigenous women from the vote tarnished the reform. Still others might say that even without Beynon Thomas's contribution making Manitoba first, the reform was inevitable, only a matter of time. After all, other provinces soon followed Manitoba's January 1916 lead: Saskatchewan in March 1916; Alberta in April 1916; British Columbia in April 1917; Ontario in April 1917; and most other provinces shortly thereafter.[920]

However, Beynon Thomas's contribution in strengthening democracy was unique. The 'votes for women' campaign that she led was the first to succeed in any Canadian federal or provincial jurisdiction after many earlier campaigns had failed. She persisted until she won, motivated by her desire to achieve other reforms, including dower, that would further women's equality. Further, in order to achieve enfranchisement, she had to invent a new way of doing politics. She came to understand that the existing system of machine politics, dominated by male power brokers like Rodmond Roblin, operating through highly partisan political par-ties and thriving on patronage distribution, could never achieve a truly representative democracy. She knew that she had to do politics differently. The result was an innovative, broadly based grassroots campaign that reached out to supporters and encouraged them to become not just voters, but politically literate participants educated in the issues that affected them. Both universal suffrage and grassroots politics, products of Beynon Thomas's leadership and organizational skills, have since become entrenched as foundational characteristics of modern democratic political life.

She also made transformative contributions in other areas of Canadian life. Although she was not among the very first of women journalists in the country, she was an early editor of a newspaper page for women and, significantly, was a pioneer in lifting her page beyond gossipy, lifestyle stories to examine substantive issues affecting women's legal, political, economic, and social role in society. Even though women had to wait several more decades before achieving full professional recognition as reporters whose stories appeared on the front page and whose editorial opinions were featured in the first section of the paper, Beynon Thomas blazed a trial with her Home Loving Hearts columns in the *Free Press* daily and weekly editions.

The same can be said of her literary efforts. Despite the fact that her numerous short stories, published in both Canada and America, have not enjoyed an enduring shelf life, they made a significant contribution to a popular genre of writing in their time. They deserve to be rediscovered. Together with her own life story, they provide a useful historical insight into rural and small-town Prairie life in early twentieth-century Canada, with all of its hopes and tribulations. Her stage dramas, which she took to both provincial and national drama festivals, played an important part in the revival of community-based theatre during the Depression years, a tradition that is still vibrant. Her interest in the arts led her to becoming an early public advocate for the development of a distinctive Canadian creative cultural tradition free from the lingering drag of British colonial influence and the powerful pull of American cultural domination. In this, she is a forerunner of today's advocates who champion the adoption of cultural content regulations designed to preserve a place for

Canadian writers and artists facing competition in markets dominated by international publishing and entertainment conglomerates.

Beynon Thomas died at home in her apartment on Saturday of the Labour Day long weekend, September 2, 1961. She was just two days shy of her 87th birthday. She had not been feeling well and had had difficulty leaving her home during the previous year.[921] She was the fourth of her siblings to die, predeceased by her older brother Manning,[922] her younger sister Francis, and her youngest brother Reuben. Surviving were a younger sister and two younger brothers. Lillian Thomas's obituary appeared in both the *Free Press* and the *Tribune*.[923] The *Tribune* carried a further story, titled "She Won the Vote for Women," that called her "a champion of women's rights" and focused on her contribution to the suffrage campaign.[924] There was also a write up in the *Selkirk Enterprise*.[925]

In 1983, the Historic Sites Advisory Board of Manitoba placed a plaque commemorating Beynon Thomas on the grounds of Laura Secord School in Winnipeg's Wolseley neighbourhood.[926] She was president of the Laura Secord Branch of the Political Equality League and had worked in Wolseley collecting petition signatures during the suffrage campaign. The plaque reads in part: "Together with other middle class women, many from Winnipeg's west-end, she helped to organize the Political Equality League in 1912. Their goal, she argued, was to show Manitobans what political equality could mean to 'women and children who were in the power of weak, coarse, unfair, sick or brutal men'."

The Beynon Thomas quote on the plaque was taken from her last article, "Reminiscences of a Manitoba Suffragette."[927] The full sentence from the article gives a more complete understanding of her position: "Those women organized 'The Political Equality League', not to fight the men and women who were opposed to 'Votes for Women', but to explain to them what it meant to women and children who were in the power of weak, coarse, unfair, sick or brutal men."

Beynon Thomas's approach to reform had been consistent throughout her time as a political advocate. As early as 1908, during her dower campaign, she explained to her newspaper readers that "This is not a struggle between men and women... It is merely an attempt to educate

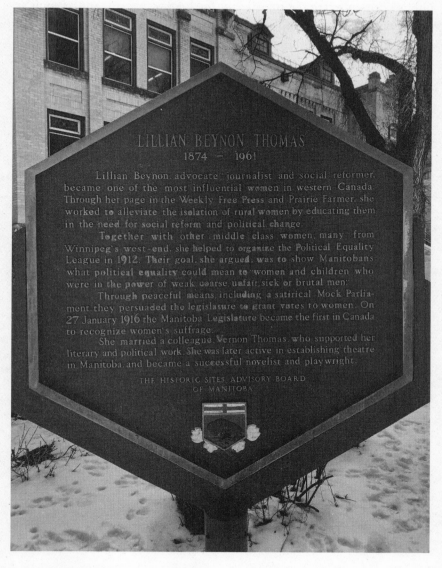

The Historical Sites Advisory Branch of Manitoba historic plaque.
Lillian Beynon Thomas, 1874-1961. Installed in 1983 outside of the Laura
Secord School, in the Wolseley area of west end Winnipeg where
Beynon Thomas lived and where, as President of the Laura Secord
Branch of the Political Equality League, she canvassed for suffrage.

public opinion to see the injustice of the present system, and as soon as public opinion is educated, there will be a change. No government can stand against public opinion."[928] She sought reform neither by confrontation nor condemnation; all her life, she preferred to persuade using reason, not sentiment."[929]

ACKNOWLEDGMENTS

The facts about, and writings of, Lillian Beynon Thomas are widely dispersed. I am very grateful for the help and encouragement that the following people have given me in locating information: Kira Baker, The United Church of Canada Archives; Sharon Bentley and Kate Gibson, King Township Public Library; Josephine Boos-Beynon; Catherine Butler, Library and Archives Canada; Monique Clement, Archives of Manitoba; Professor Ramsay Cook; Suzanne Dubeau, Clara Thomas Archives & Special Collections, York University; Nancy Girardin, Manitoba Education and Advanced Training Resources Branch; Dr. Gordon Goldsborough, Webmaster & Journal Editor, Manitoba Historical Society; Michael Hawrysh, Dictionary of Canadian Biography; Nancy E. Hawkins; Patricia C. Hawkins; Dr. Jeff Keshen, President and Vice-Chancellor, University of Regina; James Kominowski, University of Manitoba Elizabeth Dafoe Library; M. Christopher Kotecki, Jason Martin and Kevin Tarr, Archives of Manitoba; William Lahey-Ward, Library and Archives Canada; Jodi MacDonald, Manitoba Education and Advanced Learning Records; Liza Mallyon, King City Heritage and Cultural Centre; Daniel Richard Eric Matthes, Percy Miller, Canada Research Knowledge Network; University of Winnipeg Archives; Hilary B. Neary; Dr. Peter F. Neary, University of Western Ontario; Nadya Pankiw, *Winnipeg Free Press*; Linda Patterson, Manitoba Legislative Library; Prairie History Collection, Regina Public Library; Dr. M.J. Snidal; J. Snidal; Monique Vandale, Manitoba Education and Advanced Learning Financial and Administrative Services Branch; Carol Silver, Syracuse University Libraries; Dr. Chris Yost, Vice-President (Research), University of Regina.

I am grateful to Great Plains Press, Mel Marginet, Catharina de Bakker and Keith Cadieux for the production of this book, to Jessica Antony for valuable editorial assistance, and to Judy Dunlop for indexing.

I acknowledge with love and thanks the support of my family, Marie-France E. Menc and our sons Nicolas, Pierre, and François Hawkins.

Lillian Beynon Thomas's Articles, Short Stories, and Plays

Beynon Thomas was a prolific writer. In addition to her book, short stories, plays, and articles, both scholarly and journalistic, she wrote regular women's columns and editorials in the press. Of note were her "Home Loving Hearts" and "Mutual Benefit Association" columns, which appeared on the Women's Page of the *Weekly Free Press & Prairie Farmer* that she edited from 1906 to 1917 under the pen name "Lillian Laurie." Many of those columns were repeated in the daily *Manitoba Free Press* during those years. She wrote a column entitled "A Woman's Talk to Women" in the monthly *Canadian Thresherman and Farmer* during 1916–1917. She wrote columns in the monthly magazine of the New York Seaman's Institute, *The Lookout*, which she edited from 1919 to 1922. In addition, there were occasional columns in other newspapers and magazines. Apart from Beynon Thomas's regular writings as a journalist, her newspaper work ventured beyond the usual topics dealt with in the women's pages or involved a more in-depth treatment of a subject matter, which are included below.

Every effort has been made to locate her short stories and plays. Where manuscripts were found with no record of publication, it is noted below. In several instances, full citation information is not available. In a few instances titles can be identified but the work itself is missing. It is probable that some writings have been lost altogether.

Articles

"British Columbia Fishing and Fish-Life Tragedy." *The Globe and Mail*, 21 January 1911, A2.

"Westminster Abbey: Resting place of the empire's greats." *Manitoba Free Press*, (21 January 1912) woman's section—3.

"Building on Canadian Pre-Emptions." *The Christian Guardian*, (29 May 1912), 9-10.

"Canada as a British Colony" Eight Part Series including: "The Loss of the Thirteen States (where the laws, language and religion of French Canada were discussed);" "The Struggle for Representative Government;" "The Struggle of the People, (where the rebellions in Upper and Lower Canada were discussed);" The Dominion of Canada—1867; "The Northwest and the Fur Trade;" "The Situation in the West" (dealing with the current political situation); and, "The Political Situation and Woman's Suffrage." *PF,* (13, 20, 27 May, 3, 10, 17, 24 June and 8 July 1914, 2-Home Section.

"Practical Idealists." *Canada Monthly* 14.3 (London, Ontario: Vanderhoof-Gunn Company, Ltd., July 1914), 168. https://archive.org/stream/canadamonthly40westuof t#page/168/mode/2up.

"To the Visitor, the Exhibits make the Show … But to the Exhibitor, the People Present an Ever Entertaining Spectacle." *The Country Guide*. (1914), 262.

"Work of the W.C.T.U.: Pioneer of Women's Organizations in the West," *Farmer's Magazine*, January-December 1917." *Farmer's Magazine* 10.4 (Toronto: The MacLean Publishing Company, February 1917), 86. https://archive.org/stream/ farmersmagazine1917toro/farmersmagazine1917toro_djvu.txt.

"Abroad in Manitoba." *The Winnipeg Tribune Magazine* (Series running from 8 September 1934 to 3 November 1934.

"Some Manitoba Women Who Did First Things." *Transactions of the Historical and Scientific Study of Manitoba* 3.4 (1947-8): 13-25.

"I Remember." In *Hartney and District, Manitoba: 75th Anniversary Celebration 1882-1957- Souvenir Book*. Deloraine: The Deloraine Times, 1957, 57. https:// digitalcollections.lib.umanitoba.ca/islandora/object/uofm%3A3081253#page/66/ mode/2up.

"A Little Town and District Looks Back—Hartney Is Celebrating Seventy-five Years of Greatness." (Typed manuscript found in Lillian Beynon Thomas Papers, AM, 1957).

"Reminiscences of a Manitoba Suffragette." *Manitoba Pageant: Manitoba Historical Society* 5.1 (September 1959) http://www.mhs.mb.ca/docs/pageant/05/suffragette. shtml, 10. (Original typed transcript of this article titled "Manitoba Women Voted First" found in Lillian Beynon Thomas Papers, AM, P 191.)

Plays

A Women's Parliament. (Improvised) (Lillian Laurie, "Trusting All The Home Folks," *Manitoba Free Press,* 5 February 1916, 21), satirical play based on an idea by Lillian Beynon Thomas (McClung, *The Stream Runs Fast,* 113), Winnipeg: 28 January and 16 April 1914 and Brandon: 2 April 1914.

When Jack Canuck was young: a play in three acts. Mount Saint Vincent University Library: Microfilm, 1931. (no published manuscript; no record of the play being produced)

Among the Maples: a play in three acts. Mount Saint Vincent University Library: Microfilm, 1932. (no published manuscript—play ran in Winnipeg from 28 April to 4 May, 1932)

Northern Lights. (A one-act play produced in Winnipeg in January 1934—no published manuscript. See: *The Winnipeg Tribune,* 16 December 1933, 9 and 12 January 1934, 7).

Jim Barber's Spite Fence: a comedy in one act. Toronto: S. French (Canada) Ltd., 1935. (play first produced in Winnipeg from 17-19 November 1932, again as co-winner of the Manitoba Regional Drama Festival on 18 March 1933, again in Winnipeg from 31 March-1 April, 1933, following which it competed in Ottawa as part of the Dominion Drama Festival in the last week of April 1933 and subsequently in at Margaret Eaton Hall on 1 May 1933. The play was broadcast as a radio play on 15 July 1933 on the Western Regional Network of Canadian Radio Broadcasting Commission: Letter: E. Austin Weir to Mrs. Thomas, 16 May 1960, found in Lillian Beynon Thomas Papers, AM, P191; "CBC Western Regional Network Radio— Monday—15 minute drama written by Lillian Beynon Thomas," *Winnipeg Free Press,* 15 July 1933, 19. On 15 August 1960, as adapted by George Salverson, as part of the CBC "Summerfallow" series. A typed copy of the adapted radio transcript can be found in Lillian Beynon Thomas Papers, AM, P 191.)

Auld Lang Syne: a play in two acts. Mount Saint Vincent University Library: Microfilm, 1935. (no published manuscript; no record of the play being produced)

John Black: the Pioneer Minister (unpublished three-act play produced in Winnipeg on 20 November 1935: "'John Black' Remarkable Production," *The Winnipeg Tribune,* 21 November 1935, 10; "Historical Play Reveals Life of Pioneer Pastor—Story of John Black Presented by Local Actors Wednesday," *Winnipeg Free Press,* 22 November 1935, 15.) Lillian was interviewed on CBC radio on the subject of "John Black of Old Kildonan in February 1941: Peter B. Whittall, "Dial Twisting—Winnipeg Playwright To Be Guest Speaker," *Winnipeg Free Press,* 11 February 1941, 2.)

Out on the Farm. (radio serial commissioned by CBC: "Lucas Prises Radio
Playwrights In Winnipeg," *Winnipeg Free Press*, 10 March 1939, 13; Letter:
Lillian Beynon Thomas to Jennie (Mrs. Robert Macham), 17 June 1939, Lillian
Beynon Thomas Papers, AM, P 191.) (radio play)

As the Twig is Bent, (unpublished three-act play performed at the Coach House Theatre,
Oconomowoc, Wisconsin: "Week beginning August 5, AS THE TWIG IS BENT
by Lillian Beynon Thomas," *Coach House Summer Theatre Play Schedule*, found in
Lillian Beynon Thomas Papers, AM, P191.)

It Really Happened. Mount Saint Vincent Library: Microfilm, 1940. (no published
manuscript; no record of the play being produced).

"Mother Goose Rhymes for Every Age." ("A Radio Talk by Lillian Beynon Thomas,
Convenor of the Committee of Arts and Letters for the Local Council of Women,
Winnipeg:" typed transcript found in Lillian Beynon Thomas Papers, AM, P 191),
approx. 1940-1941. (radio play)

Short Stories

"The Burden of Widowhood." *Canadian Magazine* xxix.1 (Toronto: Ontario
Publishing Company Limited, May, 1907), 23. (ss) https://www.canadiana.ca/view/
oocihm.8_06911_162/16

"The Crook in the Road." *Canadian Courier: The National Weekly* vii.5 (Toronto:
Courier Press, January 1, 1910), 16. (ss) https://www.canadiana.ca/view/
oocihm.8_06251_171/57

"A Little Woman and a Little Business." *New Story Magazine* 4.6 (New York: Street &
Smith, October 1912), 161-169. (ss)

"Banking on Sam." *Canadian Courier: The National Weekly* xiv. 4 (Toronto: Courier Press,
June 28, 1913), 6. (ss) https://www.canadiana.ca/view/oocihm.8_06911_344/6

"Give and Take—But Generally Take." *New Story Magazine* 6.3 (New York: Street &
Smith, July 1913), 85-90. (ss)

"A Name for Jemima Georgina." *The Red Book Magazine* 21.4 (Chicago: The Red Book
Corporation, August 1913), 664-671.

"Reason Versus Sentiment." (unpublished manuscript with R. Oliphant reader report)
(Syracuse: Syracuse University Libraries, Special Collections Research Center, Street
& Smith Records, September 5, 1913).

"Getting There." *Collier's: The National Weekly* 52.14 (New York: P.F. Collier & Son, 20
December, 1913), 17. https://babel.hathitrust.org/cgi/pt?id=mdp.39015009286736&v
iew=1up&seq=480.

"Making New Trails." *Canadian Courier: The National Weekly* xv.12 (Toronto:
Courier Press, February 21, 1914), 8. http://eco.canadiana.ca/view/
oocihm.8_06911_378/8?r=0&s=1.

"'S. S.' for Short." *Smith's Magazine* (New York: Street & Smith Publications, Inc., 1 April 1918), 127-137.

"When Wires are Down." *The Thrill Book.* (New York: Street & Smith Publications, Inc., 1 September 1919), 53-62. https://books.google.ca/books?id=cjXpR_cllC8C&pg=PA 53&lpg=PA53&dq=when+wires+are+down+lillian+beynon+thomas&source=bl&ots= 6giOD6_Ftl&sig=ACfU3U1ADvNzOBF6M5_jUlA1e3AQhbRasA&hl=en&sa=X&v ed=2ahUKEwjRxJyMpYDjAhVCCc0KHQwhBG8Q6AEwCnoECAgQAQ#v=onep age&q=when%20wires%20are%20down%20lillian%20beynon%20thomas&f=false. Reprinted in Skene-Melvin, David, ed. *Crime When the Nights are Long.* (Toronto: Dundurn, 1999).

"Five Cents for Luck." *MacLean's Magazine* 40.18 (Toronto: The MacLean Publishing Company, Limited, 15 September 1927), 3. Reprinted in: *The American Magazine* 104.4 (Springfield: Crowell Publishing Company, October 1927). The story was broadcast on CBC radio some years later: Carbon copy of a Letter: Norma L. MacDougall to Canadian Broadcasting Co., 8 February 1960, found in, Lillian Beynon Thomas Papers, AM, P191.

"Winnowed." *The Farmer's Wife* (St. Paul: Webb Publishing Company, December 1927), 649. (Published under the pseudonym "Peter B. Thomas.")

"Rubber Heels." *MacLean's Magazine* 41.15 (Toronto: The MacLean Publishing Company, Limited, 1 August 1928), 10.

"Lights in the Windows." *MacLean's Magazine* 41.23 (Toronto: The MacLean Publishing Company, Limited, 1 December 1928), 16.

"His Wife in Secret." *Marriage Stories* (Volume and Publisher unknown, date between 1924-1925 and1928-1930), 15-24. Copy found in Lillian Beynon Thomas Papers, AM, P 191.

"Jimmy's Perfect Day." *The Country Guide* (Winnipeg: The Public Press Ltd., 15 March 1929), 4.

"Rescue from the Clouds." *Detective Story Magazine* 121.1 (23 August 1930).

"Helen Gives Notice. *The Chatelaine,* (Toronto: Maclean Pub., January 1931), 6.

"It's Not So Simple." *Wow* 1.4 (Jersey City: Wow Publications, Inc., January 1931), 49.

"Life Demanded Too Much." *True Story* (A $1,000 prize story.) (New York: Bernarr McFadden, 1935).

"Sheltered Woman." *True Story* (A $1,000 prize story.) (New York: Bernarr McFadden, June 1936), 19.

"Love the Conqueror." *True Story* (A $1,000 prize story.) (New York: Bernarr McFadden, 1936).

"Hugh Dorion Comes Home." *The Country Guide* (Winnipeg: The Public Press Ltd., October 1944), 10.

Lost Short Stories

"Money No—Pony No—Pants No—Arm Very Worse."
"Among the Willows."

Poems

"Realism." *Expressions* 6.2 (Ridgewood, NJ: The Gayren Press, Spring 1935), 21.

Books

New Secret. Toronto: T. Allen, 1946.

ENDNOTES

1   Hawkins, R.E. Dower Abolition in Western Canada: How Law Reform Failed. *Manitoba Law Journal* 24(3) (1997) 635-663; and, Hawkins, R.E. "Lillian Beynon Thomas, Woman's Suffrage and the Return of Dower to Manitoba." *Manitoba Law Journal* 27(1) (1999-2000) 45-114.

2   Catherine Cleverdon, *The Woman Suffrage Movement in Canada*, (Toronto: University of Toronto Press, 1950), 46.

3   Sarah Carter, *Ours by Every Law of Right and Justice: Women and the Vote in the Prairie Provinces*, (Vancouver: UBC Press, 2020), 36.

4   Freeman, Barbara M. *Beyond Bylines: Media Workers and Women's Rights in Canada*. Waterloo, Ontario: Wilfred Laurier University Press, 2011, 4-5, where the author states: "... Canadian women engaged in a broad range of pro-woman activism in different eras, which historians initially described as "waves" that peaked during certain time periods and around set goals."

5   Joan Sangster, *One Hundred Years of Struggle: The History of the Vote and Women in Canada*, (Vancouver: UBC Press, 2018), 8-9.

6   This phrase was used by E. Cora Hind to describe the rights claimed by women necessary for them to obtain a measure of security and economic independence. Apart from dower, these rights included such social justice reforms of the kind mentioned here. E. Cora Hind, "The Women's Quiet Hour," *The Western Home Monthly* (February 1912) 571.

7   Sarah Carter, *Ours by Every Law of Right and Justice: Women and the Vote in the Prairie Provinces*, (Vancouver: UBC Press, 2020), 37.

8   Lang, Marjory, *Women Who Made the News: Female Journalists in Canada, 1880-1945*, (Montreal & Kingston: McGill-Queen's University Press, 1999), 4

9   Carter has called for this. p.5

10   Dame Durden [Florence Lediard], "The Ingle Nook," *Farmer's Advocate and Home Journal* (Winnipeg: *Farmer's Advocate* of Winnipeg), 15 March 1911, 388.Similar observations were made by a reporter for the *New York World* magazine, who interviewed Beynon Thomas in 1920, in connection with her work in that city tracing missing seamen. He described her as a "business-like" woman and added, "Mrs. Thomas is a pleasant, quiet, efficient little woman, with bright eyes, and a firm quick-speaking voice." See: Farrar, John, *New York World Magazine*, reprinted under the headline, "Tracers For Missing Seamen: How a Former Winnipeg Woman Rescues Sailor Boys From the Limbo of Those Missing At Sea," With the Help of Captains, Crews, Seaport Dwellers and Sweethearts, Also Police, the World Over," *Manitoba Free Press*, 1920, 16 August 3.

11   "A Women's Advocate," *The Chronicle*, Shellbrook, Saskatchewan, 17 January 1914, 7, reprinted from *The Canadian Courier, Vol. 22 No. 22 (Nov. 1, 1913), Woman's Supplement, 23*. Also reprinted in *The Equity*, Shawville, Quebec, 27 November 1913.

12   Blanche Ellinthorpe, "From Teaching to Writing," *The Country Guide*, February 1953, 68. E. Cora Hind also remarked on Beynon Thomas's, "good sense of humor." See: The Woman [E. Cora Hind], "The Woman About Town: Lilian [sic] Laurie," *Winnipeg Town Topics*, 1913, Lillian Beynon Thomas Papers, Archives of Manitoba (hereafter AM), P191. The copy is undated. However, the article states that, "Two years ago, she [Lillian] was married to A.V. Thomas ..." That marriage took place on 27 September 1911. That would place this edition of *Town Topics* sometime within the three months after September and the end of 1913 when *Town Topics* ceased publication.

      Over its lifetime from 1893-1931, the sister farm weekly of the *Manitoba/Winnipeg Free Press* became the most widely circulated farm journal in Canada. At different times it was known under different names such as the *Free Press Farm Weekly* or the *Manitoba Weekly Free Press and Prairie Farmer*. However, from 1909 through 1953, the title always contained the words "Prairie Farmer." For this reason, and for ease of reference throughout, it will be referred to simply as the *Prairie Farmer*.

      The *Manitoba Free Press* was renamed the *Winnipeg Free Press* in 1931. For ease of reference, it will be referred to as the *Free Press* throughout.

13   E. Cora Hind, "The Women's Quiet Hour – Lillian Laurie," *The Western Home Monthly*, November 1911, 56.

14   Dorothy Muir, "Winnipeg Women," *C-O-A-C-H*, December 1932, 5.

15   Dave McQueen, "Writes Novel Of Atomic Age," *The Globe and Mail*, 7 September 1946, 13.

16   E. Cora Hind, "The Women's Quiet Hour," *Western Home Monthly*, November 1911, 56; also, Philistia, "Mrs. Lillian Beynon Thomas," The Canadian Courier, Vol. XIV. No. 22 (Toronto: Courier Press, Limited, November 1, 1913) 23.

17   "MacLean's $1,000 Prize Story Awards," *MacLean's Magazine*, Vol. XL, No. 9 (1 May 1927), 10; See also: "Social And Personal," *Winnipeg Free Press*, 20 August 1934, 7; Lillian Beynon Thomas, "Red River Valley Has Stirring History," *The Winnipeg Tribune Magazine*, 8 September 1934, 3.

18   "Women's Interests in the M.G.G.A.," *Farmer's Advocate and Home Journal* (Winnipeg: *Farmer's Advocate* of Winnipeg), 17 January 1917, 67.

19   W.L. Morton, *Manitoba, A History*. 2nd ed. (Toronto: University of Toronto Press, 1967), 273.

20   Lillian Beynon Thomas, "Practical Idealists: How One Man with a Dream and a Card Indexful of Facts Founded the Canadian Welfare League and What it Might Mean to Canadian Men, Women and Municipalities," *Canada Monthly* XVI, 3 (July 1914), 168.

21   Morton, 334.

22   Ellinthorpe, "From Teaching to Writing," 68.

23   The Woman [E. Cora Hind], "The Woman About Town: Lilian [sic] Laurie," *Winnipeg Town Topics*, 1913, Lillian Beynon Thomas Papers, AM, P191.

24   Letter: Lillian B. Thomas to Miss C.L. Cleverdon, 21 August 1944, Lillian Beynon Thomas Papers, AM, P191.

25   "With the C.W.P.C. Delegates," *The Winnipeg Tribune*, 22 June 1938, 9.

26   W.R.B. Jr., "Play on Lincoln Is Fourth Drama at Coach House," *Watertown Daily Times*, Watertown, Wisconsin, 6 August 1940, clipping found in Lillian Beynon Thomas Papers, AM, P191.

27   "Women Score in Drama and Debate," *Manitoba Free Press*, 29 January 1914, 20.

28   "Women Arrange Fine Program," *Manitoba Free Press*, 2 February 1916, 3.

29   S.P.L.G., "Book Review," undated clipping found in Lillian Beynon Thomas Papers, AM, P191.

30   Josephine Beynon Boos [a distant cousin of Beynon Thomas's] and Patricia C. Gallinger, *The Descendants of John Beynon*, 2nd edition, (Barrie, ON: Shenrone Enterprises, 1996), https://www.familysearch.org/search/catalog/688209?availabilit y=Family%20History%20Library.

31   Josephine Beynon Boos and Patricia C. Gallinger, *Descendants of John Beynon – Generation No. 1*, 1-2, https://books.google.ca/books/about/The_Descendants_of_ John_Beynon.html?id=ObPQAAAACAAJ&redir_esc=y.

32   Material provided to the author by Josephine Beynon Boos, "Family Tree," and "The James Barnes Beynon Family," *Beynon Family Association Newsletter*, 10th Issue (August 2007), cover page and 12.

33   Josephine Beynon Boos and Patricia C. Gallinger, *Descendants of John Beynon – Generation No. 3*: 13-14. https://books.google.ca/books/about/The_Descendants_ of_John_Beynon.html?id=ObPQAAAACAAJ&redir_esc=y; The Hartney Star, 15 April 1898, "Mother in Israel," 1.

34   Josephine Beynon Boos, *Descendants of John Beynon – Generation No. 3*,
      13-14; Letter: J.B. Beynon to Hon. Thos. Greenway, 1 March 1895, Lillian
      Beynon Thomas Papers, AM, P191; Letter: H.B. Beynon to Prof. Ramsay Cook, 19
      February 1973, Clara Thomas Archives & Special Collections, Scott Library, York
      University, where H.B. Beynon wrote: "In politics he [my father, James Barnes Jr.]
      was a grit. He had met Sir John A. MacDonald, and liked him. He said he'd like to
      vote for Sir John if he was ever right. Alas, Sir John being a tory could never be right
      in his father's eyes." Lillian Beynon Thomas, "I Remember" in *Hartney and District,
      Manitoba: 75th Anniversary Celebration 1882-1957- Souvenir Book* (Deloraine: The
      Deloraine Times, 1957), https://digitalcollections.lib.umanitoba.ca/islandora/object/
      uofm%3A3081253#page/66/mode/2up, 57-8, where Lillian wrote: "My father liked
      him [Mr. Hartney, pioneer settler in the region] too. I don't know why. It might
      have been that Mr. Hartney was grit."

35   Apart from the pseudonym, "Lillian Laurie," that she used as a journalist and
      the name, "Lillian Beynon Thomas," that she used following her 1911 marriage,
      Lillian's name was spelled in a variety of different ways on a variety of different
      documents. Unless otherwise indicated below, these documents can be found in
      Lillian Beynon Thomas Papers, AM, P191. See also: Copy of Province of Ontario
      Certificate of Birth, No. B83716, 2 April 1942 – "Lilly Kate Beynon;" 1881 Census,
      Ontario, District No. 140 Peel, Page 17, Line 11, http://data2.collectionscanada.
      gc.ca/e/e328/e008186525.pdf – "Lilli C;" 1891 Census, Manitoba, 9 Selkirk, http://
      central.bac-lac.gc.ca/.item/?app=Census1891&op=pdf&id=30953_148098-00361
      – "Lily Kate;" 1901 Census, Manitoba, http://data2.collectionscanada.ca/1901/z/
      z001/pdf/z000014258.pdf - "Lilly Beynon;" Third-Class Normal School Diploma,
      5 April, 1893 – "Lillie Beynon;" Grand Bend School 1895-6 – "Lillian Beynon;"
      Second-Class Normal School Diploma, 4 February 1897 – "Lily Beynon;" *Hartney
      Star* "Miss Lily Beynon left ... to resume control of a school near Arden..." 15
      January 1897; University of Winnipeg Archives, Wesley College Registration, 1899-
      1900 Session - "Lillie Beynon;" Letter of Recommendation, Thos D. Macdonald,
      Presbyterian Mission, Ochre River, Manitoba, 12 May 1905 – "Lillie Beynon;"
      Professional Second-Class Teacher's Certificate, 10 June 1905 - "Lillie K. Beynon;"
      Provincial Examination First-Class Teachers, July 1905 – "Lillie Beynon;"
      Interim Second- Class Certificate North-West Territories, 23 June 1906 – "Lillie
      K. Beynon;" C.W. Parker, ed., *Who's Who in Western Canada 1911* (Vancouver:
      Canadian Press Association, 1911) 109 - "Beynon, Lillian, B.A. – Editor Woman's
      Dept.;" "Certificate of Marriage, Manitoba, 27 September 1911 - Lily Kate Beynon;"
      Beynon Family Association Newsletter, 27 where it states, "Mr. Alfred Vernon
      Thomas and Miss Lillian Kathleen Beynon married Wednesday, September the
      twenty-seventh, nineteen hundred and eleven, Winnipeg, Manitoba;" A.V. Thomas,
      "Sale of Carlton School Site Recalls Noted People Who Learned 'Three R's' There,"
      The Winnipeg Tribune, 12 April 1930, 6 where Lillian's husband refers to his wife at
      a time when she was in High School as - "Lily Beynon;" Last Will and Testament,
      20 April 1954, signed - "Lillian B. Thomas."

36 Material provided to the author by Josephine Beynon Boos, "Lillian Kathleen (Lilly Kate) Beynon Thomas," *Beynon Family Association Newsletter*, 10th Issue (August 2007), 27.

37 Material provided to the author by Josephine Beynon Boos, "The James Barnes Beynon Family," *Beynon Family Association Newsletter*, 10th Issue (August 2007), 12 and 14.

38 Anne Hicks, "Francis Beynon and *The Guide*," in *First Days, Fighting Days: Women in Manitoba History*, ed. Mary Kinnear (Regina: Canadian Plains Research Center, 1987), 44; *The Grain Growers' Guide*, 2 October 1912, 24.

39 Beynon Boos, *Descendants of John Beynon – Generation No. 3*: 23-4; Letter: H.B. Beynon to Ramsay Cook, 26 February 1973.

40 Lillian Beynon Thomas, "I Remember," 57, https://digitalcollections.lib.umanitoba.ca/islandora/object/uofm%3A3081253#page/67/mode/2up

41 Ibid. 58.

42 A colourful description from the earliest of times in the Souris Valley, once home of millions of buffalo and the Assiniboine Indigenous peoples, is given in Hartney and District Historical Committee, Naomi Asper, "A Century of Living, Hartney and District 1882-1982," 1-23. https://digitalcollections.lib.umanitoba.ca/islandora/object/uofm%3A2385341#page/13/mode/2up

43 Lillian Beynon Thomas, "I Remember," 57, https://digitalcollections.lib.umanitoba.ca/islandora/object/uofm%3A3081253#page/67/mode/2up, 58.

44 Ibid. 59.

45 Ibid.

46 Hazel McDonald Parkinson, *The Mere Living: A Biography of the Hartney District* (Altona: D.W. Friesen & Sons Ltd.), 55, https://digitalcollections.lib.umanitoba.ca/islandora/object/uofm%3A2235091#page/1/mode/2up.

47 Gordon Goldsborough, Manitoba Historical Society, "Manitoba Communities: Hartney (Unincorporated Town)," http://www.mhs.mb.ca/docs/municipalities/hartney.shtml.

48 Anne Hicks, "Introduction," in Francis Marion Beynon, *Aleta Dey*, (London: Virago Modern Classics, 1988), viii.

49 E. Cora Hind, "The Women's Quiet Hour – Lillian Laurie," *The Western Home Monthly*, November 1911, 56.

50 Francis Marion Beynon, "Between the Editor and Readers," *The Grain Growers' Guide* [hereafter *GGG*], 12 June 1912, 9.

51 Francis Marion Beynon, "Sunshine," *GGG*, 21 January 1914, 22.

52 Parkinson, *The Mere Living: A Biography of the Hartney District*, 54.

53 Beynon Thomas, "I Remember," 57.

54 *The Hartney Star*, 15 January 1897.

55 Francis Marion Beynon, "Inconsistant Discipline," *GGG*, 28 October 1914, 10.

56   Francis Marion Beynon, "The Picnic," *GGG*, 14 June 1916, 10. A typical such picnic is described at, "Sunday School Picnic – 1907," *Hartney and District, Manitoba: 75th Anniversary Celebration 1882-1957- Souvenir Book* (Deloraine: The Deloraine Times, 1957), http://hartneyheritage.ca/documents/images/Hartney75th.pdf, 59-61.

57   "Hartney's Temperance Hotel," *Manitoba Daily Free Press*, 19 March 1891, 5; Brandon *Sun Weekly*, 5 March 1891, 1; 1891 Census, Manitoba, 9 Selkirk, Line 14, http://central.bac-lac.gc.ca/.item/?app=Census1891&op=pdf& id=30953_148098-00361, where J.B. Beynon is listed as an hotel proprietor.

58   "Properties For Sale," *Manitoba Daily Free Press*, 21 January 1892, 1.

59   Hazel McDonald Parkinson. *The Mere Living: A Biography of the Hartney District.* Altona: D.W. Friesen & Sons Ltd., 1957. 196.

60   *Manitoba Free Press*, 22 August 1907, 10.

61   Ibid. 124.

62   Letter: J.B. Beynon to Hon. Thos. Greenway, 1 March 1895, Lillian Beynon Thomas Papers, AM, P191; Beynon Boos, "The James Barnes Beynon Family," 12.

63   "A Mother In Israel," *The Hartney Star*, 15 April 1898, 1. Religious denomination in parenthesis in the original.

64   Advertisements placed by "M. Beynon" can be found at: "Loans at 6 ½ and 7 Per Cent and Farms In All Parts of the Province," *The Hartney Star*, 10 August 1898; "Bargains in Farms," *The Hartney Star*, 3 March 1899; "Straight Loans at 6.5% --- Samples of Champion Drills, Norwegian Plows, Scotch Diamond Clip Harrows, Detroit Disk, Now on Hand," *The Hartney Star*, 8 April 1899; "Farms Wanted," *The Hartney Star*, 8 June 1900; "Farms Wanted," 9 August 1901; and, "Farms Wanted," 23 August, 1901. Later in life, Manning sold fire engines throughout Western Canada from his home base in Saskatoon, Saskatchewan, see: "J.H. Manning Beynon Dies At Saskatoon," *The Winnipeg Tribune*, 12 March 1946, 10 where Manning is described as the owner of the Saskatoon Fire Works (i.e., "fire works," meaning fire equipment, not event "fireworks.")

65   Beynon Boos, *Descendants of John Beynon – Generation No. 3*, 23-24; Letter: H.B. Beynon to Prof. Ramsay Cook, 26 February 1973.

66   Beynon Boos, *Descendants of John Beynon – Generation No. 3*, 25; "G.W. Beynon Dead," *Portage la Prairie News* (Weekly), 28 May 1902, 3.

67   The Epworth League was a Methodist association for young adults between the ages of 18 and 35. It was founded in Cleveland, Ohio in 1889 and ten years later boasted over 1.75 million members in 19,500 chapters in Canada and the United States.

68   *The Hartney Star*, 18 July 1902, 1.

69   Application for Homestead, No. 15831, Jas B. Beynon, 19 May 1902, found in Beynon, James B, Saskatchewan Homestead Index (hereafter Homestead Index), File Number 734859, PAS.

70   Beynon, James Henry Manning, Homestead Index, File Number 589759, PAS.

71 Sworn Statement of James B. Beynon in support of his application for Homestead Patent for South West of Section 10 Township 6 Range 30 of W1 Principal Meridian, 19 May 1902 and Statutory Declaration of J.B. Beynon in the matter of his Homestead both found in Beynon, James B, Homestead Index, File Number 734859, PAS.

72 Department of the Interior, 6 March 1907 informing James B. Beynon of Antler, Sask. that a Patent had issued, 22 February 1907 and Canada, Grant of Land to James B. Beynon, 22 February 1907 both found in Beynon, James B, Homestead Index, File Number 734859, PAS.

73 Certificate of Title, James B. Beynon, 20 March 1907 found in Beynon, James B, Homestead Index, File Number 734859, PAS.

74 Certificate of Title, James B. Beynon, 20 March 1907 found in Beynon, James B, Homestead Index, File Number 734859, PAS.

75 Deaths, County of Lincoln, Division of St. Catharines, 21 June 1907, No. 92, 018290.

76 Deaths, County of Lincoln, Division of St. Catharines, 21 June 1907, No 92, 018290.

77 Barnes was born on March 22, 1835. 1901 Census of Canada, sub district: Cameron, Brandon, Manitoba, District Number: 6, sub district number: d-2, page # 2, line # 31, Archives Microfilm: T-6431, http://automatedgenealogy.com/census/ View.jsp?id=11366&highlight=31&desc=1901+Census+of+Canada+page+containing +James+B.+Beynon.

78 Transfer of Land: James B. Beynon of St. Catharines in the Province of Ontario to James Henry Manning Beynon of the Town of Estevan in the Province of Saskatchewan, 12 June 1907 and supporting affidavit sworn before William A. Beynon of the Town of Estevan, 12 June 1907 found in PAS, Homestead Index, File Number 734859, Beynon, James B.

79 "Obituary," *Manitoba Free Press*, 22 August 1907, 10.

80 Hartney and District Historical Committee, "A Century of Living, Hartney and District 1882-1982," Schools – Hartney Public School District no. 312, p. 97.

81 Beynon Boos, "Lillian Kathleen (Lilly Kate) Beynon Thomas," 27; Parkinson, *The Mere Living*, 55.

82 Lillian B. Thomas, "Abroad in Manitoba," *The Winnipeg Tribune Magazine*, 22 September 1934, 7; "Lillian Beynon Thomas," *Winnipeg Free Press*, 4 September 1961, 19; "Deaths – Thomas," *The Winnipeg Tribune*, 5 September 1961, 20.

83 "Beynon, Lillian, B.A. – Editor Woman's Dept." in C.W. Parker, *Who's Who in Western Canada 1911* (Vancouver: Canadian Press Association, Limited, 1911) 109; A.V. Thomas, Municipal Editor of *The Winnipeg Tribune*, "Sale of Carlton School Site Recalls Noted People Who Learned 'Three R's' There," *The Winnipeg Tribune*, 12 April 1930, 6 where A.V Thomas, Lillian's husband, is author of a story on the slated closure in 1930 of Maple Leaf School, a junior high school. Earlier, Maple Leaf School had been the Winnipeg Collegiate Institute, the city's first and only

high school. Thomas notes that, "Lily Beynon was a graduate of the school." Also, "Picnic To Be Held by Old Collegiate Pupils," *The Winnipeg Tribune*, 10 June 1931, 9. Lillian was a member of the committee in charge of the picnic program.

84   Michelle Swann and Veronica Strong-Boag, "Mooney, Helen Letitia (McClung)," in *Dictionary of Canadian Biography Online*, http://www.biographi.ca/en/bio/mooney_helen_letitia_18E.html; Manitoba Historical Society, "Historic Sites of Manitoba: Winnipeg Collegiate Institute/Maple Leaf School (Bannatyne Avenue, Winnipeg)," http://www.mhs.mb.ca/docs/sites/winnipegcollegiateinstitute.shtml; Reid Dickie, "Winnipeg Collegiate Institute" in *Read Reid Read*, https://readreidread.wordpress.com/2013/03/12/schools-out-forever/.

85   Leslie Gaudry, "Plain and Simple: The History of One-Room School Houses in Rural Manitoba," *The Citizen*, 2 September, 2020, https://nivervillecitizen.com/news/local/plain-and-simple-the-history-of-one-room-schoolhouses-in-rural-manitoba.

86   Letter to Dr. E.A. Blakely, Department of Ed., Report on Brandon Local Normal 1893, 30 March 1893, Normal School Records, AM.

87   Ibid.

88   Local Normal School, Manitoba, Lillie Beynon, Third-Class Normal School Diploma, Lillian Beynon Thomas Papers, AM, P191.

89   Second-Class Normal School Diploma, Lily Beynon, 4 February 1897, Lillian Beynon Thomas Papers, AM, P191; Professional Second-Class Teacher's Certificate, Lillie K. Beynon, 10 June 1905, Lillian Beynon Thomas Papers, AM, P191.

90   Michelle Swann and Veronica Strong-Boag, "Mooney, Helen Letitia (McClung)" in *Dictionary of Canadian Biography Online*, http://www.biographi.ca/en/bio/mooney_helen_letitia_18E.html.

91   "Wesley College Session 1899-1900 Cont'd – Registration No. 473," *Wesley College First Registration, 1888-1917*, University of Winnipeg Archives, WC-23-1.

92   George Siamandas, "Lillian Beynon Thomas: Writer and Social Reformer," *The Winnipeg Time Machine*, http://timemachine.siamandas.com/PAGES/people_stories/LILLIAN_BENYON_THOMAS.htm.

93   Email: Daniel Matthes, University of Winnipeg Archivist, to author, 4 March 2015; Manitoba Cultural, Heritage and Recreation, *Lillian Beynon Thomas*, 1; George Siamandas, "Lillian Beynon Thomas: Writer and Social Reformer," https://timemachine.siamandas.com/PAGES/people_stories/LILLIAN_BENYON_THOMAS.htm.

94   "University Pass List is Announced," *The Winnipeg Telegram*, 12 May 1905, 8, https://digitalcollections.lib.umanitoba.ca/islandora/object/uofm%3A2735697

95   "Our Latest Arts Alumni: An Appreciation," *Vox Wesleyana* 10.1 (Winnipeg: Wesley College, 1905), University of Winnipeg Archives, AC-9-4, 4-6.

96   Blanche Ellinthorpe, "From Teaching to Writing," *The Country Guide*, February 1953, 68.

97   Manitoba Cultural, Heritage and Recreation, *Lillian Beynon Thomas* (Winnipeg: Manitoba Culture, Heritage and Recreation, Historic Resources Branch, 1985), 1; "Winnipeg Author Adds to the List By 'Under the Maples,'" *Winnipeg Free Press*, 30 April 1932, 18.

98   Hartney-Cameron Heritage Group, Milestones: Hartney's Significant Historical Themes and Events, 14. https://heritagemanitoba.ca/images/pdfs/featuredProjects/Hartney_Milestones_Heritage_MB_Part2.pdf; The Public Schools," *The Hartney Star*, 18 January 1894, 9.

99   E. Cora Hind, "The Women's Quiet Hour – Lillian Laurie," *The Western Home Monthly*, November 1911, 56, where Hind notes that Lillian taught in country schools in many of the new districts both of Manitoba and Saskatchewan, beginning her career as a teacher when she was only 16. This is likely an error, the correct age being 18.

100 Aileen Garland, The Killarney And District Historical Committee, *Trails and Crossroads To Killarney: The story of pioneer days in the Killarney and Turtle Mountain District* (Altona: D.W. Friesen & Sons Ltd., 1967) https://digitalcollections.lib.umanitoba.ca/islandora/object/uofm%3A2233534#page/1/mode/2up, 60.

101 G.G. Phillips, *The Rise and Fall of a Prairie Town: A History of Lauder Manitoba and the Surrounding District*, Volume 3, https://digitalcollections.lib.umanitoba.ca/islandora/object/uofm%3A2386467#page/1/mode/2up, 160.

102 *The Hartney Star*, 15 January 1897, 1.

103 Parkinson, *The Mere Living*, 55.

104 The Dand Women's Institute, *Golden Memories: A History of the Dand Community*, 1882-1967 https://digitalcollections.lib.umanitoba.ca/islandora/object/uofm%3A2370402#page/4/mode/1up, 26; Census of Canada, 1901, Item Number: 184334, Province: Manitoba, District: Brandon, Sub-district: Cameron, Beynon, Lilly, Age 26, http://data2.collectionscanada.ca/1901/z/z001/pdf/z000014258.pdf; Manitoba Historical Society, "Historic Sites of Manitoba: Chain Lakes School No. 783 (RM of Cameron)," http://www.mhs.mb.ca/docs/sites/chainlakesschool.shtml; *The Hartney Star*, 16 August 1901, 1.

105 Letter: Rose to Turnbull, 14 November 1900,. Lillian Beynon Thomas Papers, AM, P191.

106 Dave McQueen, "Writes Novel of Atomic Age," *The Globe and Mail*, 7 September 1946, 13.

107 Letter: Thos. D. MacDonald, Presbyterian Mission, 12 May 1905, Lillian Beynon Thomas Papers, AM, P191.

108 John A. Cooper, "Editor's Talk," *The Canadian Courier*, Vol. XIV. No. 3 (June 21, 1913) 5.

109 Lillian Beynon Thomas, "Banking on Sam," *The Canadian Courier*, Vol. XIV, No. 4 (June 28, 1913) 6.

110 The Woman [E. Cora Hind], "The Woman About Town: Lilian [sic] Laurie,"
     Winnipeg Town Topics, 1913, Lillian Beynon Thomas Papers, AM, P191; Dorothy
     Muir, "Winnipeg Women," *C-O-A-C-H*, December 1932, 5.

111 Ellinthorpe, "From Teaching to Writing," 68.

112 Mary Ford, "The Pioneer Woman," *The Grain Growers' Guide* [hereafter *GGG*], 27
     March 1912, 23.

113 Letter: Violet McNaughton to Lillian Laurie, 19 July 1950, Violet McNaughton
     Papers, Provincial Archives of Saskatchewan [hereafter PAS].

114 S.P.L.G., "Book Review – *New Secret*," Lillian Beynon Thomas Papers, AM, P191.

115 E. Cora Hind, "The Women's Quiet Hour – Lillian Laurie," *The Western Home
     Monthly*, November 1911, 56; "MacLean's $1,000 Prize Story Awards," *MacLean's
     Magazine*, 1 May 1927, 27 where MacLean's publishes a brief autobiography
     submitted by Lillian in connection with its short story contest; Dave McQueen,
     "Writes Novel Of Atomic Age," *The Globe and Mail*, 7 September 1946, 13.

116 Mary Ford, "The Pioneer Woman," *GGG*, 27 March 1912, 23.

117 "A Women's Advocate – Mrs. Lillian Beynon Thomas Labors For Farmers' Wives,"
     The Chronicle, Shellbrook, Saskatchewan, 17 January 1914, 7 (reprinted from:
     Canadian Courier).

118 Marjory Lang, *Women Who Made the News: Female Journalists in Canada, 1880-
     1945*. (Montreal & Kingston: McGill-Queen's University Press, 1999) 108.

119 Muir, "Winnipeg Women," 5.

120 The Woman [E. Cora Hind], "The Woman About Town: Lilian [sic] Laurie,"
     Winnipeg Town Topics, 1913, Lillian Beynon Thomas Papers, AM, P191; Muir,
     "Winnipeg Women," 5; "Winnipeg Author Adds To List of Successes By 'Under the
     Maples'," *Winnipeg Free Press*, 30 April 1932, 18.

121 Ibid 265 citing, Grace Denison, *Saturday Night*, 16 November 1912, 30.

122 McQueen, "Writes Novel Of Atomic Age," 13.

123 Ellinthorpe, "From Teaching to Writing," 68.

124 Jocelyn Baker, "A Winnipeg Album – Mrs. A.V. Thomas," *The Winnipeg Tribune*, 1
     October 1932, 2 - Magazine Section. On Lillian's curiosity, see: Ellinthorpe, "From
     Teaching to Writing," 76 where Ellinthorpe, after having interviewed Lillian, wrote:
     "Lillian Thomas has through the years maintained her interest in questions of the
     day… Her interest in any live topic has always been keen." Ellinthorpe goes on to
     quote Lillian as saying, "I am glad to be living in age of perplexing problems." See
     also: Muir, "Winnipeg Women," 6, where the Muir quotes Lillian as saying, "As a
     child I often liked to imagine what period of history I would liked to have lived in."

125 Lang, 1, "… the dominant voice of the Fourth Estate was undoubtably male."

126 Murray Donnelly, *Dafoe of the Free Press*. (Toronto: McClelland and Stewart, 1966).
     Dafoe, the editor, neither smoked nor drank., 40.

127 Ibid., Lang, 92.

128 Ibid., 31.

129 Barbara M. Freeman, *Beyond Bylines: Media Workers and Women's Rights in Canada*. (Waterloo, Ontario: Wilfred Laurier University Press, 2011) 1. Some women journalists used their proper names including Beynon Thomas's sister, Francis, who edited the women's page in the *Grain Growers' Guide*. In addition to Francis's own determination, this may speak to the progressive attitudes of the newspaper's editor, George Chipman.

130 Ibid., 23

131 Ibid 27

132 Ibid., 155.

133 Ibid., Lang, 91.

134 The Woman [E. Cora Hind], "The Woman About Town: Lilian [sic] Laurie," *Winnipeg Town Topics*, 1913, Lillian Beynon Thomas Papers, AM, P191. However, later, when promoting Homemaker's Clubs for the University of Saskatchewan at rural country fairs, Lillian stressed the value of taking agricultural short courses from that University: see, Lillian K. Beynon, "Report of the Work in the University Tent," 1911, 6, SAB, Agricultural Societies File, HC, R26D, I.169. See also, Lillian Beynon Thomas, "To the Visitor, the Exhibits Make the show. But to the Exhibitor, the People Present an Ever Entertaining Spectacle," *Canada Monthly*, 1914, 262 where Lillian writes of how interesting the visitors were to the university tent at summer fairs at which the university promoted its extension courses.

135 "Women of the World – Interesting Talks at Women's Press Club Luncheon," a press clipping reporting on the 11 May 1911 meeting of the Winnipeg Branch of the Canadian Women's Press Club. The clipping can be found in *Minute Book, 22 October 1909 to 30 September 1915*, Canadian Women's Press Club Winnipeg Branch Papers, AM, P7650/2.

136 The Archives of Manitoba contain a letter dated 9 May 1960, from Mareella, Dafoe's daughter, recalling the early days when Lillian and Francis Beynon spent time with the young Mareella and her sister.

137 The entry class of women journalists and editors, well-known personalities to their many readers on isolated farm homesteads, included Kate Simpson Hayes (Mary Markwell), editor from 1899 to 1906 of the woman's page in the *Free Press*, the first newspaper in Western Canada to include such a page, and Lillian Beynon Thomas's immediate predecessor. Others who enjoyed a personal bond with their readers included the following: E. Cora Hind, Commercial and Agricultural editor of the *Free Press*; Kennethe M. Haig (Alison Craig) of the *Free Press*; Genevieve Lipsett-Skinner of *The Winnipeg Telegram*; Florence Lediard (Dame Durden) and May Clendenan (Dame Dibbins) both of *The Farmers' Advocate and Home Journal*; Mary S. Mantle (Margaret Freestone) of the *Nor'-west Farmer*; Francis Marion Beynon of *The Grain Growers' Guide*; Anne Anderson Perry of the *Winnipeg Saturday Post*; and Harriet Walker (Matinee Girl) of *Town Topics*.

138 E. Cora Hind, "The Women's Quiet Hour," *Western Home Monthly*, March 1914, 44.

139 Pearl Richmond Hamilton, "Our Winnipeg Press Women," *The Canadian Thresherman and Farmer*, July 1913, 82, https://www.canadiana.ca/view/ oocihm.8_04973_43/80?r=0&s=1

140 The Woman [E. Cora Hind], "The Woman About Town: Lilian [sic] Laurie," *Winnipeg Town Topics*, 1913, Lillian Beynon Thomas Papers, AM, P191.

141 Letters from readers were to be addressed to "Lillian Laurie, Editor, Home Loving Hearts Page, Free Press, Winnipeg, Man." See Lillian Laurie, "Home Loving Hearts – A Page Especially for Them," *PF*, 19 December 1906, 14; See also "Saskatchewan Agricultural Meetings," *GGG*, 30 November 1910, 18 where Lillian is referred to as: "Miss Lillian K. Beynon, Editor, Woman's Page, *Manitoba Free Press*."

142 Gordon Goldsborough, Manitoba Historical Society, "MHS Centennial Business: *Winnipeg Free Press (Manitoba Free Press)*," http://www.mhs.mb.ca/docs/business/ freepress.shtml; Philistia, "Mrs. Lillian Beynon Thomas," *The Canadian Courier*, Vol. XIV. No. 22 (Toronto: Courier Press, Limited, November 1, 1913) 23.

143 "A Women's Advocate – Mrs. Lillian Beynon Thomas Labors For Farmers' Wives," *The Chronicle*, Shellbrook, Saskatchewan, 17 January 1914, 7 (reprinted from: *Canadian Courier*). This article was also reprinted in the *Shoal Lake Star*, 15 January 1914, 5.

144 Freeman, 81 and Chapter 3, fn 102.

145 *PF*, 21 June 1911, 2 - Magazine Section.

146 Ibid.

147 *PF*, 29 August 1906, 15. See also R.E. Hawkins, "Lillian Beynon Thomas, Woman's Suffrage and the Return of Dower to Manitoba," *Manitoba Law Journal* 27(Issue 1 1999), 57; and Lynette Sarah Plett, "How the Vote Was Won: Adult Education and the Manitoba Woman Suffrage Movement, 1912-1916" (Winnipeg: University of Manitoba Master of Education Thesis, 2000).

148 *PF*, 22 October 1913, 2 - Home Section.

149 *PF*, 19 December 1906, 14. There is no record explaining why Lillian chose "Laurie" as the second name in her nom de plume, "Lillian Laurie." Beynon Thomas's ancestry was Irish. 'Laurie' is sometimes interpreted as the English version of the Irish name 'Lorcan' meaning 'fierce.'

150 *PF*, 9 January 1907, 20.

151 *PF*, 29 November 1911, 2 - Magazine Section.

152 *PF*, 14 October 1908, 14.

153 *PF*, 6 February 1907, 16; *PF*, 20 February 1907, 16; *PF*, 27 February 1907, 15; *PF*, 6 March 1907 16.

154 *PF*, 25 December 1907, 14.

155 Great Grandma, B.C., "Home Loving Hearts 'The page is now yours – use it,'" *Free Press Weekly Prairie Farmer*, 1 June 1960, 10.

156 Ibid.

157 Norah L. Lewis, ed. *Dear Editor and Friends: Letters from Rural Women of the North-West, 1900-1920*. (Waterloo: Wilfred Laurier University Press, 1998) 7.

158 Ibid., 5, where Norah Lewis's came to the same conclusion. She states, "Although many readers [of the newspaper columns] stated their ethnic origins or regional roots, no writers indicated that they were First Nations or Metis women. ... Missing, however, [from letter writers] were the voices of those not yet literate in English, many non-subscribers, the very poor, and those not motivated to write."

159 *Free Press Weekly Prairie Farmer*, 10 February 1960, 10 which refers to Lillian Laurie's column in, *PF*, 10 April 1912, 2 - Magazine Section. For another letter, prompted by Ashnola's letter, reminiscing about the early days of the Home Loving Hearts page see: Great Grandma, B.C., *Free Press Weekly Prairie Farmer*, 1 June 1960, 10.

160 *PF*, 25 December 1907, 14, where Beynon Thomas looked back over the column's development and the M.B.A.'s membership increase during the first year. During her time as editor of the women's page, Lillian Laurie wrote three other retrospective columns in which she described the evolution of the Home Loving Hearts page. One was at the seven-year mark of the page's existence, *PF*, 22 October 1913, 2 - Home Section, another was in the 22 April 1914, 2 Home Section, and the third was one of her final columns as she departed for New York City, *PF*, 2 May 1917, 7.

161 *PF*, 6 December 1911, 2 - Magazine Section.

162 *PF*, 10 January 1912, 3 - Magazine Section.

163 Ibid.

164 Rudimentary rural party telephone lines only started to reach rural Manitoba in the second decade of the twentieth century.

165 *PF*, 27 January 1909, 14.

166 *PF*, 25 November 1908, 14.

167 Violet McNaughton, "Jottings By The Way," *The Western Producer*, 11 December 1952, 14.

168 Pearl Richmond Hamilton, "Our Winnipeg Press Women," *The Canadian Thresherman and Farmer*, July 1918, 82, https://www.canadiana.ca/view/oocihm.8_04973_43/80?r=0&s=1

169 *Winnipeg Free Press*, 30 November 1972, 231

170 Francis Marion Beynon, "The Country Homemakers," *The Grain Grower's Guide*, 25 December 1912, 10, http://peel.library.ualberta.ca/newspapers/GGG/1912/12/25/10/

171 *PF*, 2 May 1917, 7.

172 *PF*, 22 October 1913, 2 - Home Section.

173 *PF*, 22 April 1914, 2 – Home Section.

174 Starting at "HLH," *PF*, January 14, 1914, and then weekly from May 13, 1914, to July 29, 1914, all at 2-Home Section in each issue.

175 *PF*, 9 September 1914, 1 – Home Section.

176 *PF*, 10 March 1915, 7.

177 This phrase was used by E. Cora Hind. See: E. Cora Hind, "The Women's Quiet Hour – Why Women Should Vote," *Western Home Monthly*, October 1910, 37-38 and at E. Cora Hind, "The Women's Quiet Hour," *Western Home Monthly*, February 1912, 57.

178 Lillian Laurie, "Why I Fight For Women," *Manitoba Free Press*, 16 September 1910, 9 where letters appear from women giving examples of men who had sold their homesteads and deserted their wives. See also "Surely People Will See," and "Note," *Manitoba Free Press*, 24 September 1910, 9.

179 *PF*, 17 June 1908, 14. Beynon Thomas incorrectly attributed this letter to "a woman from Alberta" when in fact it was written by "An Old Woman" from British Columbia who was complaining about the lack of a dower law in that province. See: Lillian Beynon Thomas, "Reminiscences of a Manitoba Suffragette," in Manitoba Historical Society, Manitoba Pageant 5, 1 (September 1959), http://www.mhs.mb.ca/docs/pageant/05/suffragette.shtml, 10; Catherine Cleverdon, *The Woman Suffrage Movement in Canada* (Toronto: University of Toronto Press, 1950); Letter: Lillian to Cleverdon, 21 April 1944, Lillian Beynon Thomas Papers, AM, P191; Letter: H.B. Beynon to Prof. Ramsay Cook, 19 February 1973, Clara Thomas Archives & Special Collections, Scott Library, York University.

180 An Old Woman, "A Dower Law Is Needed," *Manitoba Free Press*, 15 February 1910, 9.

181 *PF*, 28 October 1908, 14.

182 R.E. Hawkins, "Lillian Beynon Thomas, Woman's Suffrage and the Return of Dower to Manitoba," 52.

183 Dame Durden [Florence Lediard], "The Ingle Nook - A Chance To Do Something," *Farmer's Advocate and Home Journal* (Winnipeg: *Farmer's Advocate* of Winnipeg), 8 July 1908, 960; see also: "March Home Journal," *Minnedosa Tribune*, 11 March 1909, 1 where, in reference to a story in the magazine, *Canadian Home Journal*, it states: "'Western women and the Dower' is the subject of a most interesting discussion by Lillian K. Beynon of Winnipeg, and this ... gives an insight into conditions in the great west."

184 R.E. Hawkins, "Lillian Beynon Thomas, Woman's Suffrage and the Return of Dower to Manitoba." *Manitoba Law Journal* 27(1) (1999-2000), 45-114, 62-72.

185 Beynon Thomas titled one of her short stories using these words: Lillian Beynon Thomas, "Reason VS. Sentiment." (with R. Oliphant reader report) (Syracuse: Syracuse University Libraries, Special Collections Research Center, Street & Smith Records, September 5, 1913.). The story was not accepted for publication.

186 Jocelyn Baker, "A Winnipeg Album – Mrs. A.V. Thomas," *The Winnipeg Tribune*, 1 October 1932, 2 - Magazine Section.

187 *PF*, 30 September 1908, 16.

188 *PF*, 16 September 1908, 14; *PF*, 23 September 1908, 14; *PF*, 16 December 1908, 14.

189 E. Cora Hind, "The Women's Quiet Hour – The Dower Law," *The Western Home Monthly*, February 1909, 34-5; "Why Women Should Vote," *GGG*, 22 May 1912, 27; "Reply to J.P.S.," *PF* 3 February 1909, 14 and "Reply to Rose Poppy, *PF*, 10 February 1909, 14.

190 *PF*, 2 September 1908, 14; *PF*, 16 September 1908, 14; *PF*, 16 December 1908, 14.

191 "Home Loving Hearts," *PF*, 2 May 1917, 7. Manitoba passed a dower law in the 1918 spring session.

192 "Just A Word," *Manitoba Free Press*, 26 December 1908, 9. Her comments were reprinted in the weekly farm paper: *PF*, 30 December 1908, 14. See also *PF*, 20 January 1909, 14; *PF*, 27 January 1909, 14; *PF*, 4 August 1909, 14.

193 *PF*, 25 December 1907, 14.

194 Wendy Heads, "The Local Council of Women of Winnipeg, 1894-1920, Tradition and Transformation" (Winnipeg: University of Manitoba Department of History Master of Arts Thesis, 1997), http://hdl.handle.net/1993/1006, 71.

195 Lillian Laurie, "Just A Word – A Chat With Readers," *Manitoba Free Press*, 15 February 1910, 9; Isobel, "Around The Fireside - What Women Are Doing," *GGG*, 23 February 1910, 29.

196 Lillian Laurie, "Just A Word – A Chat With Readers," *Manitoba Free Press*, 24 February 1910, 9. See also R.E. Hawkins, "Lillian Beynon Thomas, Woman's Suffrage and the Return of Dower to Manitoba," 77-81.

197 "Woman's Labor League Wants Dower Law Enforced in Manitoba," *Manitoba Free Press*, 23 Nov 1910, 10; "Suffrage Organizations in Winnipeg," *Manitoba Free Press*, 14 January 1911, 20; *PF*, 22 February 1911, 44; *PF*, 11 March 1911, 5 - Women's Section; Isobel [Isobel Graham], "Around the Fireside – W.C.T.U. Convention," *GGG*, 17 May 1911, 25; Isobel [Isobel Graham], "Around the Fireside – Homesteads for Women," *GGG*, 16 August 1911, 20.

198 The 1911 lobby was well covered in the press: see, "A Plea For Better Laws," *Manitoba Free Press*, 15 February 1911, 9; "Women To Ask For Dower Law," *Manitoba Free Press*, 17 Feb 1911, 22; "Women Demand Improved Laws," *Manitoba Free Press*, 20 February 1911, 9; "Women Ask For Dower Law," *Manitoba Free Press*, 21 February 1911, 3; "Improved Laws For Women," *Manitoba Free Press*, 25 February 1911, 44; Lillian Laurie, "Women As Idols," *Manitoba Free Press*, 1 April 1911, 43 (1 - Woman's Section); "Deputation Asks For Dower Law," *Winnipeg Telegram*, 21 February 1911; "Women Plead For New Dower Law," *Winnipeg Telegram*, 14 March 1911; *PF*, 12 April 1911, 2 - Magazine Section; Isobel, "Around the Fireside - Ask For Dower Law," *GGG*, 1 March 1911, 36; Isobel, "Around The Fireside - Dower Law for Manitoba," *GGG*, 19 April 1911, 26; *The Nor'-West Farmer*, 5 May 1911, 583; E. Cora Hind, "Women's Quiet Hour - The Dower Law," *Western Home Monthly*, April 1911, 53-54.

199 Isobel, "Around The Fireside - Dower Law for Manitoba," *GGG*, 19 April 1911, 26.

200 "Women Ask For Dower Law," *Manitoba Free Press*, 21 February 1911, 3.

201 "To Consider Bill," *Manitoba Free Press*, 13 March 1911, 9.

202 Kennethe Haig (aka Alison Craig), "Over The Tea Cups," *Manitoba Free Press*, 6 April 1912, 43 (1 - Woman's Section); E. Cora Hind, "Woman's Quiet Hour - The Dower Law," *Western Home Monthly*," April 1912, 50-51; E. Cora Hind, "Woman's Quiet Hour - Acts for the Relief of Women," *Western Home Monthly*, May 1912, 62-63; "Recent Manitoba Legislation Affecting Women," *Manitoba Free Press*, 9 April 1912, 4; "Widows' And Children's Relief Act," *The Nor'-West Farmer*, 20 April 1912, 572.

203 "Recent Manitoba Legislation Affecting Women," *Manitoba Free Press*, 9 April 1912, 4.

204 Blanche Ellinthorpe, "From Teaching to Writing," *The Country Guide*, February 1953, 68.

205 "Man and Women Who Work in Words and Pictures," *The Winnipeg Tribune*, 4 March 1936, 8.

206 "Veteran Newsman Alfred V. Thomas Dies In Winnipeg," *Winnipeg Free Press*, 11 September 1950.

207 Elizabeth Blight, "In Greater Manitoba ... with A.V. Thomas," *Manitoba History* 15 (Spring 1988), http://www.mhs.mb.ca/docs/mb_history/15/thomas_av.shtml.

208 Certificate of Marriage, Alfred Vernon Thomas and Lily Kate Beynon, 27 September 1911, found in Lillian Beynon Thomas Papers, AM, P191; Province of Ontario Certificate of Birth, No. B83716, Lilly Kate Beynon, 2 April 1942, found in Lillian Beynon Thomas Papers, AM, P191.

209 Letter from Mareella to Lillian, 1 May 1960, acknowledging a letter from Lillian to the Dafoe family on Bessie Dafoe's death, found in Lillian Beynon Thomas Papers, AM, P191. See also University of Manitoba Archives and Special Collections – UMASC, TC 74 – Sheila Rabinovitch Collection, Tape 17, transcribed by Arran Jewsbury, 8, where the visits of the Beynon sisters to the Dafoe family are described.

210 Letter: Ch. Teeter, Pastor of the Beynon Family at Hartney, Manitoba, to Lillian, 26 April 1932, Lillian Beynon Thomas Papers, AM, P191.

211 *PF*, 27 September 1911, 2 - Magazine Section.

212 *PF*, 10 January 1912, 3 - Magazine Section.

213 *PF*, 25 October 1911, 2 - Magazine Section.

214 *PF*, 10 January 1912, 3 - Magazine Section.

215 "Looking Backward," *Winnipeg Free Press*, 21 January 1952, 12, recollecting Beynon Thomas's report on Westminster Abbey published in the *Free Press* 40 years earlier, see: "Westminster Abbey – Resting Place Of The Empire's Great," *Manitoba Free Press*, 20 January 1912, 43 (3 - Woman's Section).

216 Ellinthorpe, "From Teaching to Writing," 68.

217 Quill Club, "Meeting of 14 November 1908," *Minutes of Meetings 14 November 1908 – 13 November 1909*, Lillian Beynon Thomas Papers, AM, P191.

218 Quill Club, "Meeting of 20 March 1909," *Minutes of Meetings 14 November 1908 – 13 November 1909*, Lillian Beynon Thomas Papers, AM, P191.

219 There are many accounts of the formation of the P.E.L. The classic account is given by Nellie L. McClung, *The Stream Runs Fast: My Own Story*, (Toronto: Thomas Allen Limited, 1945), 101-110. That account is verified and expanded upon by Cleverdon, *The Woman Suffrage Movement In Canada*, 55.

220 "Winnipeg Author Adds To List of Successes By 'Under the Maples'," *Winnipeg Free Press*, 30 April 1932, 18. See also: Ellinthorpe, "From Teaching to Writing," 68.

221 *PF*, 10 January 1912, 3 - Magazine Section.

222 Lillian Beynon Thomas, *New Secret* (Toronto: Thomas Allen Limited, 1946), dedication page. Emphasis in the original.

223 "Canadian Authors' Group Pays Tribute to Lillian Beynon Thomas," *The Winnipeg Tribune*, 18 December 1946, 10.

224 Letter: Lillian Beynon Thomas to Jennie [Mrs. Robert Macham], 17 June 1939, Lillian Beynon Thomas Papers, AM, P191. The year of the letter can be determined by the reference in it to Beynon Thomas's upcoming trip to Boulder, Colorado.

225 E. Austin Weir was a pioneer radio broadcaster first with the Canadian National Railways network and subsequently with the early Canadian Broadcasting Corporation.

226 Letter: Lillian to Weir, 19 May 1960, Lillian Beynon Thomas Papers, AM, P191.

227 "To Organize Dramatic Club," *The Winnipeg Tribune*, 5 November 1936, 6; "Club Events", *Winnipeg Free Press*, 5 November 1936, 11; "Gordon Bell Students Will Present Play," *The Winnipeg Tribune*, 25 November 1939, 18; "2 'U' Students Win Radio Script Prizes," *The Winnipeg Tribune*, 22 April 1949, 7.

228 Baker, "A Winnipeg Album – Mrs. A.V. Thomas," 2 - Magazine Section.

229 "States Youth of Dominion must Pioneer in Arts – A.V. Thomas Speaks to the Federated Women's Institute Convention," *Winnipeg Free Press*, 8 June 1933, 6.

230 "Canadian Authors Dinner to Mark 25th Anniversary Draws Original Members," *Winnipeg Free Press*, 25 January 1950, 12.

231 Ellinthorpe, "From Teaching to Writing," 76.

232 The Woman [E. Cora Hind], "The Woman About Town: Lilian [sic] Laurie," *Winnipeg Town Topics*, 1913, Lillian Beynon Thomas Papers, AM, P191. See also letter: Lillian Beynon Thomas to W.R. Kane, Editor, *The Editor Magazine*, 19 October 1927, Lillian Beynon Thomas Papers, AM, P191.

233 For example, Florence Lediard [aka "Dame Durden"] of the *Farmer's Advocate and Home Journal* and Mary Mantle [aka Margaret Freestone] of *The Nor'-West Farmer* were among the organizers of the first Homemakers' Club convention held in Regina, in 1911. Fellow members of the Canadian Women's Press Club took part as well: Nellie McClung and E. Cora Hind gave addresses while Anne Perry of the *Saturday Post*, May Currie, and Isabel Armstrong of the *Regina Leader* registered as delegates. See Lang, *Women Who Made the News: Female Journalists in Canada, 1880-1945*, 225.

234 "Club House For Winnipeg's Women," *Manitoba Free Press*, 19 October 1911, 10.

235 Veronica Strong-Boag, "Introduction," in Nellie L. McClung, *In Times Like These* (Toronto and Buffalo: University of Toronto Press, 1972).

236 This phrase was used as the title of a regular column that was featured on the Woman's Page of the *Manitoba Free Press* from January 1913. It was authored by Kennethe Haig, under the pseudonym "Alison Craig." When Beynon Thomas left Winnipeg for New York city in 1917, Haig succeeded her as editor of the Home Loving Hearts page. Teas were frequently put on by women's organizations. They were social events meant to mark occasions such as accomplishments, anniversaries, visiting guests, and so on. Beynon Thomas was often invited to serve tea at the tea table, an indication of the status that she enjoyed in these organizations.

237 *The Winnipeg Tribune*, 19 January 1937, 5 and 27 January 1937, 7.

238 Veronica Strong-Boag, "Introduction," in Nellie L. McClung, *In Times Like These*, (Toronto and Buffalo: University of Toronto Press, 1972), x.

239 "Of Interest to Western Women," *Manitoba Free Press*, 5 February 1910, 23.

240 "Matters of Interest to Western Women," *Manitoba Free Press*, 1 December 1906, 32.

241 Marjory Lang, *Women Who Made the News: Female Journalists in Canada, 1880-1945* (Montreal & Kingston: McGill-Queen's University Press, 1999), 216-217.

242 Ibid., 217 and 224.

243 Ramsay Cook, "Francis Marion Beynon and the Crisis of Christian Reformism," in *The West and the Nation: Essays In Honour Of W.L. Morton*, eds. Carl Berger and Ramsay Cook (Toronto: McClelland and Stewart Limited, 1976), 187-208. Winnipeg's population rose from 42,300 inhabitants in 1900 to 166,553 in 1912. See: *Canadian Annual Review of Public Affairs* (Supplement) (Toronto: The Annual Review Publishing Company Limited, 1912) 81. In large part, this was the result of the efforts of Canada's Minister of the Interior, Clifford Sifton, whose immigration program attracted newcomers from the United States, Britain, and especially from eastern Europe, to the "Last Best West."

244 Ibid.

245 "Winnipeg, Grainspout of the World's Granary – The Magic City of the Great Northwest, which Expects to Wrest Supremacy from Buffalo and Duluth and Even Chicago Itself," *Manitoba Free Press*, 5 March 1910, 21-22, reprinted from *The New York Herald*, 20 February 1910.

246 Ibid., 70.

247 Morton, 297.

248 *Canadian Annual Review of Public Affairs*, 74.

249 *Manitoba Free Press*, 5 March, 1910, 21-22. The chronicler did not mention, and perhaps did not know, that the new power plant on Shoal Lake, to the east of the city, resulted in the destruction of the Anishinaabe band's water supply.

250 James S. Woodsworth, *Strangers Within Our Gates* or *Coming Canadians*, 3. The book opens with the following sentence: "Perhaps the largest and most important problem that the North American continent has before it to-day for solution is to show how the coming tides of immigrants of various nationalities and different

degrees of civilization may be assimilated and made worthy citizens of the great Commonwealths."

251 Ibid., Cook, 187. On the social gospel movement in Manitoba generally see, Richard Allen, *The Social Gospel: Religion and Social Reform in Canada 1914 – 1928* (Toronto: University of Toronto Press, 1971.

252 Cook, 188.

253 See: Ramsay Cook, "Ambiguous Heritage: Wesley College and the Social Gospel Reconsidered," *Manitoba History*, 19 (Spring 1990), http://www.mhs.mb.ca/docs/mb_history/19/wesleycollege.shtml.

254 Debbie Hathaway, "The Political Equality League of Manitoba," *Manitoba Historical Review*, 3 (1922), http://www.mhs.mb.ca/docs/mb_history/03/politicalequalityleague.shtml.

255 Katherine Ridout, "Finding Aid 2, Methodist Church (Canada), Department of Temperance, Prohibition and Moral Reform, Department of Social Service and Evangelism, Administrative History, Central Conferences Archives, The United Church of Canada Archives, Toronto.

256 Anne Hicks, "Francis Beynon and *The Guide*," in *First Days, Fighting Days: Women in Manitoba History*, ed. Mary Kinnear (Regina: Canadian Plains Research Centre, 1987), 47; Anne Hicks, "Introduction," in Francis Marion Beynon, *Aleta Dey* (London: Virago Modern Classics, 1988), x.

257 Barbara M. Freeman, *Beyond Bylines: Media Workers and Women's Rights in Canada* (Waterloo, Ontario: Wilfred Laurier University Press, 2011), 71. In 1917, when Beynon Thomas and her husband Vernon's pacifist views caused them to leave for New York City, Vernon and Woodsworth frequently exchanged letters discussing their opposition to the War.

258 Manitoba Historical Society, "Timelinks: The Peoples' Forum" (2009), http://www.mhs.mb.ca/docs/features/timelinks/reference/db0043.shtml; Manitoba Historical Society, "Timelinks: All Peoples' Mission" (2011), http://www.mhs.mb.ca/docs/features/timelinks/reference/db0061.shtml.

259 Alexander Richard Allen, "The Social Gospel Spectrum," in "Salem Bland and the Social Gospel in Canada" (Saskatoon: University of Saskatchewan Department of History Master of Arts Thesis, 1961), https://harvest.usask.ca/handle/10388/etd-07132010-073310, Chapter 4; Katherine Ridout, "Finding Aid 2, Methodist Church (Canada), Department of Temperance, Prohibition and Moral Reform, Department of Social Service and Evangelism, Administrative History" i, found in Central Conferences Archives, The United Church of Canada Archives, Toronto; Lillian Beynon Thomas, "Building on Canadian Pre-Emptions," *The Christian Guardian*, (29 May 1912) , 9-10.

260 "The People's Forum: Questions and Discussion," (Winnipeg 1914-15) http://data2.collectionscanada.gc.ca/e/e001/e000008115.jpg.

261 Lillian Beynon Thomas, "Building on Canadian Pre-Emptions," *The Christian Guardian*, (29 May 1912) 9-10.

262 Eric MacDonald, "All Peoples' Mission And The Legacy of J. S. Woodsworth: The Myth and the Reality" (Ottawa: University of Ottawa Department of History Master of Arts Thesis, 2013), https://ruor.uottawa.ca/bitstream/10393/24340/3/MacDonald_Eric_2013_thesis.pdf , 93, 106 and generally Chapter 5.

263 "The People's Forum: Questions and Discussion," (Winnipeg 1914-15) http://data2.collectionscanada.gc.ca/e/e001/e000008115.jpg ; "Announcements," *The Winnipeg Tribune*, 27 February 1914, 8.

264 "Meetings," *The Voice*, 22 Jan 1915, 8.

265 Lillian Beynon Thomas, "Practical Idealists," *Canada Monthly* 14.3 (July 1914), 168; *Manitoba Free Press*, 17 July 1914, 11.

266 "Pamphlet," (Winnipeg: Canadian Welfare League, 1913), https://archive.org/details/canadianwelfarel00cana, 1.

267 "Pamphlet," (Winnipeg: Canadian Welfare League, 1913), https://archive.org/details/canadianwelfarel00cana, 8.

268 "Pamphlet," (Winnipeg: Canadian Welfare League, 1913), https://archive.org/details/canadianwelfarel00cana, 1; Kenneth McNaught, *A Prophet in Politics: A Biography of J.S. Woodsworth* (Toronto: University of Toronto Press, 2001), 64; "Women's Press Club – First Meeting in New Quarters in Industrial Bureau," press clipping found in, "Meeting of 17 May 1912," *Minute Book, 22 October 1909 to 30 September 1915*," Canadian Women's Press Club Winnipeg Branch Papers, AM, P7650/2; Butler, "Branch Histories – Winnipeg," 19; Susan Jackel, "First Days, Fighting Days: Prairie Presswomen and Suffrage Activism, 1906-1916," in *First Days, Fighting Days: Women in Manitoba History*, ed. Mary Kinnear (Regina: Canadian Plains Research Centre, 1987), 63.

269 Lillian Beynon Thomas, "Practical Idealists," *Canada Monthly* 14, 3 (July 1914) 169.

270 Effie Butler, "Branch Histories – Winnipeg," in *Golden Jubilee 1904-1954 – Newspacket* (Toronto: Canadian Women's Press Club, 1954), 19; Harry and Mildred Gutkin, "Give us our due! How Manitoba Women Won the Vote," *Manitoba History*, 32 (Autumn 1996) where under the heading, "The Power of the Press; the Beynon Sisters," the authors point out that, "Eligibility for Club membership was extended to women who had published books or contributed to periodicals." http://www.mhs.mb.ca/docs/mb_history/32/womenwonthevote.shtml.

271 *Who's Who and Why 1913*, Vol. 1 (Vancouver) 9.

272 Beynon Thomas wrote a brief biography about her friend Harriet Walker, singer, actress, theatrical promoter, journalist and co-owner, with her husband, of Winnipeg's Walker Theatre: "For years there was a little sheet called Town Topics, published every Saturday. To many of us the most interesting part was the dramatic section, reviews and comments on plays and players. It was written by Hattie Walker, Mrs. C.P. Walker. ... Mrs. Walker assisted her husband, C.P. Walker, who had built the Walker Theatre and was bringing many of the world's outstanding actors and actresses to Winnipeg. That was the golden age of the theatre in Winnipeg, although we did not know it." Harriet Walker was a strong supporter of Manitoba's suffrage campaign. In 1914, she donated the Walker

theatre for performances of the suffrage play, *A Women's Parliament*, conceived by Beynon Thomas, that marked a turning point in the suffrage campaign. Historical and Scientific Society of Manitoba Transactions," Series III, 4 (1947- 48), http:// www.mhs.mb.ca/docs/transactions/3/firstwomen.shtml, 24. See also: Skene, Reg. "Harriet Walker". The Canadian Encyclopedia, 16 December 2013, Historica Canada., https://www.thecanadianencyclopedia.ca/en/article/harriet-walker and, "Harriet Anderson 'Hattie' Walker (1865-1943)," MHS Resources: Memorable Manitobans, http://www.mhs.mb.ca/docs/people/walker_ha.shtml.The Walker Theatre advertised itself as "Canada's Finest Playhouse." For advertisements see: *Manitoba Free Press*, 20 January 1914, 7 and 15 April 1914, 8 and *The Winnipeg Tribune*, 14 April 1914, 8.

273 Butler, "Branch Histories – Winnipeg," 19.

274 "Meeting of 28 December 1910 containing press clipping," *Minute Book, 22 October 1909 to 30 September 1915*, Canadian Women's Press Club Winnipeg Branch Papers, AM, P7650/2.

275 "Minutes of meeting of 21 October 1915," found in *Minute Book, 22 October 1909 to 30 September 1915*, Canadian Women's Press Club Winnipeg Branch Papers, AM, P7650/2.

276 Invitation: "Winnipeg Branch of the Canadian Women's Press Club on Friday, 29 April 1932, from eleven until twelve o'clock a.m. at the Free Press Club Rooms," Lillian Beynon Thomas Papers, AM, P191; "Playwright Honored At Reception," *The Winnipeg Tribune*, 30 April 1932, 14.

277 "Annual Dinner of the Woman's Press Club," a press clipping reporting on the Annual Dinner of the Winnipeg Branch of the Canadian Women's Press Club held on 17 December 1912. The clipping is found in the minutes of the Winnipeg Branch meeting held the next day, on 18 December 1912. See: *Minute Book, 22 October 1909 to 30*.

278 279 "Women's Press Club Holds Birthday Dinner," *The Winnipeg Tribune*, 31 December 1930, 4.

279 "Local Newspaper Women And Free Lances Dramatize the News at Annual Dinner," *The Winnipeg Tribune*, 5 January 1935, 9.

280 "Annual Work Form, Canadian Women's Press Club, Mrs. A.V. Thomas," Associate Membership since 1955, found in Lillian Beynon Thomas Papers, AM, P191; "CWPC Receipt," National membership fees for year beginning June 1, 1959, and ending May 31, 1960, $5.00, found in Lillian Beynon Thomas Papers, AM, P191.

281 "Authors' Association Reviews Twenty-Five Years of Work," *The Winnipeg Tribune*," 20 January 1950, 12.

282 *PF*, 24 March 1909, 14; "Few Opportunities in Professional Life For Wives, Says President," *The Winnipeg Tribune*, 13 January 1923, 35, Garbutt, Dorothy, "The Nasty Men Actually Smoked!" *Winnipeg Free Press*, 16 May 1959, 21.

283 "Quarter Century Milestone Marked by University Club," *The Winnipeg Tribune*, 8 February 1934, 6.

284 Winnipeg Women Authors to be Program Subject At University Club," *The Winnipeg Tribune*, 19 January 1937, 5; "Anecdotes and Poems Are In Order When Authors Meet At University Women's Club," *The Winnipeg Tribune*," 27 January 1937, 7. The authors who studied with Beynon Thomas included Mrs. C.L. Broley, Miss Pearl Snyder, Miss Margaret Bemister, Mrs. Gertrude Jean Elliot, Mrs. Margaret McLeod, Mrs. Irene Chapman Benson, Miss Eva Calder, Mrs. Alberta C. Trimble and, perhaps the best known, Mrs. H.G.L. Strange.

285 "Society News," *The Winnipeg Tribune*, 4 September 1916, 6.

286 *The Winnipeg Tribune*, 18 November 1936, 6.

287 Lillian Beynon Thomas Papers, AM, P191.

288 Kerrie A. Strathy, "Saskatchewan Women's Institutes: The Rural Women's University, 1911-1986," (Saskatoon: University of Saskatchewan Department of Communications, Continuing and Vocational Education Master of Continuing Education Thesis, 1987), https://harvest.usask.ca/handle/10388/6705, 18, and generally Chapter 2, 15-40; Dean Rutherford, "AHCS 6th Annual Convention Report, 1916, 23; Women's Institutes of Saskatchewan , *Legacy: A History of Saskatchewan Homemakers' Clubs and Women's Institutes, 1911-1988* (Saskatoon: Saskatchewan Women's Institute, 1988), Chapter 1.

289 Letter: Auld to Lillian Beynon, 28 June 1910, SAB, Agricultural Societies File #120.

290 Strathy, "Saskatchewan Women's Institutes, 18.

291 Letter: Auld to Lillian Beynon, 28 June 1910.

292 Letter: Lillian Beynon to Auld, 1 July 1910, SAB, Agricultural Societies File #120; Dean Rutherford, "AHCS 6th Annual Convention Report, 1916," 23.

293 Letter: Auld to Lillian Beynon, 4 July 1910, SAB, Agricultural Societies File #120.

294 Letter: Lillian Beynon to Auld, 18 October 1910, SAB, Agricultural Societies File Ag. Soc., HC, R26D, I. 169; Letter: Auld to Lillian Beynon, 3 November 1912, SAB, Agricultural Societies File Ag. Soc., HC, R26D, I. 169. Beynon Thomas had written a series of four newspaper stories in the fall of 1910 on organizing rural women's clubs or institutes. See: "Women's Clubs Or Institutes," *Manitoba Free Press*, 17 September 1910, 29; "Method Of Procedure," *Manitoba Free Press*, 1 October 1910, 31; "How One Institute Started," 8 October 1910, 31; and "Subjects For Women's Clubs, *Manitoba Free Press*, 15 October 1910, 46.

295 Beynon Thomas took a leave from the *Manitoba Free Press* in order to do this work. See: Women's Institutes of Saskatchewan, *Legacy*, Chapter 1.

296 On the history of the Homemakers' Clubs, see: Women's Institutes of Saskatchewan, *Legacy*, Chapter 1; Strathy, "Saskatchewan Women's Institutes, 18; Jennifer Milne, "Cultivating Domesticity: The Homemakers' Clubs of Saskatchewan, 1911 To 1961" (Saskatoon: University of Saskatchewan Department of History Master of Arts Thesis, 2004), https://harvest.usask.ca/bitstream/handle/10388/etd-07112005-100045/JMilne_FinalThesis.pdf?sequence=1&isAllowed=y; Michael B. Welton, "Pioneers And Progressive Pedagogues: Carrying The University To The People Of Saskatchewan, 1905-1928," *The Canadian Journal for the Study of Adult Education*

17. (November 2003), 59-83. See also: "First Annual Convention Of Saskatchewan Women's Clubs," *Regina Leader*, 1 February 1911, 4; "Saskatchewan Women's Clubs Discuss Organization Matters," *Regina Leader*, 3 February 1911, 10; "Homemakers Clubs Get Away To Splendid Start," *Regina Leader*, 4 February 1911, 8; "After the Convention," *Regina Leader*, 4 February 1911, 8; "Saskatchewan Homemakers' Clubs," *Regina Leader*, 15 April 1911, 10; "Saskatchewan Homemakers' Clubs," *Regina Leader*, 29 April 1911, 10; "Saskatchewan Homemakers' Clubs Report Great Progress - The Homemakers' Page 1st Birthday," *Regina Leader*, 20 April 1912, 8.

297   Strathy, "Saskatchewan Women's Institutes, 20.

298   "First Annual Convention Of Saskatchewan Women's Clubs," *Regina Leader*, 1 February 1911, 4; Women's Institutes of Saskatchewan, Legacy, Chapter 1.

299   "Saskatchewan Homemakers' Clubs," *Regina Leader*, 15 April 1911, 10; Beynon Thomas also started a club at Pense in January 1911, see: "Own their Club Room And The Lot Where It Stands," *GGG*, 15 October 1913, 10.

300   "Saskatchewan Convention of Women – Big Programme for Regina Meeting – Many Prominent Women Speakers – Local Council to Entertain," *Manitoba Free Press*, 17 January 1911, 8; "Women's Institutes in Saskatchewan," *Manitoba Free Press*, 12 December 1910, 9; "First Annual Convention Of Saskatchewan Women's Clubs," *Regina Leader*, 1 February 1911, 4.

301   "Saskatchewan Convention of Women – Big Programme for Regina Meeting – Many Prominent Women Speakers – Local Council to Entertain," *Manitoba Free Press*, 17 January 1911, 8; "Homemakers look back over years," *PF*, undated clipping found in Lillian Beynon Thomas papers, AM P191, likely June 1961.

302   Ellinthorpe, "From Teaching to Writing," 68; Isobel, "Around The Fireside – Homemakers' Clubs," *GGG*, 15 February 1911, 35.

303   "First Annual Convention Of Saskatchewan Women's Clubs," *Regina Leader*, 1 February 1911, 4.

304   "First Annual Convention Of Saskatchewan Women's Clubs," *Regina Leader*, 1 February 1911, 4; "Saskatchewan Homemakers' Clubs," *Regina Leader*, 15 April 1911, where the Homemakers' Clubs stated their objects to be, "to promote the interests of the home and community and to improve the conditions surrounding rural life by disseminating a greater knowledge of domestic and sanitary science and household art, and by imparting to the young knowledge of these subjects."; Isobel, "Around The Fireside – Homemakers' Clubs," *GGG*, 15 February 1911, 35; see also: Isobel, "Around The Fireside – Homemakers' Clubs," *GGG*, 5 April 1911, 28.

305   "First Annual Convention Of Saskatchewan Women's Clubs," *Regina Leader*, 1 February 1911, 4.

306   Strathy, "Saskatchewan Women's Institutes, 20-22; Milne, "Cultivating Domesticity, 35; Beynon, "Association of Homemakers' Clubs of Saskatchewan 1st Annual Convention Report, 1911, "23-5; Violet McNaughton, "Jottings By The Way," *The Western Producer*, 11 December 1952, 14.

307   "Woman's Work," *Regina Leader*, 25 January 1911, 8.

308 "Saskatchewan Homemakers' Clubs," *Regina Leader*, 15 April 1911, 10.

309 "Homemakers Clubs Get Away To Splendid Start," *Regina Leader*, 4 February 1911, 8.

310 Ibid.; Isobel, "Around The Fireside – Homemakers' Clubs," *GGG*, 15 February 1911, 35.

311 "Saskatchewan Women's Clubs Discuss Organization Matters," *Regina Leader*, 3 February 1911, 10.

312 Violet McNaughton, "Jottings By The Way," *The Western Producer*, 11 December 1952, 14.

313 Ibid. McNaughton wrote that at this time Beynon Thomas was, "president of the newly formed Political Equality League." In fact, the League was only launched in early 1912. McNaughton's error is easily forgiven. As she wrote, she was remembering events from four decades earlier.

314 Florence Lediard [aka Dame Durden], "The Ingle Nook – The Heart Of The Meeting," *The Farmers' Advocate and Home Journal*, 15 February 1911, 233. Emphasis in the original.

315 "Homemakers Clubs Get Away To Splendid Start," *Regina Leader*, 4 February 1911, 8.

316 Ibid.

317 Ellinthorpe, "From Teaching to Writing," 68.

318 Florence Lediard [aka Dame Durden], "The Ingle Nook – The Heart Of The Meeting," *The Farmers' Advocate and Home Journal*, 15 February 1911, 233.

319 "Saskatchewan Women's Clubs Discuss Organization Matters," *Regina Leader*, 3 February 1911, 10; "The Homemakers' Page 1st Birthday," *Regina Leader*, 20 April 1912, 8; Strathy, "Saskatchewan Women's Institutes, 21.

320 Ibid.

321 Women's Institutes of Saskatchewan, *Legacy*, Chapter 1.

322 Lillian K. Beynon, "Report of the Work in the University Tent," 1911, 6, SAB, Agricultural Societies File, HC, R26D, I.169; Violet McNaughton, "Jottings By The Way," *The Western Producer*, 11 December 1952, 14; "Saskatchewan Homemakers' Clubs," *Regina Leader*, 15 April 1911, 10; *Legacy: A History of Saskatchewan Homemakers' Clubs and Women's Institutes, 1911-1988*, Chapter 1.

323 Lillian Beynon Thomas, "To the Visitor, the Exhibits Make the Show. But to the Exhibitor, the People Present an Ever Entertaining Spectacle," *Canada Monthly*, (1914), 262.

324 "Saskatchewan Homemakers' Clubs," *Regina Leader*, 29 April 1911, 10.

325 Letter: Lillian Beynon to Auld, August 1911, SAB, Agricultural Societies File, HC, R26D, I.169; Lillian K. Beynon, "Report of the Summer's Work Among the Homemakers Clubs of Saskatchewan Along the Main Line," July 31 '11," SAB, Agricultural Societies File, HC, R26D, I.169; Women's Institutes of Saskatchewan, *Legacy*, Chapter 1.

326 "Saskatchewan Homemakers Convention – Great Gathering of Women discusses Vital Problems at Saskatoon," *GGG*, 28 February 1912, 8; *Farmer's Advocate and Home Journal*, 21 February 1912, 271.

327 Francis Marion Beynon, "The Country Homemakers – Women Grain Growers' Clubs," *GGG*, 3 July 1912, 9.

328 *PF*, 7 June 1914, 2 - Home Section.

329 Francis Marion Beynon, "The Country Homemakers – Homemakers' Convention," *GGG*, 10 June 1914, 9.

330 *PF*, 7 June 1914, 2 - Home Section.

331 Ibid.

332 Francis Marion Beynon, "Homemakers in Convention," *GGG*, 26 May 1915, 4 and 23.

333 Violet McNaughton, "Jottings By The Way," *The Western Producer*, 15 July 1954, 11.

334 "States Youth Of Dominion Must Pioneer In Arts – Mrs. A.V. Thomas Speaks To Federated Women's Institute Convention," *Winnipeg Free Press*, 8 June 1933, 6; "Institute Workers Protest Cuts in Extension Service AT Mid-Week Session," *The Winnipeg Tribune*, 8 June 1933, 6.

335 Home Economics Societies were referred to by different names. Sometimes they were called Household Science Associations, sometimes Ladies Mutual Benefit Societies. In 1919 a new national organization was formed under the name Federated Women's Institutes of Canada. At that point, the Manitoba societies adopted the name Women's Institutes of Manitoba. See: TimeLinks, "Women's Institutes of Manitoba (Home Economics Societies)," Manitoba Historical Society (2009), http://www.mhs.mb.ca/docs/features/timelinks/reference/db0023.shtml; Anonymous, "The Great Human Heart: History of the Manitoba Women's Institute 1910-1980," (Brandon: Manitoba Women's Institute, 1980).

336 "Extension Service At Mid-Week Session," *The Winnipeg Tribune*, 8 June 1933, 7; Jackel, "First Days, Fighting Days, 62-3.

337 Isobel, "Around The Fireside – Manitoba Women's Convention," *GGG*, 22 Feb 1911, 35.

338 P.R.H., "Convention of Manitoba Household Science Association," *Canadian Thresherman and Farmer*, March 1911, 70.

339 "Women's Clubs in the West," *Manitoba Free Press*, 20 July 1912, 1 - Woman's Section.

340 "Work of Home Economics Societies," *Manitoba Free Press*, 18 January 1913, 1 - Woman's Section.

341 E. Cora Hind, "The Women's Quiet Hour – The H.E.S. and W.G.G.s," *The Western Home Monthly*, March 1915, 21.

342 E. Cora Hind, "The Women's Quiet Hour," *The Western Home Monthly*, February 1912, 57.

343 Lillian Laurie, "Women's Clubs In The West," *Manitoba Free Press*, 20 July, 1912, 1 - Woman's Section.

344 E. Cora Hind, "The Women's Quiet Hour – Another Step Onward," *The Western Home Monthly*, October 1915, 25; "Mrs. Leslie Named On College Board," *The Winnipeg Tribune*, 18 May 1917, 17.

345 E. Cora Hind, "The Women's Quiet Hour – Another Step Onward," *The Western Home Monthly*, October 1915, 25; Francis Marion Beynon, "The Country Homemakers – Honor Conferred on Mrs. Thomas," *GGG*, 22 September 1915, 10.

346 E. Cora Hind, "The Women's Quiet Hour – Another Step Onward," *The Western Home Monthly*, October 1915, 25.

347 "Resolutions Passed at Regina," *GGG*, 28 February 1912, 14.

348 "Saskatchewan Farmers' Parliament," *GGG*, 26 February 1913, 7, 10.

349 Mary Ford, "The Home – Manitoba Grain Growers' Resolution," *GGG*, 7 Feb 1912, 23.

350 The motion was carried unanimously. "Votes for Women," *Manitoba Free Press*, 27 January 1912, 31; Mary Ford, "The Home – Equal Suffrage," *GGG*, 7 February 1912, 23.

351 "Manitoba Farmers' Parliament," *GGG*, 22 January 1913, 7; "Grain Growers and Suffrage," *GGG*, 29 January 1913, 21.

352 Alison Craig, "Over the Tea-Cups," *Manitoba Free Press*, 17 January 1914, 1 - Women's Section; "Manitoba Farmers' Parliament," *GGG*, 14 January 1914, 4.

353 "Manitoba Farmers' Parliament," *GGG*, 22 January 1913, 7; "Grain Growers and Suffrage," *GGG*, 29 January 1913, 21.

354 Francis Marion Beynon, "The Country Homemakers – How You Can Help Along Woman's Suffrage," *GGG*, 8 Jan 1913, 10; Francis Marion Beynon, "The Country Homemakers – 'After Us, The Deluge,'" *GGG*, 12 February 1913, 10.

355 Georgina M. Taylor, "'Ground for Common Action': Violet McNaughton's Agrarian Feminism and the Origins of the Farm Women's Movement in Canada" (Ottawa: Carleton University Department of History Doctor of Philosophy Thesis,1997), https://www.collectionscanada.gc.ca/obj/s4/f2/dsk2/ftp03/NQ26870. pdf , 249 – 250; Letter: F.W. Green to McNaughton, 23 December 1913, SAB, McNaughton Papers, A1 C1, n.d.

356 In 1912, Beynon Thomas was elected a member of the Executive Board of the Press Association of the Congress; in 1913 and again in 1914 she was elected First Vice President of the Press Association of the Congress. "Official Proceedings of the First International Congress of Farm Women, Colorado Springs, Colorado, October 17-20, 1911" (Lethbridge: The International Dry-Farming Congress, 1911), http:// memory.loc.gov/service/gdc/scd0001/2008/20080222001in/20080222001in.pdf, 62; https://idnc.library.illinois.edu/?a=d&d=FFW19121201.2.15&srpos=6&e=-------en-20-FFW-1--img-txIN-lillian+thomas---------; *The Farmer's Wife*, 1 December 1913, "Third International Congress Of Farm Women" (Illinois Digital Newspaper Collections), 219; Taylor, "'Ground for Common Action'," 249 – 250.

357 See generally: Mary P. McCallum, "Women as an Organized Force," *GGG*, 26 June 1918, 10 extracted in The Saskatchewan Grain Growers' Association Limited Women's Section, *The Women's Section – Past Present Future*, (Regina: April, 1923).

358 Fred W. Green, "Saskatchewan," *GGG*, 29 January 1913, 11.

359 Beynon Thomas wrote a series of four columns for her Home Loving Hearts page in the *Manitoba Free Press* in the fall of 1910: "Ontario Women's Institutes," 17 Sept 1910, 29; "Procedure for a Club Meeting," 1 Oct. 1910, 31; "How to Start a Club," 8 Oct. 1910, 31; and "Subjects for Club Meetings," 15 Oct. 1910," 46.

360 Francis Marion Beynon, "The Country Homemakers," *GGG*, 22 January 1913, 10.

361 Francis Marion Beynon, "The Country Homemakers," *GGG*, 26 February 1913, 8; Taylor, "'Ground for Common Action'," 249 – 250.

362 Letter: McNaughton to 'My dear Lillian Laurie," 19 July 1950, SAB, McNaughton Papers, A1 C1.

363 Homemakers' Clubs of Saskatchewan, *Retrospect and Prospect: The Silver Cord and the Golden Chain* (Saskatoon: University of Saskatchewan, Extension Division, 1939), 10 cited in Milne, "Cultivating Domesticity, 41, fn. 48; Violet McNaughton, "Jottings By The Way," *The Western Producer*, 11 December 1952, 14.

364 Catherine Cleverdon, *The Woman Suffrage Movement in Canada* (Toronto: University of Toronto Press, 1974) [1950].

365 Francis Marion Beynon, "The Country Homemakers - Women Grain Growers In Convention," *GGG*, 26 February 1913, 17.

366 Francis Marion Beynon, "The Country Homemakers – Homemakers Convention," *GGG*, 26 May 1915, 4, 23.

367 Francis Marion Beynon, "The Country Homemakers – Women Grain Growers In Convention," *GGG*, 26 February 1913, 17; Taylor, "'Ground for Common Action'," 255– 256.

368 "Saskatchewan Farmers' Parliament," *GGG*, 26 February 1913, 7.

369 Mary P. McCallum, "Women as an Organized Force," *GGG*, 26 June 1918, 10.

370 E. Cora Hind, "The Women's Quiet Hour – At Saskatoon," *The Western Home Monthly*, March 1913, 38; E. Cora Hind, "The Women's Quiet Hour – Women Grain Growers," *The Western Home Monthly*, March 1914, 43.

371 Violet McNaughton, "Jottings By The Way," *The Western Producer*, 11 December 1952, 14.

372 Taylor, "'Ground for Common Action'," 264.

373 Francis Marion Beynon, "The Country Homemakers – The Women Grain Growers' Convention," *GGG*, 14 January 1914, 10.

374 Taylor, "'Ground for Common Action'," 277 – 278.

375 E. Cora Hind, "The Women's Quiet Hour – Women Grain Growers," *The Western Home Monthly*, March 1914, 43; Georgina M. Taylor, "'Ground for Common Action'," 275 – 276.

376 Lillian Beynon Thomas, "A Woman's Talk to Women – Developing Leaders," *The Canadian Thresherman and Farmer*, March 1917, 44.

377 Violet McNaughton, "Jottings By The Way," *The Western Producer*, 11 December 1952, 14.

378 "Meeting of 11 May 1911" containing press clipping 'Women of the World – Interesting Talks at Women's Press Club Luncheon,' *Minute Book, 22 October 1909 to 30 September 1915*, Canadian Women's Press Club Winnipeg Branch Papers, AM, P7650/2.

379 Letter: Lillian Beynon to Auld, 1 July 1910, SAB, Agricultural Societies File #120.

380 Violet McNaughton, "Jottings By The Way," *The Western Producer*, 15 July 1954, 11.

381 *The Evening Province & Standard*, Regina, Saskatchewan, 15 February 1915, clipping found in PAS, Violet McNaughton papers.

382 On the occasion of Canada's centennial year in 1967, the *Winnipeg Free Press* published a fulsome account of the fight for suffrage in the province dating back its beginnings the late 1880s to the denouement in 1916. See: Edith Pajerson, "Long, Exciting Battle Won the Vote for Manitoba Women, *Winnipeg Free Press*, 27 June 1967, 98 (Centennial Edition). The *Free Press* has published detailed historical accounts of the Manitoba suffrage movement on three other occasions. On the occasion of Manitoba's centennial, see: "Once Ignored, Women Now Express Own Viewpoint, 30 November 1972, 231; marking the centennial of Manitoba's entry into Confederation, see: Linda Scharf Taylor, "Manitoba Women's Vote 60 Years Old," *Winnipeg Free Press*, 28 January 1976, 1 and 84.

383 Anne Anderson Perry, "Winning the Franchise," *GGG*, 7 July 1920, 19; and on the centenary of Manitoba women being enfranchised see: "The Advancement of Women," *Winnipeg Free Press*, 30 January 2016, 9.

384 Lillian Beynon Thomas, "Some Manitoba Women who did First Things," in *Historical and Scientific Society of Manitoba Transactions*," Series III, 4 (1947- 48), http://www.mhs.mb.ca/docs/transactions/3/firstwomen.shtml, 25, where Lillian described Hind as follows: "It was no accident that made Cora Hind the first woman typist in Winnipeg, the first woman agricultural editor, one of the first workers for the franchise for women. She was made of the stuff that was forever reaching out for new horizons."

385 "Just A Word," *Manitoba Free Press*, 22 April 1910, 9.

386 Bess, 9 August 1908, *PF*, 14.

387 Trilby, 26 August 1908, *PF*, 14; See also Lover of Justice, *Manitoba Free Press*, 7 March 1910, 9 and Oliver King, *Manitoba Free Press*, 2 September 1910, 9.

388 "Do You Want a Vote?", *Manitoba Free Press*, 11 November 1909, 10. See also "What Western Women Are Doing," *Manitoba Free Press*, 3 April 1909, 21; and "Women For Women," *Manitoba Free Press*, 22 April 1910, 9.

389 Quill Club, "Meeting of 14 November 1908," *Minutes of Meetings 14 November 1908 – 13 November 1909*, Lillian Beynon Thomas Papers, AM, P191.

390 Quill Club, "Meeting of September 1909," *Minutes of Meetings 14 November 1908 – 13 November 1909*, Lillian Beynon Thomas Papers, AM, P191, "profitably" underlined in the original.

391 Ibid., Cock Robin is a reference to a rather dark, very old English nursery rhyme which speculates on which of the other birds killed the Robin. The author of the Minutes was metaphorically indicating that the reason for the demise of the club was a mystery.

392 E. Cora Hind, "The Women's Quiet Hour – The Franchise," *The Western Home Monthly*, March 1910, 61; E. Cora Hind, "The Women's Quiet Hour – Why Women Should Vote," *Western Home Monthly*, October 1910, 38.

393 E. Cora Hind, "The Women's Quiet Hour – Why Women Should Vote," *Western Home Monthly*, October 1910, 38.

394 Philistia, "Mrs. Lillian Beynon Thomas," *The Canadian Courier*, Vol. XIV. No. 22 (Toronto: Courier Press, Limited, November 1, 1913) 23.

395 "About Women and Men, Especially Women: Asking for the Franchise," *Manitoba Free Press*, 9 May 1910, 9. "Franchise was used interchangeably with suffrage or 'the vote.'

396 *PF*, 25 May 1910, 16 and 11 May 1910, 15; See also E. Cora Hind, "The Right to Vote," *Western Home Monthly*, August 1912, 28.

397 Letter: Lillian to Cleverdon, 21 April 1944, Lillian Beynon Thomas Papers, AM, P191.

398 Lillian Beynon Thomas, "Reminiscences of a Manitoba Suffragette," in Manitoba Historical Society, *Manitoba Pageant* 5, 1 (September 1959), http://www.mhs. mb.ca/docs/pageant/05/suffragette.shtml, 10. Nellie McClung gave a different account of the genesis for the suffrage campaign. In her autobiography, she described how, "the seed germ of the suffrage association was planted" over tea at weekly meetings of the Winnipeg Branch of the Canadian Women's Press Club. Although she did not reference dower reform, she did give an example of laws which treated women inadequately: "The immediate cause of our desire to organize was the plight of women workers in small factories." She and a colleague had earlier toured Premier Roblin through several squalid factories where women worked long hours, for small wages, and in distressing conditions. It is likely that many different reform demands came together to form the inspiration for the suffrage campaign.

399 Olive Schreiner, *Woman and Labour* (New York: Frederick A. Stokes, 1911).

400 Lillian Laurie, "Olive Schreiner's Brilliant Book," *Manitoba Free Press*, 1 April 1911, 43 (1 - Woman's Section).

401 Francis Marion Beynon, "Explanatory," *GGG*, 10 July 1912, 9.

402 Lillian Beynon Thomas, "Study 15: The Woman Movement – Equal Suffrage," in *Studies in Rural Citizenship*, J.S. Woodsworth, ed. (Winnipeg: Canadian Council of Agriculture, c.1914), 83-84.

403 Catherine L. Cleverdon, *The Woman Suffrage Movement in Canada*, (Toronto, University of Toronto Press, 1950), 46.

404 Ramsay Cook, "Introduction," in The Woman Suffrage Movement in Canada, Catherine Cleverdon (Toronto: University of Toronto Press, 1950) xvi.

405 "Legislature Is Prorogued By Lieut.-Governor," Winnipeg Tribune, 6 March 1918, 2.

406 Lillian Laurie, "M.B.A.," Prairie Farmer, 25 May 1910, 15; Lillian Laurie, "Why I Fight For Women," Manitoba Free Press, 16 September 1910, 10.

407 "Great Ovation for Representatives of Equality League – Monster Audience of Delegates Rises and Cheers Mrs. McClung and Mrs. Thomas – First Time in History of Canada that Women Had Addressed Political Convention," Manitoba Free Press, 28 March 1914, 12.

408 Nellie L. McClung, The Stream Runs Fast: My Own Story, (Toronto: Thomas Allen Limited, 1946), 106; also: McClung, The Stream Runs Fast, 101-110 cited by Catherine Lyle Cleverdon, The Woman Suffrage Movement In Canada (Toronto: University of Toronto Press, 1950), 55 and fn 24.

409 Sarah Carter, Ours by Every Law of Right and Justice: Women and the Vote in the Prairie Provinces, (Vancouver: UBC Press, 2020), 76.

410 Ramsay Cook, "Introduction," in The Woman Suffrage Movement in Canada, Catherine Cleverdon (Toronto: University of Toronto Press, 1950) xv.

411 Cited by Jennifer Ditchburn, The Canadian Press, in, "A century ago, a savvy Manitoba political campaign won some women the right to vote," Canadian Broadcasting Corporation, 28 January 1916, https://www.cbc.ca/news/canada/manitoba/a-century-ago-a-savvy-manitoba-political-campaign-won-some-women-the-right-to-vote-1.3417599.

412 In 1913 the League ordered one hundred 'Votes for Women' banners and placed them on Winnipeg streetcars. Linda McDowell, "The Political Equality League (1912-1916)," The Nellie McClung Foundation, http://www.ournellie.com/womens-suffrage/political-equality-league/; Edith Paterson, "Long, Exciting Battle Won The Vote For Manitoba Women," Winnipeg Free Press, 27 June 1967, 50; Lynette Sarah Plett, "How the Vote Was Won: Adult Education and the Manitoba Woman Suffrage Movement, 1912-1916," (Winnipeg: University of Manitoba Master of Education Thesis, 2000), file:///C:/Users/Robert/Downloads/Plett_How_the.pdf, 48; Irene Craig, "Those Women!" in Manitoba Historical and Scientific Society, Manitoba Pageant 5, 1 (September 1959), http://www.mhs.mb.ca/docs/pageant/05/thosewomen.shtml, 8.

413 Plett, "How the Vote Was Won," 65 (Streetcars decorated in yellow banners carried delegates to the first Woman Suffrage Convention at the Industrial Bureau, Winnipeg on 18 February 1915); "Personal and Social," Manitoba Free Press, 20 February 1915, 9 (On 19 February 1915, the delegates to the Manitoba Political Equality League convention were entertained at a tea hosted by Jane Hample who decorated the tables with centrepieces of violets and buttercups, representing the votes for women colors); Manitoba Free Press, 14 August 1915, 2 (Political Equality League cars were decorated in purple and yellow flowers in the congratulatory parade welcoming newly-elected Premier Norris); "Women, In Autos, Hail New

Premier," *The Winnipeg Tribune*, 10 August 1915, 1-2 (There were 285 cars in the parade led by a car carrying Lillian).

414   "Great Ovation For Representatives Of Equality League," *Manitoba Free Press*, 28 March 1914, 12; "Great Ovation for Equality League," *PF*, 1 April 1914, 12 (Lillian concluded her speech to the Manitoba Liberal Convention, "amid a storm of applause, with the words, 'Let Manitoba be first.'"); "Manitoba Women's Opportunity," *Manitoba Free Press*, 14 August 1915, 4; Barbara Roberts, *A Reconstructed World: A Feminist Biography of Gertrude Richardson*, (Montreal & Kingston: McGill-Queen's University Press) 1996, 146 where Lillian's is cited as reporting during the September 1915 suffrage campaign, "OUR MOTTO: MANITOBA FIRST." (capitals in original); "Trusting All The Home Folks," *Manitoba Free Press*, 5 February 1916, 21 (Lillian sums up the suffrage campaign stating, "Manitoba has been first to trust all the people."); "Manitoba First," *Farmer's Advocate and Home Journal*, 9 February 1916, 207.

415   *PF*, 27 August 1913, 2 - Home Section.

416   Beynon Thomas referred to the members of her M.B.A. as having banded together. *PF*, 25 December 1907, 14.; Prairie Fanner (19 August 1908) 14.

417   Lillian wrote a series of four columns in the fall of 1910 on organizing rural women's clubs or institutes. See: "Women's Clubs Or Institutes," *Manitoba Free Press*, 17 September 1910, 29; "Method Of Procedure," *Manitoba Free Press*, 1 October 1910, 31; "How One Institute Started," 8 October 1910, 31 and "Subjects For Women's Clubs, *Manitoba Free Press*, 15 October 1910, 46.

418   *PF*, 25 February 1914, 2 - Home Section; Plett, "How the Vote Was Won," 93-94.

419   See: R.E. Hawkins, "Lillian Beynon Thomas, Woman's Suffrage and the Return of Dower to Manitoba," 27 *Man. L. J.* 45 (1999-2000), 52 and 57-72.

420   Plett, "How the Vote Was Won," 79.

421   Plett, "How the Vote Was Won," 97.

422   Plett, "How the Vote Was Won," 79.

423   *PF*, 27 August 1913, 2 - Home Section, where Lillian wrote, "The women of our province need a lot of education – not only to teach them the value of the franchise, but to lead them to a broader outlook on life so that they will take some interest in public questions."

424   Blanche Ellinthorpe, "From Teaching to Writing," *The Country Guide*, February 1953, 68 where the interviewer wrote, "Lillian's was the intellectual approach. She was far from being a militant suffragette."

425   Barbara Roberts, *A Reconstructed World: A Feminist Biography of Gertrude Richardson* (Montreal: McGill-Queen's University Press, 1996) 106 and chapter 3, fn. 65, citing "Minitonas," *Swan River Star*, 12 September 1913.

426   *The Evening Province & Standard*, Regina, Saskatchewan, 15 February 1915, SAB, McNaughton Papers A1 C1.

427   McClung, *The Stream Runs Fast*, 133.

428 Historical accounts treat the meeting at Hample's house without mentioning the small preparatory gatherings that Lillian put together earlier. For these preparatory gatherings see: "Manitoba First," *Farmer's Advocate and Home Journal*, 9 February 1916, 207; Francis Marion Beynon, "The Country Homemakers – The Conclusion Of A Big Struggle," *GGG*, 9 February 1916, 10; Anne Anderson Perry, "Winning the Franchise," *GGG*, 7 July 1920, 19; "Obituary - Lillian Beynon Thomas," *Winnipeg Free Press*, 4 September 1961, 19; "Deaths - Thomas," *The Winnipeg Tribune*," 5 September 1961, 20.

429 "Minutes – 12 April 1912," Political Equality League of Manitoba Papers, AM, P192/1.

430 Lillian Beynon Thomas, "Reminiscences," 10; Beynon Thomas, "Some Manitoba Women who did First Things," 23, where Beynon Thomas wrote the following about Hample: "Coming down to more modern times, a woman who must have a place in this paper is Mrs. Jane Hample. It was in the home of Mrs. Hample that the Political Equality League of Manitoba was organized. Mrs. Hample stood back of that organization like a rock, in its moments of discouragement. Her home was always open for meetings. Her purse was always open for anything that might help the cause of women. We owed Mrs. Hample more than we were ever able to express."

431 "Minutes – 29 March 1912," Political Equality League of Manitoba papers, AM, P 192/1.

432 Beynon Thomas, "Some Manitoba Women who did First Things," 24.

433 Susan Jackel, "First Days, Fighting Days: Prairie Presswomen and Suffrage Activism, 1906-1916," in *First Days, Fighting Days: Women in Manitoba History*, ed. Mary Kinnear (Regina: Canadian Plains Research Centre, 1987), 58. McClung left Winnipeg for Edmonton in November 1914, before the end of the suffrage campaign, when her husband took a job there.

434 Linda McDowell, "Political Equality League 1912-116," The Nellie McClung Foundation, https://www.ournellie.com/learn/political-equality-league/. See: "Minutes – 12 April and 13 April, 1912," Political Equality League of Manitoba Papers, AM, P192/1.

435 *GGG*, "Why Women Should Vote," 22 May 1912, 27.

436 "Political Equality League," *The Winnipeg Tribune*, 10 May 1912, 6; "Votes For Women Theme Of Speeches," *Manitoba Free Press*, 15 May 1912, 2.

437 "Political Equality Meeting," *The Winnipeg Tribune*, 28 June 1912, 5; *Manitoba Free Press*, "To Wage Fight For Political Equality," 28 June 1912 9.

438 "Minutes - 30 April 1912," Political Equality League of Manitoba Papers, AM, P192/1.

439 Jocelyn Baker, "A Winnipeg Album – Mrs. A.V. Thomas," *The Winnipeg Tribune Magazine*, 1 October 1932, 2.

440 "Political Equality," *Manitoba Free Press*, 15 April 1912, 28.

441 Beynon Thomas, "Reminiscences," 10. These words are cited on a plaque commemorating Lillian placed outside Laura Secord School, Winnipeg, by the Manitoba Heritage Council in 1983.

442 Perry, "Winning the Franchise," 19.

443 The militant English suffragettes that Lillian referred to in her letter to Cleverdon were Emmeline Pankhurst who spoke in Winnipeg on 16 December, 1911 and Barbara Wylie, who made speeches in Regina, Moose Jaw and Maple Creek while on a 1912 Christmas visit to her brother, David Wylie, a Conservative MLA in the Saskatchewan legislature; Letter: Lillian to Cleverdon, 21 April 1944, Lillian Beynon Thomas Papers, AM, P191; "Political Equality Meeting," *The Winnipeg Tribune*, 28 June 1912, 5 for a report on the PEL meeting at which it was decided to favour peaceful methods; "Men For Business Women After Good Of All Humanity," *The Winnipeg Tribune*, 10 January 1913, 3 for a report on Lillian's speech to the 1913 Manitoba Grain Growers' Association Annual Convention in which she rejected the use of violent methods; and "HLH," *PF*, 1 April 1914, 12 where it is reported that Lillian, in her address to the Manitoba Liberal Convention, pointed out that there was a plank in the Political Equality League constitution prohibiting the use of militant methods and that the League's policy was one of education.

444 "Minutes – 7 June 1912," Political Equality League of Manitoba Papers, AM, P192/1; "Political Equality Meeting," *The Winnipeg Tribune*, 28 June 1912, 5; "To Wage Fight For Political Equality," *Manitoba Free Press*, 28 June 1912, 9.

445 For the growth and constitutional evolution of the League generally, see: Perry, "Winning the Franchise," 19.

446 "Minutes - 13 March 1913 and December 1913", Political Equality League of Manitoba papers, AM, P192/1; "Annual Meeting Of Equality League," *Manitoba Free Press*, 1 April 1913, 28; "Hear Arguments On Woman Suffrage," *Manitoba Free Press*, 16 February 1914, 9; Wendy Heads, "The Local Council of Women of Winnipeg, 1894-1920, Tradition and Transformation," (Winnipeg: University of Manitoba Department of History Master of Arts Thesis, 1997), where the author states that Lillian gave up the presidency of the Political Equality League, "to free herself for work behind-the-scenes as chief organizer of the League and to enable her to carry out speaking engagements in which she supported the more spectacular suffragist platform performer, Nellie McClung."

447 For the growth and constitutional evolution of the League in 1913-14, see: "Minutes - 21 and 25 March 1914 and 2 April 1914 (League 1914 annual meeting)," Political Equality League of Manitoba Papers, AM, P192/1; "Announcements," *The Winnipeg Tribune*, 10 March 1914, 8 (Lillian and McClung speak to city groups organizing new branches); "Woman Suffrage in Manitoba," *GGG*, 22 July 1914, 6 (six Winnipeg branches exist by mid-1914).

448 The Political Equality League of Manitoba, "Constitution 1914," Lillian Beynon Thomas Papers, AM, P191.

449 The Political Equality League of Manitoba, "Constitution 1914," "Article I - NAME," Lillian Beynon Thomas Papers, AM, P192.

450 Ibid. p.3

451 "Minutes of Meeting of the Political Equality League of Manitoba, held in the Industrial Bureau, March 21, 1914 and April 2, 1914," and "Order of Proceedings at the Special Meeting of the Representatives of the Branches of the Political Equality League of Manitoba, Held Friday Evening April 24, 1914, in the Board Room of the Bible House Alexander Avenue," Political Equality League of Manitoba Papers, AM, P192/1.

452 "HLH," PF, 15 July 1914, 2 - Home Section.

453 For growth and constitutional evolution of League in 1915, see: "The Woman Suffrage Convention," GGG, 24 February 1915, 22; "First Suffrage Convention," Farmer's Advocate & Home Journal, 24 February 1915, 230.

454 The Evening Province & Standard, Regina, Saskatchewan, 15 February 1915, Violet McNaughton papers, PAS; Plett, "How the Vote Was Won," 65.

455 Lillian Laurie, "Trusting All The Home Folks," Manitoba Free Press, 5 February 1916, 21.

456 "Minutes – 6 April 1913", Political Equality League of Manitoba Papers, AM, P192/1; "The Campaign For Woman Suffrage," Manitoba Free Press, 9 July 1914, 4.

457 For example, see: Lillian Laurie, "Why I Fight for Women," Manitoba Free Press, 16 September 1910, 10.

458 Lillian Beynon Thomas, "The Homeless and Childless Women of Manitoba," in Winnipeg Trades and Labour Council, The Voice, 23 April 1915, 6.

459 "Minutes - 26 April 1913," Political Equality League of Manitoba Papers, AM, P192/1.

460 "The Campaign for Woman Suffrage," Manitoba Free Press, 9 July 1914, 4:3 (Material Supplied to the Manitoba Free Press by the Political Equality League of Manitoba).

461 Winnipeg's population in 1911 was 136,035 making it the third largest city in Canada. 1911 Census of Canada, https://en.wikipedia.org/wiki/List_of_largest_Canadian_cities_by_census.

462 Bruce Cherney, "Whatever happened to the Winnipeg Industrial Exhibition," Winnipeg Realtors, Real Estate News, 24 August 2007, http://www.winnipegrealestatenews.com/Resources/Article/?sysid=687.

463 "Winnipeg Stampede Tremendous Event," The Winnipeg Tribune, 16 July 1913, 6.

464 "HLH," PF, 27 August 1913, 2 - Home Section; Lillian Laurie, "Trusting All The Home Folks," Manitoba Free Press, 5 February 1916, 21; Francis Marion Beynon, "The Exhibition Board Anti-Suffragists," GGG, 16 July 1913, 9; Plett, "How the Vote Was Won," 52.

465 Tony Seskus, "Calgary Stampede: The Beginning – Guy Weadick's Grand Vision – Chapter 1," Calgary Herald, 11 July 2016, http://calgaryherald.com/news/local-news/calgary-stampede-the-complete-story-and-wild-history-of-the-greatest-

outdoor-show-on-earth-2; Tony Seskus, "Who is Guy Weadick? Well, buckaroo, let us tell you ...," *Calgary Herald*, 8 July 2016, http://calgaryherald.com/news/local-news/who-is-guy-weadick-well-buckaroo-let-us-tell-you.

466 "HLH," *PF*, 27 August 1913, 2 - Home Section.

467 Lillian Laurie, "Trusting All The Home Folks," *Manitoba Free Press*, 5 February 1916, 21.

468 "HLH," *PF*, 27 August 1913, 2 - Home Section.

469 Craig, "Those Women!" 8; Francis Marion Beynon, "Working For An Unpopular Cause," *GGG*, 27 August 1913, 9.

470 Beynon Thomas, "Reminiscences," 10.

471 Francis Marion Beynon, "The Conclusion of a Big Struggle," *GGG*, 9 February 1916, 10.

472 "Minutes – 31 March 1913", Lillian Beynon Thomas Papers, AM, P192/1; Cleverdon, *The Woman Suffrage Movement in Canada*, 56.

473 "Minutes – 7 September 1912", Political Equality League of Manitoba Papers, AM, P192/1.

474 "Over The Tea Cups," *Manitoba Free Press*, 25 January 1913, 51 (1 - Woman's Section); "Over The Tea Cups," *Manitoba Free Press*, 22 February 1913, 47 (1 - Woman's Section); "Annual Meeting of Equality League," *Manitoba Free Press*, 1 April 1913, 28.

475 Francis Marion Beynon, "How Can You Help Along Woman's Suffrage," *GGG*," 8 January 1913, 10; "Annual Meeting Of Equality League," The *Manitoba Free Press*, 1 April 1913, 28; Perry, "Winning the Franchise," 19; McClung, *The Stream Runs Fast*, 106.

476 Some reports of these events included: "Public Meeting," *Manitoba Free Press*, 15 May 1912, 2; "Minutes - 6 November 1913" (public debate), Political Equality League of Manitoba Papers, AM, P192/1; "Reception for home nursing course students from out of town," *Manitoba Free Press*, 16 February 1914, 9; "Sectional suffrage tea," *Manitoba Free Press*, 16 March 1914, 9; "People's Forum Adult Education," *Manitoba Free Press*, 25 January 1915, 16; "Home Economics Section of the Brandon Winter Fair –The New Old Women," *Farmer's Advocate and Home Journal*, 19 March 1913, 433; "Woman's Section of the Brandon Winter Fair," *Western Home Monthly*, April 1914, 50.

477 Lillian Laurie, "Trusting All The Home Folks," *Manitoba Free Press*, 5 February 1916, 21.

478 Perry, "Winning the Franchise," 19.

479 "Hear Arguments On Woman Suffrage," *Manitoba Free Press*, 16 February 1914, 9.

480 "Discussing Vote For Women," *The Winnipeg Tribune*, 7 May 1914, 8.

481 "Brandon Begins Campaign For Women's Votes," *The Winnipeg Tribune*, 3 September 1915, 6.

482 "Men For Business Women After Good Of All Humanity," *The Winnipeg Tribune*, 10 January 1913, 3; "Manitoba Farmers' Parliament," *GGG*, 22 January 1913, 7.

483 "Mrs. Pankhurst's Address," *GGG*, 3 January 1912, 22, continued at *GGG*, 17 January 1912, 8 and 18.

484 "Men For Business Women After Good Of All Humanity," *The Winnipeg Tribune*, 10 January 1913, 3; Craig, "Those Women!" 8.

485 Lillian was here referring to the rude conduct of the members of the Law Amendment Committee who killed the 1911 dower Bill proposed by Harvey Simpson and who insulted the delegation of women as they were leaving after having presented arguments in favour of the Bill. "Improved Laws For Women," *Manitoba Free Press*, 11 March 1911, 45 (5 - Woman's Section); Lillian Laurie, "Women as Idols," *Manitoba Free Press*, 1 April 1911, 43 (1 - Woman's Section).

486 J. Castel Hopkins, The Canadian Annual Review of Public Affairs 1914 (Toronto: The Annual Review Publishing Company Limited, 1914) 588.

487 At this time, the typewriter was becoming common and was offering women one of the rare opportunities to work outside of the home in a non-domestic, non-traditional female role. E. Cora Hind, Lillian's colleague at the *Manitoba Free Press*, was one of the first women in western Canada to be employed as a typist. In 1901, her ability to type helped her to get a permanent job at the Free Press at a time when journalism was not considered suitable work for a woman. Harry Gutkin and Mildred Gutkin, "'Give us our due!' How Manitoba Women Won the Vote – E. Cora Hind, Pioneer 'Typewriter'," *Manitoba History*, Number 32, Autumn 1996, http://www.mhs.mb.ca/docs/mb_history/32/womenwonthevote.shtml.

488 "Men for Business Women After Good of All Humanity," *The Winnipeg Tribune*, 10 January 1913, 3; "Manitoba Farmers' Parliament," *GGG*, 22 January 1913, 7.

489 Ibid.

490 Ibid.

491 Ibid.

492 E. Cora Hind, "The Women's Quiet Hour – Manitoba GGA" *Western Home Monthly*, February 1913, 40.

493 "Saskatchewan Farmers' Parliament - Annual Convention of the Saskatchewan Grain Growers' Association, Saskatoon, Feb12-14, 1913" *GGG*, 26 February 1913, 10.

494 "Saskatchewan Farmers' Parliament," *GGG*, 26 February 1913, 10.

495 Francis Marion Beynon, "Program for Women's Section Brandon Winter Fair – Thursday: 2.15, address 'The old new woman,' Mrs. A.V. Thomas (Lillian Laurie)," *GGG*, 5 March 1913, 14; "Home Economics Section of the Brandon Winter Fair –The New Old Women," *Farmer's Advocate and Home Journal*, 19 March 1913, 433; E. Cora Hind, "The Women's Quiet Hour, *Western Home Monthly*, April 1913, 32A. Francis Beynon and E. Cora Hind each reported that the title of Lillian's address was "The Old New Woman" whereas the *Farmer's Advocate* reported it as "The New Old Woman." It is more likely that Lillian's sister and friend were correct.

496 "Home Economics Section of the Brandon Winter Fair –The New Old Women," *Farmer's Advocate and Home Journal*, 19 March 1913, 433.

497 Lillian Laurie, "HLH," *PF*, 6 January 1909, 14.

498 Lillian Laurie, "Mrs. J.P.S.," *PF*, 3 February 1909, 14; Lillian Laurie, "Rose Poppy," *PF*, 10 February 1909, 14.

499 "Why Women Should Vote," *GGG*, 22 May 1912, 27.

500 "HLH," *PF*, 7 May 1913, 2 - Magazine Section and 21 May 1913, 2 - Magazine Section; Plett, "How the Vote Was Won," 54; "Minutes – 12 April 1913," Political Equality League of Manitoba Papers, AM, P192/1.

501 "HLH," *PF*, 7 May 1913, 2 - Magazine Section and 21 May 1913, 2 - Magazine Section.

502 Political Equality League, "Minutes – 9 October 1913," Political Equality League of Manitoba Papers, AM, P192/1.

503 Plett, "How the Vote Was Won," 56; Timelinks, "Political Equality League," Manitoba Historical Society, 30 May 2014, http://www.mhs.mb.ca/docs/features/timelinks/reference/db0001.shtml.

504 "The Campaign for Woman Suffrage," *Manitoba Free Press*, 9 July 1914, 4 ("The matter in this column is supplied by the PEL of Manitoba.")

505 Letter: Lillian to Cleverdon, 21 April 1944, Lillian Beynon Thomas Papers, AM, P191; Lillian Laurie, "Trusting All The Home Folks," *Manitoba Free Press*, 5 February 1916, 21. See also, Kym Bird, ed. *Recovered and Reanimated Plays by Early Canadian Women Dramatists, 1870-1920* (Montreal & Kingston: McGill-Queen's University Press, 2020), 132 n5 and 6.
    Lillian was probably aware of an earlier mock parliament put on Winnipeg in 1893 by the WCTU, see: Anne Anderson Perry, "Winning the Franchise," *GGG*, 7 July 1920, 19. There was also a mock parliament put on in Toronto, in 1896, by Dr. Stowe, Canada's first female practicing doctor. See: Veronica Strong-Boag, "Introduction," in Nellie L. McClung, *In Times Like These*, (Toronto and Buffalo: University of Toronto Press, 1972), vii. What was unique about the 1914 mock parliament was its use of humour.

506 Plett, "How the Vote Was Won, 58.

507 Lillian Laurie, "Trusting All The Home Folks," *Manitoba Free Press*, 5 February 1916, 21; Nellie L. McClung, *The Stream Runs Fast*, 113.

508 Francis Marion Beynon, "Suffrage Movement Moving," *GGG*," 11 February 1914, 10, citing Miss Kennethe Haig's speech in the play. This phrase was used by A.A. Perry, acting the role of Attorney-General in the play. See: Francis Marion Beynon, "Suffrage Movement Moving," *GGG*, 9 February 1916, 10; "A One-Eyed Parliament," *Farmer's Advocate and Home Journal*, 11 February 1914, 192; Anne Anderson Perry, "Winning the Franchise," *GGG*, 7 July 1920, 19.

509 Lillian Beynon Thomas, "Reminiscences," 10; For Lillian's description of Harriet Walker see: Lillian Beynon Thomas, "Some Manitoba Women who did First Things," 13. For the Walker Theatre advertisement for the evening see: "How the

Vote Was Won followed by A Women's Parliament," prices 50 cents and 25 cents, *The Winnipeg Tribune*, 16 January 1914, 9.

510 McClung, *The Stream Runs Fast*, 113.

511 Ibid."

512 Theatre historian Kym Bird has written a book in which she recovers the work of overlooked Canadian women playwrights from the period between 1870 and 1920 who used theatre as a means of advocating for women's equality and social justice. Professor Bird deals extensively with mock parliaments staged in several Canadian cities by women's organizations. She makes the following general observations applicable also to the 1914 Winnipeg play: "The most spectacular, the most high-profile, and the most important theatrical phenomena to emerge out of the Canadian women's movement were *The Mock Parliament* suffrage plays. ...The *Mock Parliaments* express the contradiction – one with which nineteenth-century feminists were happy to live – between equality and maternal feminism." Kym Bird, ed., *Recovered and Reanimated Plays by Early Canadian Women Dramatists, 1870-1920* (Montreal & Kingston: McGill-Queen's University Press, 2020), 125 and 127. Beynon Thomas's plays, staged in the 1930s and 1940s, also overlooked, will be considered subsequently. It is important to recognize the early suffragettes not only for their work in the political arena but also for their lifetime contributions in diverse fields.

513 "How The Vote Was Not Won-Burlesqued in Women's Parliament," *The Winnipeg Tribune*, 29 January 1914, 6.

514 Gutkin, "'Give us our due!' How Manitoba Women Won the Vote – Nice Women Don't Want to Vote," http://www.mhs.mb.ca/docs/mb_history/32/womenwonthevote.shtml.

515 "Suffragists To Attack Legislature With Petition," *The Winnipeg Tribune*, 26 January 1914, 7.

516 Hopkins, The Canadian Annual Review of Public Affairs 1914, 588.

517 "Premier Roblin Says Home Will Be Ruined by Votes for Women," *Free Press*, 28 January 1914, 5; "Premier Roblin Is Against Franchise," *The Winnipeg Tribune*, 27 January 1914, 1.

518 Hopkins, The Canadian Annual Review of Public Affairs 1914, 588.

519 "Premier Roblin Says Home Will Be Ruined by Votes for Women," *Manitoba Free Press*, 28 January 1914, 5; Hopkins, The Canadian Annual Review of Public Affairs 1914, 588.

520 "The Women's Delegation," *Manitoba Free Press*, 28 January 1914, 11; "Sir Rodmond Roblin and the Women's Delegation," *Manitoba Free Press*, 31 January 1914, 35 (1 - Woman's Section).

521 "Premier Roblin Says Home Will Be Ruined by Votes for Women," *Manitoba Free Press*, 28 January 1914, 5; "Premier Roblin Is Against Franchise," *The Winnipeg Tribune*, 27 January 1914, 1; Cleverdon, *The Woman Suffrage Movement In Canada*, 58 citing, *inter alia*, at fn 30, the P.E.L. Minute Book, 1914 and the *Platform of the*

Manitoba Liberals, 1914, 51; Gutkin, "'Give us our due!' How Manitoba Women Won the Vote – The Political Equality League; Nellie McClung," http://www.mhs. mb.ca/docs/mb_history/32/womenwonthevote.shtml.

522 Nellie L. McClung, *The Stream Runs Fast*, 140.

523 Francis Marion Beynon, "Suffrage Movement Moving," *GGG*, 11 February 1914, 10.

524 "Walker – Canada's Finest Theatre," *The Winnipeg Tribune*, 6 January 1914, 6 (Theatre advertisement). The theatre presentations were described in detail the next day: "How the Vote Was Not Won—Burlesqued In Women's Parliament," *The Winnipeg Tribune*, 29 January 1914, 6; "Women Score In Drama and Debate," *Winnipeg Free Press*, 29 January 1914, 20.

525 Francis Marion Beynon, "Suffrage Movement Moving," *GGG*, 11 February 1914, 10; Cicely Hamilton and Christopher St. John, "How the Vote Was Won,", Naomi Paxton, ed., Drama Online, http://www.dramaonlinelibrary.com/plays/how-the-vote-was-won-ed-paxton-iid-134035. This play was first performed in London, England on 13 April 1909; Plett, "How the Vote Was Won, 151-2 where the historian notes, "'How the vote was won' (Lacey and Hayman, 1985) was a popular British suffrage play. It was performed several times by the Manitoba women's suffrage movement. Most notably, a performance of "How the vote was won" preceded the well-known performance of "Women's Parliament" at the Walker Theatre in 1913."

526 Lillian Laurie, "Trusting All The Home Folks," *Manitoba Free Press*, 5 February 1916, 21.

527 Ibid.

528 Anne Anderson Perry, herself in the play as the Leader of the Opposition, wrote three years later that Lillian was the opposition member for North Winnipeg while Lillian's sister, Francis, was the opposition member from Brandon: Perry, "Winning the Franchise,"19. The Tribune reported that Lillian played the opposition member for Brandon when the play was later staged later in that city. "Mock Parliament," *The Winnipeg Tribune*, 14 April 1914, 8.

529 "Members of Mock Parliament Announced," *The Winnipeg Tribune*, 20 January 1914, 7 and "Mock Parliament," 14 April 1914, 8.

530 "Women Score In Drama and Debate," *Manitoba Free Press*, 20 January 1914, 20; Francis Marion Beynon, "The Suffrage Movement Moving," *GGG*, 11 February 1914, 10; Anne Anderson Perry, "Winning the Franchise," *GGG*, 7 July 1920, 19.

531 "Women Score In Drama and Debate," *Manitoba Free Press*, 20 January 1914, 20; Cleverdon, *The Woman Suffrage Movement In Canada* 59; Gutkin, "'Give us our due!' How Manitoba Women Won the Vote - The Political Equality League; Nellie McClung," http://www.mhs.mb.ca/docs/mb_history/32/womenwonthevote.shtml.

532 Cleverdon, *The Woman Suffrage Movement In Canada*, 59; "Women Score In Drama And Debate," *Manitoba Free Press*, 29 January 1914, 20; Nellie L. McClung, *The Stream Runs Fast*, 122.

533 "How The Vote Was Not Won Burlesqued in Women's Parliament," *The Winnipeg Tribune*, 29 January 1914, 6.

534 Letter: Lillian B. Thomas to Miss C.L. Cleverdon, 21 April 1944, Lillian Beynon Thomas Papers, AM, P191.

535 "Sidelights on Shows Billed for the Coming Week," *The Winnipeg Tribune*, 4 April 1914, 2 (Second Section).

536 For the Walker Theatre advertisement for the evening see: "'How the Vote Was Won,' 'A Women's Parliament' and 'The Assiniboine Male Quartet Will Sing Suffrage Songs - $1.00, 75, 50 and 25 cents,'" *The Winnipeg Tribune*, 14 April 1914, 8. For this performance, the cast appeared to have changed roles. *The Winnipeg Tribune* reported as follows: "The honourable first minister, Mrs. Nellie L. McClung; leader of the opposition, Mrs. W.C Perry; member for Brandon, Mrs. A.V. Thomas; Dr. Mary Crawford, Mrs. Lipsett-Skinner and Mrs. C.P. Walker as ministers of education, of agriculture and of public works." 14 April 1914, 8.

537 "Mock Parliament," *The Winnipeg Tribune*," 14 April 1914, 8.

538 Lillian Laurie, "HLH," *PF*, 29 April 1914, 2 - Women's Section; Plett, "How the Vote Was Won," 69.

539 Letter: Lillian to Cleverdon, 21 April 1944, Lillian Beynon Thomas Papers, AM, P191; *The Evening Province & Standard*, Regina, Saskatchewan, 15 February 1915, clipping found in the Violet McNaughton Papers, PAS.

540 Perry, "Winning the Franchise," 19; Lillian Laurie, "Trusting All The Home Folks," *Manitoba Free Press*, 5 February 1916, 21.

541 McClung, *The Stream Runs Fast*, 117.

542 Lillian Laurie, "Trusting All The Home Folks," *Manitoba Free Press*, 5 February 1916, 21.

543 Francis Marion Beynon, "The Conclusion Of A Big Struggle," *GGG*, 9 February 2016, 10.

544 Francis Marion Beynon, "The Conclusion Of A Big Struggle," *GGG*, 9 February 2016, 10; Lillian Laurie, "Trusting All The Home Folks," *Manitoba Free Press*, 5 February 1916, 21.

545 Perry, "Winning the Franchise," 19; Cleverdon, *The Woman Suffrage Movement In Canada*, 59, at fn.32, where letters to Cleverdon from Lillian (21 April 1944), and from Violet McNaughton (17 November 1943), and an interview with Francis Marion Beynon (27 April 1944), are cited.

546 "Great Ovation for Representatives of Equality League – Monster Audience of Delegates Rises and Cheers Mrs. McClung and Mrs. Thomas – First Time in History of Canada that Women Had Addressed Political Convention," *Manitoba Free Press*, 28 March 1914, 12.

547 Ibid.

548 Hopkins, The Canadian Annual Review of Public Affairs 1914, 590.

549 This was not the first time that Simpson had been frustrated in his attempts to champion laws that would protect women. In 1911 and again in 1912 he had seen

his proposed bills to reform property laws affecting women defeated or watered down.

550 "Solid Against Woman Suffrage – Government Members Line Up Against Resolution of Opposition Member – Simpson Not Present – Conservative Who Introduced the Motion Last Year Not on Hand for Vote," *Winnipeg Free Press*, 4 February 1914, 1; "Woman Suffrage In Manitoba," *GGG*, 22 July 1914, 6.

551 Cleverdon, *The Woman Suffrage Movement In Canada*, 60; Record of the Roblin Government, 1900-1914, Winnipeg, 1914, 168-170.

552 "Women's Rights Discussed," *The Winnipeg Tribune*, 5 May 1914, 8; "Discussing Votes for Women," *The Winnipeg Tribune*, 7 May 1914, 8.

553 "Will Support Dixon," *The Winnipeg Tribune*, 1 May 1914, 6.

554 Ibid.; Gutkin, "'Give us our due!' How Manitoba Women Won the Vote – The Political Equality League; Nellie McClung" http://www.mhs.mb.ca/docs/mb_history/32/womenwonthevote.shtml.

555 "Dixon Holds Meeting," *The Winnipeg Tribune*, 8 May 1914, 6; Gutkin, "Give us our due!' How Manitoba Women Won the Vote – The Political Equality League; Nellie McClung," http://www.mhs.mb.ca/docs/mb_history/32/womenwonthevote.shtml

556 Francis Marion Beynon, "Suffrage Week In Manitoba," *GGG*, 1 July 1914, 14; "The Campaign for Woman Suffrage," *Manitoba Free Press*, 9 July 1914, 4.

557 Francis Marion Beynon, "The Country Homemakers – Suffrage Week In Manitoba," *GGG*, 1 July 1914, 14.

558 "The Campaign For Woman Suffrage," *Manitoba Free Press*, 9 July 1914, 4.

559 Francis Marion Beynon, "Suffrage Week In Manitoba," *GGG*, 1 July 1914, 14.

560 Hopkins, The Canadian Annual Review of Public Affairs 1914, 605.

561 *The Winnipeg Tribune*, 16 November 1914, 5; Cleverdon, *The Woman Suffrage Movement In Canada*, 62.

562 "Young Men's Club Hears About Women," *The Winnipeg Tribune*, 9 January 1915, 1 (Second Section).

563 "Women Should Have Some Voice in War," *The Winnipeg Tribune*, 20 January 1915, 6.

564 "The Woman Suffrage Convention," *GGG*, 24 February 1915, 22.

565 "Mrs. Nellie McClung On Woman's Suffrage," *Manitoba Free Press*, 20 February 1915, 17.

566 "The Woman Suffrage Convention," *GGG*, 24 February 1915, 22; "Should President Be Man Or Woman?" *Manitoba Free Press*, 19 February 1915, 16.

567 Ibid.; "The Woman Suffrage Convention," *GGG*, 24 February 1915, 22.

568 "Not Yet Time For Votes For Women," *Manitoba Free Press*, 20 February 1915, 4.

569 Ibid.

570 "The Woman Suffrage Convention," *GGG*, 24 February 1915, 22.

571 "Not Yet Time For Votes For Women," *Manitoba Free Press*, 20 February 1915, 4.

572 "The Woman Suffrage Convention," *GGG*, 24 February 1915, 22.

573 "Not Yet Time For Votes For Women," *Manitoba Free Press*, 20 February 1915, 4.

574 Ibid.; "The Woman Suffrage Convention," *GGG*, 24 February 1915, 22.

575 "First Suffrage Convention," *Farmer's Advocate and Home Journal*, 24 February 1915, 230.

576 M. MacLean, Clerk of the Executive Council of Manitoba, "Certificate," Lillian Beynon Thomas Papers, AM, P191. Several sources, including the *GGG*, incorrectly wrote that 17,000 signatures were required. In the end, given that more than twice the number of signatures were collected, that slight mistake proved immaterial. See: "Manitoba Suffrage Petition," *GGG*, 6 October 1915, 5.

577 Francis Marion Beynon, "Will You Help With Petitions?" *GGG*, 28 July 1915, 10.

578 Lillian Laurie, "Women And Public Questions," *Manitoba Free Press*, 5 June 1915, 32 (2 - Woman's Section).

579 "Dixon Opens Up Vote Campaign," *The Winnipeg Tribune*, 6 July 1915, 5.

580 Cleverdon, *The Woman Suffrage Movement In Canada*, 62.

581 "Surprisingly Heavy Vote In The Winnipeg Constituencies," *Manitoba Free Press*, 7 August 1915, 14; Gutkin, "'Give us our due!' How Manitoba Women Won the Vote – 'It's All Over Now': A First for Manitoba Women," http://www.mhs.mb.ca/docs/mb_history/32/womenwonthevote.shtml.

582 "Odds and Ends of the Suffrage Campaign," Lillian Beynon Thomas Papers, AM, P191; "Women, In Autos, Hail New Premier," *The Winnipeg Tribune*, 10 August 1915, 1-2.

583 "Odds and Ends of the Suffrage Campaign," Lillian Beynon Thomas Papers, AM, P191.

584 Lillian Laurie, "Manitoba Women's Opportunity," *Manitoba Free Press*, 14 August 1915, 21.

585 "Brandon Begins Campaign For Women's Votes," *The Winnipeg Tribune*, 3 September 1915, 6.

586 Lillian Laurie, "Manitoba Women Wide Awake," *Manitoba Free Press*, 11 September 1915, 22 (2 - Woman's Section).

587 "Women Rush To Sign Petition," *Manitoba Free Press*, 18 September 1915, 1.

588 "Announcements," *The Winnipeg Tribune*, 23 September 1915, 6.

589 "Self-Respect of Women Would be Aided by Votes," *The Winnipeg Tribune*, 15 November 1915, 6; "Good Effect Of The Vote On Women," *Manitoba Free Press*, 15 November 1915, 7.

590 "Announcements," *The Winnipeg Tribune*, 29 November 1915, 4.

591 Lillian Laurie, "Manitoba Women Wide Awake," *Manitoba Free Press*, 11 September 1915, 22 (2 - Woman's Section).

592 Cleverdon, *The Woman Suffrage Movement In Canada*, 63.

593 Lillian Laurie, "Forty Thousand Women Want To Vote," *Manitoba Free Press*, 9 October 1915, 20.

594   Letter: Lillian to Cleverdon, 21 April 1944, Lillian Beynon Thomas Papers, AM, P191.

595   Beynon Thomas, "Reminiscences," 11. A stone-boat is a wooden flat-bottomed sled, pulled by horses, usually used for moving heavy objects such as stones.

596   Lillian Laurie, "Manitoba Women Wide Awake," *Manitoba Free Press*, 11 September 1915, 22 (2 - Woman's Section).

597   Lillian Laurie, "The Last Call For Petitions," *Manitoba Free Press*, 18 December 1915, 5.

598   J.H. Menzies, Chartered Accountant, "I certify that I have examined the several sheets conveying a Petition to the Government and Legislative Assembly of the Province of Manitoba signed by women of the province praying that a measure be enacted extending the franchise to them, …" 22 December 1915, Lillian Beynon Thomas Papers, AM, P191.

599   J. Castel Hopkins, *The Canadian Annual Review of Public Affairs 1916* (Toronto: The Annual Review Publishing Company Limited, 1917), 658.

600   Rollason, Kevin, "Lives that mattered," *Winnipeg Free Press*, 7 April 2018, 25.

601   "Manitoba Women Promised The Vote," *GGG*, 29 December 1915, 3; "Manitoba Women Want The Vote," *GGG*, 29 December, 1915, 6; Francis Marion Beynon, "Nearly Forty Thousand Signatures," *GGG*, 5 January 1916, 8.

602   "Manitoba Women Want The Vote," *GGG*, 29 December 1915, 6; Francis Marion Beynon, "Nearly Forty Thousand Signatures," *GGG*, 5 January 1916, 8.

603   Letter: Lillian to Cleverdon, 21 April 1944, Lillian Beynon Thomas Papers, AM, P191.

604   Ellinthorpe, "From Teaching to Writing," 68.

605   The incident was reported in: "Manitoba's Legislative Program," *GGG*, 29 March 1916, 7. It was also described in unsigned, typed notes, apparently not written by LBT, entitled 'Odds and Ends of the Suffrage Campaign,' Lillian Beynon Thomas Papers, AM, P191. The incident was also recounted in Cleverdon, *The Woman Suffrage Movement In Canada*, 63, where the account was based on a letter from Lillian to Cleverdon dated 21 April 1944. There was also an account in the 1953 Ellinthorpe interview: Ellinthorpe, "From Teaching to Writing," 148-9. The various accounts differ slightly in immaterial details.

606   Letter: Lillian to Cleverdon, 21 April 1944, Lillian Beynon Thomas Papers, AM, P191. One of the five Conservative members of the House, Joseph Hamelin, was the last member to speak against the suffrage bill but in an act of chivalry he abstained from voting on Third Reading so that the Bill would pass unanimously.

607   "Women Of The Province Are Given The Vote," *Manitoba Free Press*, 28 January 1916, 1.

608   Ibid.

609   "Manitoba Women Enfranchised," *GGG*, 2 February 1916, 22.

610   The play was staged on 28 January 1914; the Bill was given Royal Assent on 28 January 1916. This was noted in Lillian's summary of the campaign: Lillian Laurie,

"Trusting All The Home Folks," *Manitoba Free Press*, 5 February 1916, 21, and in her sister's summary: Francis Marion Beynon, "Conclusion Of A Big Struggle," *GGG*," 9 February 1916, 10.

611 "Women Of The Province Are Given The Vote," *Manitoba Free Press*, 28 January 1916, 1.

612 "Tribune Trumps," "Society," and "The Legislative Mirror," *The Winnipeg Tribune*, 28 January 1916, 1, 6 and 11; Cleverdon, *The Woman Suffrage Movement In Canada*, 64; "Women Of The Province Are Given The Vote," *Manitoba Free Press*, 28 January 1916, 1; "Personal and Social," *Manitoba Free Press*, 28 January 1916, 3.

613 Lillian Laurie, "The Women Of Manitoba Celebrate," *The Manitoba Free Press*, 29 January 1916, 19.

614 Ibid.

615 Ellinthorpe, "From Teaching to Writing," 68; Lillian Laurie, "The Women Of Manitoba Celebrate," *The Manitoba Free Press*, 29 January 1916, 19.

616 Letter: Lillian to Cleverdon, 21 April 1944, Lillian Beynon Thomas Papers, AM, P191.

617 Craig, "Those Women!"; "Women's Victory Is Celebrated," *Manitoba Free Press*, 2 February 1916, 1.

618 "Women's Victory Is Celebrated," *Manitoba Free Press*, 2 February 1916, 1.

619 "Women's Victory Is Celebrated," *Manitoba Free Press*, 2 February 1916, 3.

620 Ibid.

621 Ibid.

622 Lillian Laurie, "Trusting All The Home Folks," *Manitoba Free Press*, 5 February 1916, 21.

623 Ibid.

624 Beynon Thomas, "Reminiscences," 10.

625 William Shakespeare, *Julius Caesar*, Act 4, Sc. III, L. 217: "There is a tide in the affairs of men. Which, taken at the flood, leads on to fortune."

626 McClung, *The Stream Runs Fast*, 109.

627 Sarah Carter, *Ours by Every Law of Right and Justice: Women and the Vote in the Prairie Provinces*, (Vancouver: UBC Press, 2020), 21, 96.

628 Ibid., 21.

629 Ibid., Carter, 22.

630 Ibid.

631 Ibid.

632 L.K. Beynon, "The Burden of Widowhood," *The Canadian Magazine*, Vol. 29. No.1 (Toronto: Ontario Publishing Company Limited, May 1907) 23. https://www.canadiana.ca/view/oocihm.8_06251_171/57

633 Ibid., 99.

634 Ibid., p.22, citing F.J. Dixon, "Let the Women Vote," *GGG*, 26 May 1915, p. 7.

635 Lillian Beynon Thomas, "Abroad in Manitoba, *The Winnipeg Tribune Magazine*, 8 September 1934, 3. For an additional reference indicating that Beynon Thomas had written about, "the character of the Canadian Indian showing the Indian's wrath because the white man had made him weaker," see: Lillian Beynon Thomas, "Woman's Talk," *The Canadian Thresherman and Farmer*," April 1916, 82.

636 Hawkins, Return of Dower, 88-101; Carter, p. 65

637 Carter, 24 and 65.

638 Ramsay Cook, "Introduction," in *The Woman Suffrage Movement in Canada*, Catherine Cleverdon (Toronto: University of Toronto Press, 1950) xx.

639 Anne Anderson Perry, "Winning the Franchise," *GGG*, 7 July 1920," 24.

640 "HLH", *PF*, 23 May 1917, 7.

641 "Want Changes In Present Laws," *Manitoba Free Press*, 12 December 1916, 7; Lillian Laurie, "Current Comment for Women – Laws Concerning Women," *Manitoba Free Press*, 23 December 1916, 14.

642 Lillian Beynon Thomas, "Woman's Talk to Women – The Laws Concerning Women," *The Canadian Thresherman and Farmer*, January 1917, 36.

643 "Monday's Calendar," *The Winnipeg Tribune*, 1 April 1916, 4; "Announcements," *The Winnipeg Tribune*, 15 November 2016, 6 reporting that the Ladies' Auxiliary of the Winnipeg Lodge, No. 650, Independent order B'nay Brith, held a meeting at which Beynon Thomas made an address titled, "New Canada." E. Cora Hind, "Women Appoint District Directors," *Manitoba Free Press*, 12 January 1917, 2 where it is reported that Beynon Thomas addressed the Women's auxiliary of the Grain Growers' Association which was meeting in convention in Brandon; "Women Grain Growers Elect," *The Winnipeg Tribune*, 12 January 1917, 2; "Women's Work At Big Convention," *Manitoba Free Press*, 13 January 1917, 11.

644 "Saskatchewan Homemaker's Convention," *GGG*, 28 June 1916, 27.

645 "What Laws Do Women Want?" *Farmer's Advocate and Home Journal*, 17 January 1917, 67.

646 Francis Marion Beynon, "Reorganization Of The P.E.L.," *GGG*, 1 March 1916, 12.

647 "Want Changes In Present Laws," *Manitoba Free Press*, 12 December 1916, 7; "What Laws Do Women Want?" *Farmer's Advocate and Home Journal*, 24 January 1917, 135.

648 "Dr. Mary Crawford Made President," *Manitoba Free Press*, 18 February 1916, 3.

649 "What Laws Do Women Want?" *Farmers' Advocate & Home Journal*, 24 January 1917, 135; Francis Marion Beynon, "Re-Making Laws," *GGG*, 13 December 1916, 10.

650 Beynon Thomas was made Honorary President of the PEdL's City Executive on 14 April 1916: "Society and the Home," *The Winnipeg Tribune*, 15 April 1916, 6.

651 "Want Changes In Present Laws," *Manitoba Free Press*, 12 December 1916, 7.

652 Ibid.; "What Laws Do Women Want?" *Farmer's Advocate and Home Journal*, 24 January 1917, 135.

653 Lillian Beynon Thomas, "The Laws Concerning Women," *The Canadian Thresherman and Farmer*, January 1917, 36; Lillian Laurie, "Laws Concerning Women," *Manitoba Free Press*, 23 December 1916, 14.

654 "Women's Work At Big Convention," *Manitoba Free Press*, 13 January 1917, 11; "Women Grain Growers Elect," The Winnipeg Evening Tribune, 12 January 1917, 2; "What Laws Do Women Want?" *Farmers' Advocate & Home Journal*, 24 Jan 1917, 135.

655 "Women in Plea For Equality," The Winnipeg Evening Tribune, 23 January 1917, 1; "Want Better Laws," *Manitoba Free Press*, 24 January 1917, 4; "Women Ask For Entire Privileges," *The Winnipeg Telegram*, 23 January 1917, 1.

656 The Torrens system required that all interests in land be registered in order to facilitate secure land transfers.

657 "Women Grain Growers Elect," *The Winnipeg Tribune*, 12 January 1917, 2; Beynon Thomas Laurie, "Current Comment for Women – The Married Woman's Property Act," *Manitoba Free Press*, 23 December 1916, 14.

658 "Legislature Is Prorogued By Lieut.-Governor," Winnipeg Tribune, 6 March 1918, 2.

659 For an excellent explanation of the issues with respect to women voting federally, see: Barbara Roberts, *A Reconstructed World: A Feminist Biography of Gertrude Richardson*, (Montreal & Kingston: McGill-Queen's University Press, 1996), Chapter 2.

660 E. Cora Hind, "Women Appoint District Directors," *Manitoba Free Press*, 12 January 1917, 2.

661 Francis Marion Beynon, "An Explanation," GGG, 2 August 1916, 9 and Francis Marion Beynon, "More About Voting," GGG, 2 August 1916, 9. Beynon Thomas wrote "The Country Homemakers" column while Francis, the column's regular author, was on summer vacation in New York City where she was enrolled in a story writing course at Columbia University. See: Minutes of meeting of October 1916, "Minute Book 1915 to 1922," Canadian Women's Press Club Winnipeg Branch Papers, AM, P7650/2.

662 Francis Marion Beynon, "An Important Admission," GGG, 18 October 1916, 9.

663 Francis Marion Beynon, "The Foreign Woman's Franchise," GGG, 27 December 1916, 10; Beynon Thomas Laurie, "Mrs. McClung For All Women," *Manitoba Free Press*, 20 January 1917, 20; Francis Marion Beynon, "Mrs. McClung's Reply," GGG, 24 January 1917, 10; "Federal Franchise For Women Asked," *Manitoba Free Press*, 6 January 1917, 8; *Manitoba Free Press*, 20 Jan 1917, 20.

664 Barbara M. Freeman, *Beyond Bylines: Media Workers and Women's Rights in Canada* (Waterloo, Ontario: Wilfred Laurier University Press, 2011), 79.

665 Beynon Thomas Laurie, "Mrs. McClung and the Dominion Franchise," *Manitoba Free Press*, 16 December 1916, 24; Beynon Thomas Beynon Thomas, "The Federal Franchise," *The Canadian Thresherman and Farmer*, February 1917, 46.

666 "HLH," *PF*, 3 January 1917, 7.

667 Letter: Beynon Thomas to McNaughton, 21 December 1916, Violet McNaughton Papers, PAS.

668 Francis Marion Beynon, "The Foreign Woman's Franchise," *GGG*, 27 December 1916, 10.

669 Nellie McClung, "Mrs. McClung's Letter – Dear Beynon Thomas Laurie," *Manitoba Free Press*, 6 January 1917, 18; Francis Marion Beynon, "Mrs. McClung's Reply,' *GGG*, 24 January 1917, 10.

670 Francis Marion Beynon, "Mrs. McClung's Reply,' *GGG*, 24 January 1917, 10.

671 Beynon Thomas Laurie, "Mrs. McClung For All Women," *Manitoba Free Press*, 20 January 1917, 20.

672 Francis Marion Beynon, "Mrs. McClung's Reply,' *GGG*, 24 January 1917, 10.

673 Letter: Beynon Thomas to McNaughton, 21 December 1916, Violet McNaughton Papers, PAS; Beynon Thomas Beynon Thomas, "The Federal Franchise," *The Canadian Thresherman and Farmer*, February 1917, 46.

674 Freeman, *Beyond Bylines*, 78.

675 Letter: Beynon Thomas to McNaughton, 17 September 1916, Violet McNaughton Papers, PAS. At the time that this letter was written, women in the three Prairie provinces had won the right to vote. The vote was granted in Saskatchewan on 14 March 1916 and in Alberta on 12 April 1916. The other provinces adopted the reform after the letter was written: British Columbia on 5 April 1917, Ontario on 4 December 1917, Nova Scotia on 26 April 1918, New Brunswick on 17 April 1919 and Quebec on 25 April 1940.

676 Letter: Beynon Thomas to McNaughton, 21 December 1916, Violet McNaughton Papers, PAS.

677 "Lively Discussion At Women's Meeting," *Manitoba Free Press*, 16 February 1917, 5.

678 Letter: Beynon Thomas to McNaughton, 21 December 1916, Violet McNaughton Papers, PAS.

679 "HLH," *PF*, 18 April 1917, 7.

680 Ibid.

681 E. Cora Hind, "Women Appoint District Directors," *Manitoba Free Press*, 12 January 1917, 2.

682 Beynon Thomas, "The Federal Franchise," *The Canadian Thresherman and Farmer*, February 1917, 46.

683 "The Social Side of Life," *The Winnipeg Tribune*, 25 January 1917, 6.

684 "Women's Political League Will Meet Thursday Afternoon," *The Winnipeg Tribune*, 14 February 1917, 7.

685 Roberts, *A Reconstructed World*, 158.

686 "Lively Discussion At Women's Meeting," *Manitoba Free Press*, 16 February 1917, 5; Sybil Oldfield, ed., *International Woman Suffrage - Jus Suffragii*, II (Nov 1914 – Sept 1916), 375; Perry, "Winning the Franchise," 19.

687 Roberts, *A Reconstructed World*, 155-56.

688 "Dixon Speech Draws Crowd," *The Winnipeg Tribune*, 18 January 1917, 1; "Dixon Defends His Attitude - Tells Why He Opposes War - Would Not 'Die For a Myth'," *The Winnipeg Tribune*, 18 January 1917, 3 and "Dixon Raps Norris For Jail Threat," *The Winnipeg Tribune*, 19 January 1917, 11.

689 "Dixon Speech Draws Crowd*Silence Greets Utterances*Several Members To Reply," *The Winnipeg Tribune*, 18 January 1917, 1.

690 Freeman, *Beyond Bylines*, 81.

691 "Bid Farewell To Mrs. A.V. Thomas," *Manitoba Free Press*, 3 May 1917, 7.

692 Letter: Beynon Thomas to McNaughton, 20 February 1917, Violet McNaughton Papers, PAS.

693 Ibid.

694 "Women In Plea For Equality," *The Winnipeg Tribune*, 23 January 1917, 1.

695 Blanche Ellinthorpe, "From Teaching to Writing," *The Country Guide*, February 1953, 68; Letter: Beynon Thomas to Cleverdon, 21 April 1944, Beynon Thomas Beynon Thomas Papers, AM, P191.

696 Minutes - 27 April, 1917, Canadian Women's Press Club: Winnipeg Branch, *Minute Book 1915 -1922*, AM, P7650/2.

697 Minutes - 5 October 1916, Canadian Women's Press Club: Winnipeg Branch, *Minute Book 1915-1922*, AM, P7650/2.

698 Francis Marion Beynon, "Good-Bye," *GGG*, 27 June 1917, 9.

699 Examples include: "A Little Woman and a Little Business," *New Story Magazine*, v. 4, #6, October 1912 (Street & Smith) 161-169; Beynon Thomas, "Give and Take – But Generally Take," *New Story Magazine*, v. 6, #3, July 1913, 85-90; Beynon Thomas, "A Name for Jemima Georgina," *The Red Book Magazine*," v. 21, #4, August 1913 (The Red Book Corporation) 664-671; Beynon Thomas, "Getting There, "*Collier's*," 20 December 1913; see also: "Bid Farewell To Mrs. A.V. Thomas," *Manitoba Free Press*, 3 May 1917, 7.

700 Letter: Nellie L. McClung to Mrs. A.V. Thomas, 21 April 1917, Beynon Thomas Beynon Thomas Papers, AM, P191.

701 "Society News – Personals - Club Affairs," *The Winnipeg Tribune*, 27 April 1917, 6; Minutes - 27 April, 1917, Canadian Women's Press Club: Winnipeg Branch, *Minute Book 1915 - 1922*, AM, P7650/2.

702 Minutes - 27 April, 1917, Canadian Women's Press Club: Winnipeg Branch, *Minute Book 1915-22*, AM, P7650/2 and CWPC Reel M 613, Canadian Women's Press Club: Winnipeg Branch Guest Book with Beynon Thomas's entry for 26 April 1917, AM.

703 "Announcements," *The Winnipeg Tribune*, 25 April 1917, 6.

704 "Society News – Personals – Club Affairs," *The Winnipeg Tribune*, 2 May 1917, 6.

705 Scroll, "Dear Mrs. Thomas," signed: Mary E. Crawford, Ex-President, P.P.E.L., Alice A Holding, President, P.P.E.L., Agnes Munro, Recording Secretary, P.P.E.L., May Stuart Clendenan, Ex-Recording Secretary, P.P.E.L., Beynon Thomas Beynon Thomas Papers, AM, P191.

706 Beynon Thomas, "HLH," *PF*, 2 May 1917, 7. Even though Beynon Thomas told her Home Loving Hearts column readers that she was saying "good-bye," a month earlier she had signed the Minute Book at the farewell party for her sponsored by the Canadian Women's Press Club by writing that this was, "not good-bye." Perhaps she was signalling her intention to maintain her close friendships but not to continue her career as a journalist. She may have already planned to realize her dream of becoming an author.

707 "Bid Farewell To Mrs. A.V. Thomas," *Manitoba Free Press*, 3 May 1917, 7.

708 Francis Marion Beynon, "Crossing An Imaginary Line," *GGG*, 16 May 1917, 9.

709 Freeman, *Beyond Bylines*, 81.

710 Letter: Alfred Vernon Thomas to J.S. Woodsworth, 13 May 1917, Library and Archives Canada, J.S. Woodsworth (MG27111C7), Finding Aid 159, 43.

711 Letter: Alfred Vernon Thomas to J.S. Woodsworth, 28 June 1917, Library and Archives Canada, J.S. Woodsworth (MG27111C7), Finding Aid 159, 43.

712 Letter: Alfred Vernon Thomas to J.S. Woodsworth, 15 August 1917, Library and Archives Canada, J.S. Woodsworth (MG27111C7), Finding Aid 159, 43.

713 Dorothy Muir, "Winnipeg Women," *C-O-A-C-H*, December 1932, 5.

714 A. Vernon Thomas to "Dear Woodsworth," 28 June 1917, Library and Archives Canada, J.S. Woodsworth (MG27111C7), Finding Aid 159, 43.

715 Roberts, *A Reconstructed World*, 208.

716 Jocelyn Baker, "A Winnipeg Album – Mrs. A.V. Thomas," *The Winnipeg Tribune Magazine*, 1 October 1932, 2; A.R. Mansfield, "Mrs. Thomas Leaves Us," *The Lookout*, New York: Seamen's Church Institute of New York, vol. 13, no. 6, June 1922, http://seamenschurch-archives.org/sci/items/show/823, 8.

717 "Why the Institute?" *The Lookout*, New York: Seamen's Church Institute of New York, vol. 12, no. 11, November 1921, http://seamenschurch-archives.org/sci/items/show/816, 1.

718 John Farrar, *New York World Magazine*, reprinted under the headline, "Tracers For Missing Seamen," *Manitoba Free Press*, 16 August 1920, 3.

719 Letter: Alfred Vernon Thomas to J.S. Woodsworth, 18 June 1918, Library and Archives Canada, J.S. Woodsworth (MG27111C7), Finding Aid 159, 43.

720 Letter: Alfred Vernon Thomas to J.S. Woodsworth, 13 May 1917, 18 June 1918 and 1 August 1920, Library and Archives Canada, J.S. Woodsworth (MG27111C7), Finding Aid 159, 43.

721 Letter: Alfred Vernon Thomas to J.S. Woodsworth, 1 August 1920, Library and Archives Canada, J.S. Woodsworth (MG27111C7), Finding Aid 159, 43.

722 Ibid.

723 Canada Immigration Service Border Entry, Form 30, 1919-1924, Microfilm t-15335, Mikan number 161377, pages 100-101, 20 August 1921, http://www.bac-lac.gc.ca/eng/discover/mass-digitized-archives/border-entry/Pages/item.aspx?EntryName=Thistle%2c+Le+Baron+C.+-+Todd%2c+Harold&PageId=4901520.

724 "A.V. Thomas, Former City Hall Editor Dies," *The Winnipeg Tribune*, 9 November 1950, 15.

725 Letter of Condolence from Beynon Thomas B. Thomas to Lucy [Woodworth], March 21, 1942, Public Archives of Canada, J.S. Woodsworth Papers, 1942 (M.G. 27, III, C 7, Volume 4) page 1218.

726 A.R. Mansfield, "Mrs. Thomas Leaves Us," *The Lookout*, New York: Seamen's Church Institute of New York, vol. 13, no. 6, June 1922, http://seamenschurch-archives.org/sci/items/show/823, 8.

727 "Social And Personal," *Winnipeg Free Press*, 20 August 1934, 7.

728 Lillian Beynon Thomas, "Abroad in Manitoba." *The Winnipeg Tribune Magazine*, 8 September 1934, 3; 15 September 1934, 5; 22 September 1934, 7; 29 September 1934, 6; 6 October 1934, 6; 13 October 1934, 7; 20 October 1934, 6; 27 October 1934, 3; and 3 November 1934, 3.

729 "Winnipeg Author Adds To List of Successes By 'Under the Maples'," *Winnipeg Free Press*, 30 April 1932, 18.

730 Blanche Ellinthorpe, "From Teaching to Writing," *The Country Guide*, February 1953, 76.

731 "Short Story Course," *The Winnipeg Tribune*, 18 September 1922, 19.

732 "Want Ads – Educational," *The Winnipeg Tribune*, 10 October 1947, 21.

733 André Vanasse and Darcy Dunton, *Gabrielle Roy: A Passion for Writing*, English Translation (Montreal: XYZ Publishing, 2007) 129 where the authors notes that Roy took literary composition classes from Beynon Thomas, (http://books.google.ca/books?id=Cxbd1arUKPAC&pg=PA129&lpg=PA129&dq=lillian+beynon+thomas&source=bl&ots=J3Zw35H8Lh&sig=3NFN9TwJWBnRdSgl7FxoOsL7A8M&hl=en&sa=X&ei=1eJqqU5bbCKigyAGJm4DADw&ved=0CDgQ6AEwAzgo#v=onepage&q=lillian%20beynon%20thomas&f=false. There were parallels between Roy's life and Beynon Thomas's such that it is not surprising that Roy became interested in taking classes from Beynon Thomas. Roy was born in St. Boniface, Manitoba, the 11th child of a family with financial difficulties. In childhood her health was frail. From an early age she was interested in writing. She trained as a teacher at the Winnipeg Normal School and then, between 1929-1937, she taught in small town Manitoba and rural schools.

734 Ellinthorpe, "From Teaching to Writing," 76.

735 Letter: Lillian Beynon Thomas to WR Kane, Editor, of *The Editor Magazine*, 19 October 1927, Lillian Beynon Thomas Papers, AM, P191.

736 "Anecdotes and Poems are in Order When Authors Meet at University Women's Club," *The Winnipeg Tribune*, 27 January 1937, 7.

737 Muir, "Winnipeg Women," 6.

738 Ellinthorpe, "From Teaching to Writing," 76.

739 "Canadian Authors' Group Pays Tribute to Lillian Beynon Thomas," *The Winnipeg Tribune*, 18 December 1946, 10.

740 "Prairies Inspire Writers, Says Authors' President," *The Winnipeg Tribune*," 28 April 1927, 9.

741 Press reports of club activities can be found at: "Short Story Club Formed," *The Winnipeg Tribune*, 31 May 1924, 10; "Authoress Is Entertained by Short Story Group," *The Winnipeg Tribune*," 4 May 1932, 6; "City Briefs," *The Winnipeg Tribune*, 3 June 1932, 2 (J.W. Dafoe was guest speaker at the joint banquet of the Writers' Club and the Short Story Club); "Presentation to Playwright," *The Winnipeg Tribune*, 21 April 1933, 7; "Inkslingers Entertain At Annual Dinner," *The Winnipeg Tribune*, 27 May 1933, 7; "Authors' Club Closes Season With Dinner At Lower Fort Garry," *The Winnipeg Tribune*, 6 June 1934, 6; "Writers Give Farewell Tea For Miss Irwin at Southwood Country Club," *The Winnipeg Tribune*, 26 June 1934, 7; "Members of Writers' Club Are Guests Tonight of Short Story Class," *The Winnipeg Tribune*, 22 February 1935, 6; "Writers' Club Holds "Wordlurers' Banquet on Wednesday Evening ," *The Winnipeg Tribune*, 28 May 1936, 9; "Writers' Club Enjoys Annual Christmas Party," *The Winnipeg Tribune*, 27 December 1937, 5.

742 "Pen-Handlers Club is 25 years old," *The Winnipeg Tribune*, 24 April 1965, 16.

743 "Gordon Bell Students Will Present Play," *The Winnipeg Tribune*, 25 November 1939, 18.

744 "Individuality Features in Kelvin High Year Book," *The Winnipeg Tribune*, 9 May 1928, 4; "Kelvin Year Book," *Winnipeg Free Press*, 25 June 1935, 11; "Puritanism Seen Bane of Canadian Authors," *Winnipeg Free Press*, 29 April 1947, 3.

745 The colloquial name for mass market magazines was 'pulp' fiction magazines, a term which referenced the cheap quality paper on which they were printed in order to keep the price of the magazine within reach of the mass market.

746 "Short Story Still in Morning of Life," *The Winnipeg Tribune*, 19 February 1925, 12.

747 E. Cora Hind, "Lillian Laurie," *Western Home Monthly*, October 1913, 41.

748 "Byrne Hope Sanders Tells Group of Writers Needs of Women's Magazines," *The Winnipeg Tribune*, 5 November 1936, 5.

749 Jocelyn Baker, "A Winnipeg Album – Mrs. A.V. Thomas," *The Winnipeg Tribune Magazine*, 1 October 1932, 2.

750 Dorothy Muir, "Winnipeg Women," *C-O-A-C-H*, December 1932, 5.

751 "Winnipeg Woman's Novel Is 'Tense...Dramatic'," Winnipeg Tribune, 26 October 1946, 12; Dave McQueen, "Writes Novel Of Atomic Age," *The Globe and Mail*, 7 September 1946, 13.

752 "New Secret By Lillian Beynon Thomas," *The Winnipeg Tribune*, 26 October 1946, 12; S.P.L.G., "Book Review – *New Secret*," Lillian Beynon Thomas Papers, AM, P191; "School of Canadian Writers Urged at Authors' Dinner," *Winnipeg Free Press*, 18 December 1946, 9.

753 Ellinthorpe, "From Teaching to Writing," 76; Muir, "Winnipeg Women," 6.

754 Muir, "Winnipeg Women," 5.

755 E. Calder, "Among the Maples," in The Winnipeg Little Theatre, *The Bill*, Vol. 4, No. 5 (April 1932), 2.

756 "Play About Boy Lincoln, By Local Writer, Hailed," *The Winnipeg Tribune*, 13 August 1940, 3.

757 "Elizabeth Norrie, "Under the Shadow of the Bomb,", undated clipping, possibly taken from the *Montreal Gazette*, found in the Lillian Beynon Thomas Papers, AM, P191.

758 Dave McQueen, "Writes Novel Of Atomic Age," *The Globe and Mail*, 7 September 1946, 13.

759 M.K., "Truly Winnipeg Play is accorded Hearty Reception – Lillian Beynon Thomas' 'Among the Maples' Wildly Applauded After 'Premiere' Presentation," *Winnipeg Free Press*, 30 April 1932, 31.

760 "Winnipeg Women's Page Editor Is Writer of Play," unattributed Winnipeg newspaper clipping dated 25 June 1932 found in Lillian Beynon Thomas Papers, AM, 191.

761 "MacLean's $1,000 Prize Story Awards," *MacLean's Magazine*, 1 May 1927, 10.

762 Lillian Beynon Thomas, "Five Cents for Luck," *MacLean's Magazine*, (Toronto: The Maclean Publishing Company, Limited, 15 September 1927) 3. https://archive.org/details/Macleans-Magazine-1927-09-15/page/n1/mode/2up

763 Letter: Lillian Beynon Thomas to W.R. Kane, Editor, *The Editor Magazine*, 19 October 1927, Lillian Beynon Thomas Papers, AM, P191. (emphasis in original)

764 "Short Story Still in Morning of Life," *The Winnipeg Tribune*, 19 February 1925, 12.

765 Lillian Beynon Thomas, "Five Cents for Luck," *MacLean's Magazine*, 15 September 1927, 3; Lillian Beynon Thomas, *Among the Maples: A Play in Three Acts*, 1932, unpublished manuscript found in Lillian Beynon Thomas Papers, AM, P 191.

766 "Anecdotes and Poems are in Order When Authors Meet at University Women's Club," *The Winnipeg Tribune*, 27 January 1937, 7.

767 Letter: Lillian Beynon Thomas to W.R. Kane, Editor, *The Editor Magazine*, 19 October 1927, Lillian Beynon Thomas Papers, AM, P191.

768 Letter: B. Macfadden to Mrs. Thomas, 6 November 1935, Lillian Beynon Thomas papers, AM, P191.

769 *True Story Magazine*, June 1936, 19.

770 Prize Award Payment Slip: Macfadden Publications, Inc. to Lillian B. Thomas, 6 November 1935, Lillian Beynon Thomas Papers, AM P191/4c.

771 "MacLean's $1,000 Prize Story Awards," *MacLean's Magazine*, 1 May 1927, 10; "Prairies Inspire Writers, Says Authors' President," *The Winnipeg Tribune*, 28 April 1927, 9.

772 *MacLean's Magazine*, 15 September 1927, 3.

773 Letter: H. Napier Moore, Editor, *MacLean's Magazine* to Miss [sic] Lillian Beynon Thomas, Lillian Beynon Thomas Papers, AM, P191; *Lethbridge Herald*, 30 April 1927, 14.

774 "MacLean's $1,000 Prize Story Awards," *MacLean's Magazine*, 1 May 1927, 10.

775 "Story Contest Won By Winnipeg Woman," *The Globe*, 26 April 1927, 12.

776 Letter: Lillian Beynon Thomas to W.R. Kane, Editor, *The Editor Magazine*, 19 October 1927, Lillian Beynon Thomas Papers, AM, P191.

777 Anne Hicks, "Introduction," viii in Francis Marion Beynon, *Aleta Dey*, (London: Virago Modern Classics, 1988).

778 Ibid.

779 *The American Magazine*, October 1927.

780 H. Napier Moore, "In the Editor's Confidence," *MacLean's Magazine*, 1 June 1927, 104.

781 *MacLean's Magazine*, 1 August 1928, 10.

782 *MacLean's Magazine*, 1 December 1928, 16.

783 *The Country Guide*, 15 March 1929, 4.

784 *The Country Guide*, October 1944, 10. A copy can be found in the Lillian Beynon Thomas Papers, AM, P 191/4c.

785 Ibid.

786 Ibid.

787 Lillian Beynon Thomas, *New Secret* (Toronto: Thomas Allen Limited, 1946).

788 "Elizabeth Norrie, "Under the Shadow of the Bomb," possibly from the *Montreal Gazette*, undated clipping found in Lillian Beynon Thomas Papers, AM, P191.

789 The Canadian Press, "Problem of Atomic Bomb Basis For Story by Winnipeg Woman," 29 October 1946, Lillian Beynon Thomas Papers, AM, P191. Beynon Thomas wrote one other play, *It Really Happened*, in three acts, in 1940.

790 Dave McQueen, "Writes Novel Of Atomic Age," *The Globe and Mail*, 7 September 1946, 13; R.C.H., "A New 'First' By a Canadian: Lillian B. Thomas Presents 'New Secret'," *Montreal Star*, 2 November 1946.

791 "Canadian Authors' Group Pays Tribute to Lillian Beynon Thomas," *The Winnipeg Tribune*, 18 December 1946, 10.

792 "A.V. Thomas, Former City Hall Editor Dies," *The Winnipeg Tribune*, 9 November 1950, 15.

793 Dave McQueen, "Writes Novel Of Atomic Age," *The Globe and Mail*, 7 September 1946, 13.

794 "Canadian Novel Stresses Challenge of Atomic Age," *The Observer*, undated clipping found in Lillian Beynon Thomas Papers, AM, P191.

795 C.S., "New Secret by Lillian Beynon Thomas," undated clipping found in Lillian Beynon Thomas Papers, AM, P191.

796 Elizabeth Norrie, "Under the Shadow of the Bomb." possibly from the *Montreal Gazette*, undated clipping found in Lillian Beynon Thomas Papers, AM, P191.

797 *Edmonton Journal*, undated clipping found in Lillian Beynon Thomas Papers, AM, P191.

798 Nellie McClung submitted a "guest editorial" to the editor of *Home & School, Alberta* magazine. In an "Editor's Note," the following appeared: "With Mrs. McClung's article came her recommendation of a Canadian book which she

urges all adults and teenagers to read. ... This book, "New Secret" is by Lillian Beynon Thomas of Winnipeg." The "Editor's Note" undated and unattributed, can be found in Lillian Beynon Thomas Papers, AM, P191.

799 "Spiritual Reply," *The Globe and Mail*, 2 November 1946, 12.

800 I.L.M., "Winnipeg Novelist – New Secret," *Winnipeg Free Press*, undated clipping found in Lillian Beynon Thomas Papers, AM, P191.

801 *Quill & Quire*, "More Wind Without Rain," undated clipping found in Lillian Beynon Thomas Papers, AM, P191.

802 *Edmonton Journal*, undated clipping found in Lillian Beynon Thomas Papers, AM, P191.

803 "Canadian is Author Atomic Bomb Novel" undated clipping found in Lillian Beynon Thomas Papers, AM, P191.

804 "Ottawa Casts And Directors Are Honored," *The Winnipeg Tribune*, 9 May 1933, 7.

805 "Manitoba Drama League," *Winnipeg Free Press*, 30 April 1932, 27.

806 Grant Dexter, "The Revival of Canadian Drama," *Winnipeg Free Press*, 15 April 1933, 4 - Magazine Section.

807 Ibid.

808 "Expressing Canada," *The Winnipeg Tribune*," 4 March 1933, 17; Grant Dexter, "The Revival of Canadian Drama," *Winnipeg Free Press*, 15 April 1933, 4 - Magazine Section.

809 Letter: Lillian Beynon Thomas to W.R. Kane, Editor, *The Editor Magazine*, 19 October 1927, Lillian Beynon Thomas Papers, AM, P191.

810 Lillian Beynon Thomas. *Northern Lights*. (A one-act play performed at Little Theatre Members Night, Winnipeg, January 1934 – no published manuscript). See: *The Winnipeg Tribune*, 16 December 1933, 9 and 12 January 1934, 7).

811 The typed manuscript of the play that is contained in the Lillian Beynon Thomas Papers, AM, P191 is titled, *Among the Maples: A Play in Three Acts*. U.S copyright registered by the author, Winnipeg, 1932. This was the name that also appeared in the playbill. However, some review headlines referred to the play as "Under the Maples": see, "Winnipeg Author Adds To List of Successes By 'Under the Maples'," *Winnipeg Free Press*, 30 April 1932, 18.

812 "Little Theatre To Open Season Friday Night," *The Winnipeg Tribune*, 15 October 1932, 14.

813 Lillian Beynon Thomas, "Among the Maples – Act III, 24," Unpublished manuscript found in Archives of Manitoba, Lillian Beynon Thomas papers, AM, P191.

814 "Men For Business Women After Good Of All Humanity," *The Winnipeg Tribune*," 10 January 1913, 3; "Manitoba Farmers' Parliament," *GGG*, 22 January 1913, 7.

815 "University Women Plan to Aid Development of Canada's Native Drama," *Winnipeg Free Press*, 16 May 1932, 10.

816 "New Canadian Comedy Will Be Presented," *The Winnipeg Tribune*, 15 January 1932, 7.

817 Ibid.

818 "Lillian B. Thomas Play Next Friday," *Winnipeg Free Press*, 23 April 1932, 27; "Truly Winnipeg Play is Accorded Hearty Reception – Lillian Beynon Thomas' 'Among the Maples' Wildly Applauded After 'Premiere' Presentation," *Winnipeg Free Press*, 30 April 1932, 31.

819 The Winnipeg Little Theatre, *The Bill*, Vol. 4, No. 5 (April 1932), 2.

820 "Truly Winnipeg Play is Accorded Hearty Reception – Lillian Beynon Thomas' 'Among the Maples' Wildly Applauded After 'Premiere' Presentation," *Winnipeg Free Press*, 30 April 1932, 31; "Premiere of Canadian Play Gets Ovation – 'Among the Maples,' At The Little Theatre, Creates Pleasurable Picture," *The Winnipeg Tribune*, 30 April 1932, 30.

821 "Little Theatre To Open Season Friday Night," *The Winnipeg Tribune*, 15 October 1932, 14.

822 "Premiere of Canadian Play Gets Ovation – 'Among the Maples,' At The Little Theatre, Creates Pleasurable Picture," *The Winnipeg Tribune*," 30 April 1932, 30.

823 Ibid.

824 "Truly Winnipeg Play is Accorded Hearty Reception – Lillian Beynon Thomas' 'Among the Maples' Wildly Applauded After 'Premiere' Presentation," *Winnipeg Free Press*, 30 April 1932, 31.

825 "Among the Maples," *Ottawa Citizen*, 7 May 1932, found in Lillian Beynon Thomas Papers, AM, P191.

826 Ibid.

827 *Winnipeg Free Press*, 7 August 1970, 3.

828 "Winnipeg Little Theatre Comes Into Its Own," *The Winnipeg Tribune Magazine*," 30 April 1932, 2.

829 "University Women's Club Entertains Guest Speakers At Annual Luncheon," *The Winnipeg Tribune*, 16 May 1932, 6; "University Women Plan to Aid Development of Canada's Native Drama," *Winnipeg Free Press*, 16 May 1932, 10; "Expressing Canada," *The Winnipeg Tribune*," 4 March 1933, 17; "The Revival of Canadian Drama," Grant Dexter, *Winnipeg Free Press*, 15 April 1933, 4 - Magazine Section.

830 M.K., "Truly Winnipeg Play is accorded Hearty Reception – Lillian Beynon Thomas' 'Among the Maples' Wildly Applauded After 'Premiere' Presentation," *Winnipeg Free Press*, 30 April 1932, 31; "Winnipeg Little Theatre Comes Into Its Own," *The Winnipeg Tribune Magazine*, 30 April 1932, 2.

831 "Little Theatre To Open Season Friday Night," *The Winnipeg Tribune*, 15 October 1932, 14; Irene June Karasick, "Early English Playwrights," (Winnipeg: University of Manitoba Department of English Master of Arts Thesis, 1979), https://mspace. lib.umanitoba.ca/xmlui/bitstream/handle/1993/6301/Karasick_Early_Winnipeg. pdf?sequence=1&isAllowed=y.

832 "Little Theatre To Open Season Friday Night," *The Winnipeg Tribune*, 15 October 1932, 14.

833 Ibid.

834 Telegram: Frances Beynon, F.E. Thomas [Beynon Thomas's sister-in-law] and Mrs. Janet Roper [House Mother of the Seamen's Church Institute] to Mrs. Lillian B. Thomas, 6 May 1932, Lillian Beynon Thomas Papers, AM, P191.

835 "Local One-Act Play Will Be Given On Bill," Winnipeg Tribune, 12 November 1932, 21; "Highlights Of The Drama, Stage and Screen in Review," *Winnipeg Free Press*, 1 April 1933, 14.

836 "Two Winnipeg Plays Will Be Seen At Ottawa," *The Winnipeg Tribune*, 25 March 1933, 13.

837 Lillian Beynon Thomas, *Jim Barber's Spite Fence: A Comedy in One Act* (Toronto: Samuel French (Canada) Limited, 1935), 27.

838 "Expressing Canada," *The Winnipeg Tribune*, 4 March 1933, 17.

839 "Programme of Plays by THE MASQUERS' CLUB of Winnipeg and Members Night Committee of THE WINNIPEG LITTLE THEATRE," Margaret Eaton Hall, Toronto, 1 May 1937, Lillian Beynon Thomas Papers, AM, P191.

840 "Two One-Act Plays Tie For First Place," *The Winnipeg Tribune*, 20 March 1933, 5.

841 "Two Winnipeg Plays Will Be Seen At Ottawa," Winnipeg Tribune, 25 March 1933, 13.

842 "Citizens To See Winning Plays," *Winnipeg Free Press*, 25 March 1933, 30; "Under the Auspices Of The Women's Canadian Club, The Drama Festival Committee Presents ..." *Winnipeg Free Press*, 31 March 1933, 6.

843 "Highlights Of The Drama, Stage and Screen in Review," *Winnipeg Free Press*, 1 April 1933, 4. The Tribune critic agreed: "Spite Fence has been made brisker and more dramatic by the playwright than it was at its premiere. "Prize Winners At Festival Are Honored," *The Winnipeg Tribune*, 1 April 1933, 15.

844 "Masquers Club Comes First In Drama Festival," *The Winnipeg Tribune*, 1 May 1933, 3, 4; "Institute Workers Protest Cut in Extension Service at Mid-Week Session," *The Winnipeg Tribune*, 8 June 1933, 7.

845 "Notice: Tonight Margaret Eaton Hall ... The Members Night Committee of Winnipeg Little Theatre will present 'Jim Barber's Spite Fence' by Lillian Beynon Thomas," *The Globe*, 1 May 1933, 16.

846 "Broadcast Winning Play Friday Night," *The Leader Post*, Regina, 3 May 1933, 15.

847 "Institute Workers Protest Cut in Extension Service at Mid-Week Session," *The Winnipeg Tribune*, 8 June 1933, 7.

848 "States Youth Of Dominion Must Pioneer In Arts – A.V. Thomas Speaks to Federated Women's Institute Convention," *Winnipeg Free Press*, 8 June 1933, 6.

849 "Institute Workers Protest Cut in Extension Service at Mid-Week Session," *The Winnipeg Tribune*, 8 June 1933, 7

850 Lillian Beynon Thomas, *Jim Barber's Spite Fence: A Comedy In One Act*. (Toronto: Samuel French (Canada) Limited, 1935).

851 "Nine Groups To Offer Plays In Province Tests," *The Winnipeg Tribune*, 29 May 1937, 20. Also, the University of Manitoba drama students staged the play over two nights, 7 – 8 August, 1970: *Winnipeg Free Press*, 7 August 1970, 3.

852 Larry Honnor, "From Stage And Screen," *The Winnipeg Tribune*, 16 December 1933, 9.

853 "'Woodcarver's Wife' Features One-Acter Bill," *The Winnipeg Tribune*, 12 January 1934, 7.

854 Lillian Beynon Thomas, *Auld Lang Sang! A Play in Two Acts*, U.S. copyright registered by the author, Winnipeg, 1935.

855 "'John Black' Remarkable Production," *The Winnipeg Tribune*, 21 November 1935, 10; "Historical Play Reveals Life of Pioneer Pastor – Story of John Black Presented by Local Actors Wednesday," *Winnipeg Free Press*, 22 November 1935, 15.

856 "Ten Manitoba Dramatic Groups Will Compete at Regional Festival Here," *The Winnipeg Tribune*, 15 February 1936, 8.

857 "Receives Drama Awards," *The Winnipeg Tribune*, 15 October 1936, 10; The Canadian Drama Award – 1936, Lillian Beynon Thomas Papers, AM, P191.

858 "Writers Group Entertains for Lillian Thomas," *The Winnipeg Tribune*, 21 May 1946, 8.

859 G.H.K., "Play About Abe Lincoln is Coach House High Light," *Waukesha Daily Freeman*, Waukesha, Wisconsin, 6 August 1940, press clipping found in Lillian Beynon Thomas Papers, AM, P191.

860 "Week beginning August 5, AS THE TWIG IS BENT by Lillian Beynon Thomas," *Couch House Summer Theatre Play Schedule*, found in Lillian Beynon Thomas Papers, AM, P191.

861 W.R.B. Jr., "Play on Lincoln is Fourth drama At Coach House," *Watertown Daily Times*, Watertown, Wisconsin, 6 August 1940, press clipping found in Lillian Beynon Thomas Papers, AM P191; "Writers Group Entertains for Lillian Thomas," *The Winnipeg Tribune*," 21 May 1946, 8.

862 "Couch House Play Review," *Oconomowoc Enterprise*, 6 August 1940, Oconomowoc, Wisconsin, press clipping found in Lillian Beynon Thomas Papers, AM P191.

      Beynon Thomas wrote a final play which does not appear to have ever been produced: Lillian Beynon Thomas, *It Really Happened*, Mount Saint Vincent Library: Microfilm, 1940. U.S. copyright registered by author, Winnipeg, 1940 (no published manuscript; no record of the play being produced).

863 Letter: E. Austin Weir to Mrs. Thomas, 16 May 1960, found in Lillian Beynon Thomas Papers, AM, P191; "CBC Western Regional Network Radio – Monday – 15 minute drama written by Lillian Beynon Thomas," *Winnipeg Free Press*, 15 July 1933, 19.

864 *The Winnipeg Tribune*, 18 June 1938, 12.

865 *The Winnipeg Tribune*, 21 June 1938, "Interesting Delegates Come For Women's Press Club Meet," 6. In addition to taking in 'Radio Day,' the delegates, including Nellie McClung and Beynon Thomas, went on an airplane excursion from Winnipeg to Edmonton to tour a gold mine.

866 "Lucas Praises Radio Playwrights In Winnipeg," *Winnipeg Free Press*, 10 March 1939, 13; *The Leader Post*, 27 July, which reported that Beynon Thomas was busy writing 13 rural dramas for the CBC under the direction of Rupert Lucas.

867 Letter: Lillian Beynon Thomas to Jennie (Mrs. Robert Macham), 17 June 1939 (year determined by Beynon Thomas's reference in her letter to her upcoming trip to Boulder, Colorado and by Lucas's announcement on 10 March 1939 of Beynon Thomas's commission to write the radio serial.) On 27 July, 1939, *The Leader Post*, Regina, 17, reported that, "Lillian Beynon Thomas, of the Press Club, was busy writing a series of 13 dramas for CBC to be given under the direction of Rupert Lucas.

868 Peter B. Whittall, "Dial Twisting – Winnipeg Playwright To Be Guest Speaker," *Winnipeg Free Press*, 11 February 1941, 2.

869 Typed transcript for a radio talk entitled, "Mother Goose Rhymes for Every Age – A Radio Talk by Lillian Beynon Thomas, Governor of the Committee of Arts and Letters for the Local Council of Women, Winnipeg," found in Lillian Beynon Thomas Papers, AM, P191.

870 "'U' Students Win Radio Script Prizes," *The Winnipeg Tribune*, 22 April 1949, 7.

871 Carbon copy of a Letter: Norma L. MacDougall to Canadian Broadcasting Co., 8 February 1960, found in Lillian Beynon Thomas Papers, AM, P191.

872 Typed radio transcript: "Summerfallow – 'The Spite Fence'" by L.B. Thomas adapted by George Salverson, Monday, 15 Aug. 1960, 8:30-9:00 pm," found in Lillian Beynon Thomas Papers, AM, P191. Also: "Programming Schedule: '8:30 – CBO [local CBC radio affiliate] – Summer Fallow,'" *The Ottawa Journal*, 15 August 1960.

873 W.R.B. Jr., "Play on Lincoln is Fourth Drama at Coach House," *Watertown Daily Times*, August 6, 1940.

874 A copy of the letter was supplied by the *Dictionary of Canadian Biography*. For the copy of the newspaper article see: Gillian Gibbons, "She Won The Vote For Women," *The Winnipeg Tribune*, 5 September 1961, 15. For a copy of the obituary see: *The Winnipeg Tribune*, "Deaths -Thomas," 5 September 1961, 20. Very similar language describing Beynon Thomas's interest in television is found in the obituary and the letter leading to the possibility that Green Ellis wrote both. See: Gillian Gibbons, "She Won The Vote For Women," *The Winnipeg Tribune*, 5 September 1961, 15.

875 "University Women Plan to Aid Development of Canada's Native Drama," *Winnipeg Free Press*, 16 May 1932, 10.

876 "Writers' Club Holds 'Wordlurers' Banquet' on Wednesday," *The Winnipeg Tribune*, 28 May 1936, 9.

877 "Mrs. Strange New Leader of Writers' Club," *Winnipeg Free Press*, 26 May 1936, 8.

878 "Book Group Guild Plans Central Meet For Late January," *The Winnipeg Tribune*, 16 January 1940, 9; "Short Story Contribution to Canadian Life Stressed by Mrs. Lillian B. Thomas," *Winnipeg Free Press*, 31 January 1940, 9.

879 "University Women to Hear Lillian B. Thomas," *The Winnipeg Tribune*, 31 October 1946, 9; "Let Canadian Art Be Guided By Its Own North Star," *The Winnipeg Tribune*, 18 November 1946, 10; "Lillian Thomas Speaks On Art At U. Luncheon," *Winnipeg Free Press*, 19 November 1946, 10.

880 "Let Canadian Art Be Guided By Its Own North-Star," *The Winnipeg Tribune*, 18 November 1946, 10.

881 "School of Canadian Writers Urged at Authors' Dinner," *Winnipeg Free Press*, 18 December 1946, 9; "Canadian Authors' Group Pays Tribute to Lillian Beynon Thomas," *The Winnipeg Tribune*, 18 December 1946, 10.

882 "States Youth of Dominion must Pioneer in Arts – A.V. Thomas Speaks to the Federated Women's Institute Convention," *Winnipeg Free Press*, 8 June 1933, 6; see also, "Institute Workers Protest Cut in Extension Service at Mid-Week Session," *The Winnipeg Tribune*, 8 June 1933, 7.

883 "Authors Association Reviews Twenty-Five Years of Work," *The Winnipeg Tribune*, 20 January 1950, 12.

884 "Canadian Authors Dinner to Mark 25th Anniversary Draws Original Members," *Winnipeg Free Press*, 23 January 1950, 12.

885 Letter: Lillian Beynon Thomas to Jennie Macham, 17 June 1939, Lillian Beynon Thomas Papers, AM, P191; Jocelyn Baker, "A Winnipeg Album – Mrs. A.V. Thomas," *The Winnipeg Tribune*, 1 October 1932, 2; Dorothy Muir, "Winnipeg Women," *C-O-A-C-H*, December 1932, 5; Letter: Lillian Beynon Thomas to W.R. Kane, Editor, *The Editor Magazine*, 19 October 1927, Lillian Beynon Thomas Papers, AM, P 191.

886 Violet McNaughton, "Jottings By The Way," *The Western Producer*, 11 December 1952, 14 and "Jottings By The Way," *The Western Producer*, 15 July 1954, 11; Letter: Miriam Green Ellis to "Kay," 5 September 1961, copy provided by the *Dictionary of Canadian Biography*.

887 "Historical Group to Hear Mrs. A.V. Thomas," *The Winnipeg Tribune*, 24 November 1947, 13; "Women of Early Manitoba Were Valiant and Resourceful!" *The Winnipeg Tribune*, 27 November 1947, 16.

888 Lillian Beynon Thomas, "Some Manitoba Women who did First Things," *Historical and Scientific Society of Manitoba Transactions*, Series 3, Number 4, 1947-1948. A condensed version appears at, http://www.mhs.mb.ca/docs/transactions/3/firstwomen.shtml, 13.

889 Ibid. "Manitoba Women who did First Things," 13.

890 Ibid. 23.

891 A detailed exploration of the permutations to which these uncertain facts give rise, and the possibility that Lillian's interpretation is questionable, is examined

by Cherney, Bruce in: "Extraordinary affair at Pembina, Part One" (25 November 1911), https://www.winnipegrealestatenews.com/publications/real-estate-news/1415 and "Part Two" (2 December 2011), https://www.winnipegrealestatenews.com/publications/real-estate-news/1421.

892　Ibid. "Manitoba Women who did First Things," 14.

893　Ibid., 20.

894　Lillian Beynon Thomas, "Practical Idealists," *Canada Monthly* 14, 3 (July 1914), 168. Beynon Thomas titled that article *Practical Idealists* and subtitled it, *How One Man with a Dream and a Card Indexful of Facts Founded the Canadian Welfare League and What it Might Mean to Canadian Men, Women and Municipalities.*

895　Ibid, "Manitoba Women who did First Things," 24-25.

896　Lillian Beynon Thomas, "I Remember" in *Hartney and District, Manitoba: 75th Anniversary Celebration 1882-1957- Souvenir Book* (Deloraine: The Deloraine Times, 1957), 57-8, https://digitalcollections.lib.umanitoba.ca/islandora/object/uofm%3A3081253#page/66/mode/2up.

897　Lillian Beynon Thomas, "A Little Town and District Looks Back: Hartney is Celebrating Seventy-five Years of Greatness," unpublished manuscript, Lillian Beynon Thomas Papers, AM, P191, (MG 10 C3).

898　Lillian Beynon Thomas, "Reminiscences," *Manitoba Pageant: Manitoba Historical Society* 5.1 (September 1959) http://www.mhs.mb.ca/docs/pageant/05/suffragette.shtml, 10.

899　Copy of a letter from Beynon Thomas to "Cousin Charles," 10 June 1951, Beynon Thomas Beynon Thomas Papers, AM, P191; "Veteran Newsman Alfred V. Thomas Dies In Winnipeg," *Winnipeg Free Press*, 11 September 1950.

900　"Men and Women Who Work in Words and Pictures," *The Winnipeg Tribune*, 4 March 1936, 8; "A.V. Thomas, Former City Hall Editor Dies," *The Winnipeg Tribune*, 9 November 1950, 15; *The Winnipeg Tribune*, "News, Civic Heads Honor A.V. Thomas," 11 September 1950, 15.

901　Letter: Nellie McClung to "My Dearest Lillian", 14 September [1950], Lillian Beynon Thomas Papers, AM, P191.

902　Nellie L. McClung, *The Stream Runs Fast: My Own Story* (Toronto: Thomas Allen Limited, 1945).

903　"That Dappled Horse Was a Great Present – Says Nellie McClung," *The Winnipeg Tribune*, 22 December 1938, 9.

904　Dave, McQueen, Canadian Press Staff Writer, "Writes Novel of Atomic Age," *The Globe & Mail*, 6 September 1946, 13.

905　McClung's letter is cited in 'Editor's Note' in *Home & School, Alberta* magazine, found in an undated clipping in Lillian Beynon Thomas Papers, AM, P191.

906　Letter: Nellie McClung to "My Dearest Lillian", 14 September [1950], Lillian Beynon Thomas Papers, AM P191.

907　In her 1988 play, 'The Fighting Days,' Wendy Lill portrays in a semi-fictional manner the disagreement between McClung and Francis Beynon over the selective franchise issue. Beynon Thomas is portrayed as someone caught in the middle trying to mediate between her friend and her sister. In fact, Beynon Thomas's and her sister's views on this issue were very similar. See: Wendy Lill, *The Fighting Days* (Vancouver: Talonbooks, 1985).

908 Kurt Korneski, *Race, Nation, and Reform Ideology in Winnipeg, 1880s-1920s*, (Madison*Teaneck: Farleigh Dickinson University Press, 2015), 193.

909 Ramsay Cook, "Francis Marion Beynon and the Crisis of Christian Reformism," in *The West and the Nation: Essays In Honour Of W.L. Morton*, eds. Carl Berger and Ramsay Cook (Toronto: McClelland and Stewart Limited, 1976), 191.

910 Lynette Sarah Plett, "How the Vote Was Won: Adult Education and the Manitoba Woman Suffrage Movement, 1912-1916," (Winnipeg: University of Manitoba Master of Education Thesis, 2000), citing Howard Beynon's diaries as follows: "Francis was ill with cancer when she returned home ... she'd had an operation in New York."

911 Copy of a letter Lillian to "Cousin Charles," 10 June 1951, Lillian Beynon Thomas Papers, AM, P191.

912 Letter: H.B. Beynon to Prof. Ramsay Cook, 19 February 1973, Clara Thomas Archives & Special Collections, Scott Library, York University, Toronto.

913 "Dies in Hospital," *Winnipeg Free Press*, 6 October 1951, 33; Gordon Goldsborough, "Memorable Manitobans: Francis Marion Beynon (1884 – 1951)," Manitoba Historical Society, http://www.mhs.mb.ca/docs/people/beynon_fm.shtml. 'Francis' was misspelt with an 'e' in the report of her death in the *Winnipeg Free Press* and on her gravestone in Brookside cemetery. It is possible that the plot beside Vernon had been intended for Beynon Thomas, his wife.

914 There is a statue of the grounds of the Manitoba legislative building depicting the Famous Five, including Nellie McClung, acknowledging their victory in the Persons case. In 1929, the Privy Council ruled that women were "persons" under the Canadian constitution with a right to sit in the Canadian Senate. There is no statue for Lillian Beynon Thomas recognizing her role in initiating, organizing and participating in all aspects of the campaign that won the right to vote for Manitoba women, the first Canadian jurisdiction to recognize such a right.

915 Irene Craig, "Those Women!" in Manitoba Historical Society, *Manitoba Pageant* 5, 1 (September 1959), http://www.mhs.mb.ca/docs/pageant/05/thosewomen.shtml, 8; See also McManus, Brie, "Francis Marion Beynon: The Forgotten Suffragist," *Manitoba History* 28, (Autumn 1994), http://www.mhs.mb.ca/docs/mb_history/28/beynon_fm.shtml, where McManus states: "Nellie McClung ... is now considered a 'leading figure in the early rights movement in Canada, and one of the most dynamic, energetic, and influential women in Canada's history.'" McManus cites, at fn. 27, the book cover of Mary Hallett and Marilyn Davis, *Firing the Heather*, (Saskatchewan: Fifth House Ltd., 1993).

916 Lillian Laurie, "Manitoba Women Wide Awake," *Manitoba Free Press*, 11 September 1915, 22 (2 - Woman's Section); Lillian Beynon Thomas, "Reminiscences of a

Manitoba Suffragette," in Manitoba Historical Society, *Manitoba Pageant* 5, 1 (September 1959), http://www.mhs.mb.ca/docs/pageant/05/suffragette.shtml, 10.

917 Rollason, Kevin, "Lives that Mattered, "*Winnipeg Free Press*, 7 April 2018, 25.

918 Letter: H.B. Beynon to Prof. Ramsay Cook, 26 March 1973, Clara Thomas Archives & Special Collections, Scott Library, York University, Toronto.

919 Mary Ann Loewen, "McClung Was Not Alone," *Winnipeg Free Press*, 3 April 2010, 19.

920 It was only in 1960 that First Nations men and women were given the right to vote in Canada without conditions.

921 Letter: Miriam Green Ellis to Kay, 5 September 1961.

922 James Howard Manning Beynon died in Saskatoon in March 1946 at the age of 72.

923 "Lillian Beynon Thomas," *Winnipeg Free Press*, 4 September 1961, 19; "Deaths – Thomas," *The Winnipeg Tribune*, 5 September 1961, 20. The *Winnipeg Free Press* and *The Winnipeg Tribune* obituaries are the same except the *Free Press* gives 1912 as the date of the meeting at Lillian's house, held at the suggestion of Lillian's husband, to discuss the formation of the organization that several weeks later became the Political Equality League. The *Tribune* gives the date as 1913, a typo.

924 "She Won The Vote For Women," *The Winnipeg Tribune*, 5 September 1961, 15.

925 Elsie McKay, "Women's Rights Champion Lillian Beynon Thomas," *Selkirk Enterprise*, 4 October 1961, 15.

926 Manitoba Heritage Council Commemorative Plaques, http://www.gov.mb.ca/chc/hrb/plaques/plaq1217.html.

927 The plaque reads in full:

"Installed 1983, Laura Secord School, 960 Wolseley Avenue, Winnipeg

Lillian Beynon, advocate journalist and social reformer, became one of the most influential women in western Canada. Through her page in the "Weekly Free Press and Prairie Farmer", she worked to alleviate the isolation of rural women by educating them in the need for social reform and political change.

Together with other middle class women, many from Winnipeg's west-end, she helped to organize the Political Equality League in 1912. Their goal, she argued, was to show Manitobans what political equality could mean to "women and children who were in the power of weak, coarse, unfair, sick or brutal men."

Through peaceful means, including a satirical Mock Parliament, they persuaded the legislature to grant votes to women. On 27 January 1916 the Manitoba Legislature became the first in Canada to recognize women's suffrage.

She married a colleague, Vernon Thomas, who supported her literary and political work. She was later active in establishing theatre in Manitoba and became a successful novelist and playwright.

928 *PF*, 16 December 1908, 14.

929 She titled an unpublished short story manuscript "Reason VS. Sentiment," Syracuse University Libraries, Special Collections Research Center, Street & Smith Records, September 5, 1913.

BIBLIOGRAPHY

Archives:

Archives of Manitoba:
- · Alfred Vernon Thomas Papers
- · Canadian Women's Press Club: Winnipeg Branch Papers
- · Lillian Beynon Thomas Papers
- · National Council of Women Wpg Branch Papers
- · Normal School Records

Census of Canada 1881, 1891, 1901, 1911, 1921
Census of the Prairie Provinces 1916, 1926
Harbord Collegiate Archives
Library and Archives Canada
J.S. Woodsworth Fonds
Mount St. Vincent Archives
Canadian Drama Collection Special Collections
Portage la Prairie School Division Archives
Regina Public Library Prairie History Room
Saskatchewan Archives Board
Violet McNaughton Papers
Saskatchewan Archives Board
University of Saskatchewan Newspaper Collection

United Church Archives
University of Winnipeg Archives
University of Manitoba Libraries
York University Archives

Newspapers:

Brandon Sun Weekly
Brandon Daily Sun
Canada Monthly
The Canadian Courier
The Canadian Magazine
The Canadian Thresherman and Farmer
  · Lillian Beynon Thomas [Lillian Laurie], "Woman's Talk to Women"
The Chronicle, Shellbrook, Saskatchewan
C-O-A-C-H
The Country Guide
The Equity, Shawville, Quebec
Farmer's Advocate & Home Journal (Winnipeg)
  · Florence Lediard [Dame Durden], "The Ingle Nook"
The Farmer's Wife—Third International Congress of Farm Women
The Globe
The Globe and Mail
The Grain Growers' Guide
  · Isobel Graham, "Around the Fireside;"
  · Mary Ford, "The Home;"
  · Francis Marion Beynon, "The Country Homemakers;"
  · Mary P. McCallum, "The Countrywoman"
The Hartney Star, 1898-1901
The Lookout, New York: Seamen's Church Institute of New York, March
MacLean's Magazine
Manitoba Free Press / Winnipeg Free Press
Manitoba Weekly Free Press (May 1904-December 1908)
Manitoba Weekly Free Press & Prairie Farmer (January 1909-December 1920)
  · Lillian Beynon Thomas [Lillian Laurie], "Home Loving Hearts," Fall 1906-May 1917
Free Press Prairie Farmer (January 1921-December 1941)
Free Press Weekly Prairie Farmer (January 1942-December 1953)
Free Press Weekly (January 1954-December 1970)

Minnedosa Tribune

Oconomowoc Enterprise

Portage la Prairie News and Portage la Prairie Review

Regina Evening Province and Standard

Regina Leader

Steinbach Carillon News

Watertown Daily Times, Watertown, Wisconsin

Waukesha Daily Freeman, Waukesha, Wisconsin

The Western Home Monthly

  · E. Cora Hind, "The Women's Quiet Hour"

The Western Producer

The Winnipeg Telegram

The Winnipeg Tribune

Secondary Sources:

Allen, Alexander Richard. "The Social Gospel Spectrum," in "Salem Bland and the Social Gospel in Canada" (Saskatoon: University of Saskatchewan Department of History Master of Arts Thesis, 1961). https://harvest.usask.ca/handle/10388/etd-07132010-073310, Chapter 4.

Allen, Richard. *The Social Passion: Religion and Social Reform in Canada 1914–1928.* Toronto: University of Toronto Press, 1971.

Bacchi, Carol Lee. *Liberation Deferred? The Ideas of the English-Canadian Suffragists.* Toronto: University of Toronto Press, 1983.

Baker, Jocelyn. "A Winnipeg Album—Mrs. A.V. Thomas." *The Winnipeg Tribune* (1 October 1932, 2-Magazine Section).

Boos, Jodine Beynon and Patricia C. Gallinger. *The Descendants of John Beynon,* 2nd edition. Shenrone Enterprises, 1996. https://books.google.ca/books/about/The_Descendants_of_John_Beynon.html?id=ObPQAAAACAAJ&redir_esc=y.

Boos, Josephine 'Jodine.' *Beynon Family Association: Newsletter,* 10th Issue. Barrie, Ontario: Shenrone Enterprises, August, 2007.

Bryce, George. *The History and Condition of Education in the Province of Manitoba—Primary Source Edition.* Montreal: Dawson Bros., 1885.

Butler, Effie. "Branch Histories—Winnipeg." In *Golden Jubilee 1904-1954—Newspacket.* Toronto: Canadian Women's Press Club, 1954, 19.

"The Canadian Women's Press Club," *The Canadian Courier (Woman's Supplement),* Vol. XI. No. 3 (Toronto: Courier Press, Limited, December 16, 1911).

Canadian Women's Press Club. *Golden Jubilee 1904-1954: Newspacket.*

Carter, Sarah. *Ours by Every Law of Right and Justice: Women and the Vote in the Prairie Provinces*. Vancouver: UBC Press, 2020.

Cleverdon, Catherine. *The Woman Suffrage Movement in Canada*. Toronto: University of Toronto Press, 1974 [1950].

Cook, Ramsay. "Ambiguous Heritage: Wesley College and the Social Gospel Reconsidered." *Manitoba History*, #19, Spring 1990, http://www.mhs.mb.ca/docs/mb_history/19/wesleycollege.shtml.

Cook, Ramsay. "Introduction." In *The Woman Suffrage Movement in Canada*, Catherine Cleverdon, Toronto: University of Toronto Press, 1950, vi.

Cook, Ramsay. "Francis Marion Beynon and the Crisis of Christian Reformism." In *The West and the Nation: Essays in Honour Of W.L. Morton*, eds. Carl Berger and Ramsay Cook. Toronto: McClelland and Stewart, 1976, 187-208.

Craig, Irene. "Those Women!" *Manitoba Pageant: Manitoba Historical Society* 5.1 (September 1959), http://www.mhs.mb.ca/docs/pageant/05/thosewomen.shtml, 6.

The Dand Women's Institute. *Golden Memories: A History of the Dand Community, 1882-1967*. Dand Women's Institute History Committee, 1967. https://digitalcollections.lib.umanitoba.ca/islandora/object/uofm%3A2370402#page/4/mode/1up.

Dickie, Reid. "Winnipeg Collegiate Institute." In *Read Reid Read*. https://readreidread.wordpress.com/2013/03/12/schools-out-forever/.

Ditchburn, Jennifer. "A century ago, a savvy Manitoba political campaign won some women the right to vote." Canadian Broadcasting Corporation, (28 January 1916). https://www.cbc.ca/news/canada/manitoba/a-century-ago-a-savvy-manitoba-political-campaign-won-some-women-the-right-to-vote-1.3417599

Donnelly, Murray. *Dafoe of the Free Press*. Toronto: McClelland and Stewart, 1966.

Ellinthorpe, Blanche. "From Teaching to Writing." *The Country Guide*. (February 1953), 68.

Freeman, Barbara M. *Beyond Bylines: Media Workers and Women's Rights in Canada*. Waterloo, Ontario: Wilfred Laurier University Press, 2011.

Garland, Aileen. *Trails and Crossroads To Killarney: The story of pioneer days in the Killarney and Turtle Mountain District*. Altona: The Killarney and District Historical Committee, D.W. Friesen & Sons Ltd., 1967. https://digitalcollections.lib.umanitoba.ca/islandora/object/uofm%3A2233534#page/1/mode/2up

Goldsborough, Gordon. "George William Beynon (1856-1902)." *Memorable Manitobans: Manitoba Historical Society* (2015). http://www.mhs.mb.ca/docs/people/beynon_gw.shtml

Goldsborough, Gordon. "Harriet Anderson 'Hattie' Walker (1865-1943)." *Memorable Manitobans: Manitoba Historical Society* (2017). http://www.mhs.mb.ca/docs/people/walker_ha.shtml

Goldsborough, Gordon. "James Harvey Hartney (1848-1924)." *Memorable Manitobans: Manitoba Historical Society* (2018). http://www.mhs.mb.ca/docs/people/hartney_jh.shtml

Goldsborough, Gordon. "Lillian Beynon Thomas (1874-1961)." *Memorable Manitobans: Manitoba Historical Society* (2017). http://www.mhs.mb.ca/docs/people/thomas_lb.shtml

Goldsborough, Gordon. "Martha Jane Richards Hample (1859-1927)." *Memorable Manitobans: Manitoba Historical Society* (2015). http://www.mhs.mb.ca/docs/people/hample_mj.shtml

Gorham, Deborah. "English Militancy and the Canadian Suffrage Movement." *Atlantis* 1.1 (Fall 1975), 83-112. file:///C:/Users/Robert/Downloads/4108-Article%20Text-5476-1-10-20150616%20(1).pdf

Gorham, Deborah. "The Canadian Suffragists." In *Women in the Canadian Mosaic,"* ed. Gwen Matheson. Toronto: Peter Martin Associates Limited, 1976, 23-56.

Gutkin, Harry and Mildred Gutkin. "'Give us our due!' How Manitoba Women Won the Vote." *Manitoba History: Manitoba Historical Society* 32 (Autumn 1996). http://www.mhs.mb.ca/docs/mb_history/32/womenwonthevote.shtml

Hamilton, Pearl Richmond. "Our Winnipeg Press Women." *The Canadian Thresherman and Farmer* (July 1918), 82.

Harrison, Dick. "Prairie Fiction: Life on the Bibliographical Frontier." *Papers of the Bibliographical Society of Canada* (1978), Vol. 17(1), 13.

Hartney-Cameron Heritage Group. *Milestones: Hartney's Significant Historical Themes and Events.* https://heritagemanitoba.ca/images/pdfs/featuredProjects/Hartney_Milestones_Heritage_MB_complete.pdf

Hartney and District Historical Committee, "A Century of Living, Hartney and District 1882-1982," Schools—Hartney Public School District no. 312, p. 97-8: https://digitalcollections.lib.umanitoba.ca/islandora/object/uofm%3A2385341#page/698/mode/2up

Hartney Heritage Advisory Group. "Famous Daughter—Activist Lillian Beynon Thomas." In *Our Heritage: The Municipality of Grassland: We Made Hartney: Notable People from Hartney's Past.* https://heritagemanitoba.ca/images/pdfs/featuredProjects/We_Made_Hartney_Heritage_MB_complete.pdf

Hathaway, Debbie. "The Political Equality League of Manitoba." *Manitoba History: Manitoba Historical Society* 3 (1982). http://www.mhs.mb.ca/docs/mb_history/03/politicalequalityleague.shtml

Hawkins, R.E. "Dower Abolition in Western Canada: How Law Reform Failed." *Manitoba Law Journal* 24(3) (1997), 635-663. https://www.canlii.org/en/commentary/doc/1997CanLIIDocs134#!fragment//BQCwhgziBcwMYgK4DsDWsz IQewE4BUBTADwBdoByCgSgBpltTCIBFRQ3AT0otokLC4EbDtyp8BQkAGU8pAEL cASgFEAMioBqAQQByAYRW1SYAEbRS2ONWpA

Hawkins, R.E. "Lillian Beynon Thomas, Woman's Suffrage and the Return of Dower to Manitoba." *Manitoba Law Journal* 27(1) (1999-2000), 45-114. http://themanitobalawjournal.com/wp-content/uploads/articles/MLJ_27.1/Lillian%20Beynon%20Thomas,%20Woman's%20Suffrage%20and%20the%20Return%20of%20Dower%20to%20Manitoba.pdf

Heads, Wendy. *The Local Council of Women of Winnipeg, 1894-1920, Tradition and Transformation*. Winnipeg: University of Manitoba Faculty of Graduate Studies, 1997. https://www.collectionscanada.gc.ca/obj/s4/f2/dsk3/ftp04/mq23337.pdf

Hicks, Anne. "Introduction." In Francis Marion Beynon, *Aleta Dey*, Francis Marion Beynon, London: Virago Press Limited, 1988, viii. (First published in Great Britain: C.W. Daniel Ltd., 1919.)

Hicks, Anne. "Francis Beynon and The Guide." In *First Days, Fighting Days: Women in Manitoba History*, ed. Mary Kinnear. Regina: Canadian Plains Research Center, 1987, 41-52.

Hind, E. Cora. ("The Woman"). "The Woman About Town—Lillian Laurie." *Winnipeg Town Topics* (approx. Fall 1913) (Archives of Manitoba, Lillian Beynon Thomas Papers, P 191).

Homemakers' Clubs of Saskatchewan. *Retrospect and Prospect: The Silver Cord and the Golden Chain*. Saskatoon: University of Saskatchewan, Extension Division, 1939.

Hopkins, J. Castel. *The Canadian Annual Review of Public Affairs 1914*. Toronto: The Annual Review Publishing Company Limited, 1915. https://electriccanadian.com/history/annual/canadianannual14.pdf.

Hopkins, J. Castel. *The Canadian Annual Review of Public Affairs 1916*. Toronto: The Annual Review Publishing Company Limited, 1917. https://electriccanadian.com/history/annual/canadianannual16.pdf

The International Dry-Farming Congress. *Official Proceedings of the First International Congress of Farm Women, Colorado Springs, Colorado, October 17-20, 1911*. Lethbridge: The International Dry-Farming Congress, 1911. http://memory.loc.gov/service/gdc/scd0001/2008/20080222001in/20080222001in.pdf.

Jackel, Susan. "First Days, Fighting Days: Prairie Presswomen and Suffrage Activism, 1906-1916." In *First Days, Fighting Days: Women in Manitoba History*, ed. Mary Kinnear. Regina: Canadian Plains Research Centre, 1987, 53-75.

Kalmakoff, E.A. "Woman Suffrage." In *The Encyclopedia of Saskatchewan*. Regina: Canadian Plains Research Centre, 2006. https://esask.uregina.ca/entry/woman_suffrage.jsp.

Karasick, Irene June. "Early English Playwrights." M.A. Thesis, The University of Manitoba, 1979. https://mspace.lib.umanitoba.ca/xmlui/bitstream/handle/1993/6301/Karasick_Early_Winnipeg.pdf?sequence=1&isAllowed=y.

Kelcey, Barbara E. and Angela E. Davis, eds. *A Great Movement Underway: Women and The Grain Growers' Guide, 1908-1928—Selected Letters and Editorials from the Woman's Page*. Winnipeg: The Manitoba Record Society, 1997. http://www.mhs.mb.ca/docs/books/mrs12.pdf.

Keshen, Jeffrey A. *Propaganda and Censorship During Canada's Great War*. Edmonton: The University of Alberta Press, 1996.

Korneski, Kurt. *Race, Nation, and Reform Ideology in Winnipeg, 1880s-1920s*. Madison*Teaneck: Farleigh Dickinson University Press, 2015.

Lang, Marjory. *Women Who Made the News: Female Journalists in Canada, 1880-1945*. Montreal & Kingston: McGill-Queen's University Press, 1999.

Leonard, John William, ed. *Woman Who's Who of America: a biographical dictionary of contemporary women of United States and Canada* 1914-1915. New York: American Commonwealth Co., 1914, 810. https://archive.org/details/womanswhoswhoofa00leon/page/810.

Lewis, Norah L., ed. *Dear Editor and Friends: Letters from Rural Women of the North-West, 1900-1920*. Waterloo: Wilfred Laurier University Press, 1998.

Lill, Wendy. *The Fighting Days*. Vancouver: Talonbooks, 1985.

MacDonald, Eric. "All Peoples' Mission and The Legacy of J. S. Woodsworth: The Myth and the Reality." M.A. Thesis, University of Ottawa, 2013. https://ruor.uottawa.ca/bitstream/10393/24340/3/MacDonald_Eric_2013_thesis.pdf.

Manitoba Culture, Heritage, and Recreation. *Lillian Beynon Thomas*. Winnipeg: Manitoba Culture, Heritage, and Recreation Historical Resources Branch, 1986.

Manitoba Historical Society. "Lillian Beynon Thomas." *Timelinks* 23 (August 2009). http://www.mhs.mb.ca/docs/features/timelinks/reference/db0008.shtml.

Manitoba Historical Society. "Harriet (Anderson) Walker and C.P. Walker." *Timelinks* 27 (August 2009). http://www.mhs.mb.ca/docs/features/timelinks/reference/db0050.shtml.

Manitoba Women's Institute. *The Great Human Heart: A History of the Manitoba Women's Institute 1910-1980*. Altona: Manitoba Women's Institute, 1980.

McClung, Nellie L. *Clearing in the West: My Own Story*. Toronto: Thomas Allen, 1935. https://gutenberg.ca/ebooks/mcclung-clearinginthewest/mcclung-clearinginthewest-00-h-dir/mcclung-clearinginthewest-00-h.html.

McClung, Nellie L. *The Stream Runs Fast: My Own Story*. Toronto: Thomas Allen Limited, 1945. http://peel.library.ualberta.ca/bibliography/6771.html.

McDowell, Linda. "Nellie Was Not Alone." *Association of Canadian Studies* (Fall 2016), 24-27.

McDowell, Linda. "The Political Equality League 1912-1916." *The Nellie McClung Foundation* (2018). https://www.ournellie.com/learn/political-equality-league/.

McManus, Brie. "Francis Marion Beynon: The Forgotten Suffragist." *Manitoba History* 28 (Autumn 1994), 22-30.

McNaught, Kenneth. *A Prophet in Politics: A Biography of J.S. Woodsworth*. Toronto: University of Toronto Press, 2001.

McNaughton, Violet. "Jottings By The Way." *The Western Producer* (11 December 1952), 14 and (15 July 1954), 11.

McQueen, Dave. "Writes Novel of Atomic Age." *The Globe and Mail* (7 September 1946), 13.

Milne, Jennifer. "Cultivating Domesticity: The Homemakers' Clubs of Saskatchewan, 1911 To 1961" (Saskatoon: University of Saskatchewan Department of History Master of Arts Thesis, 2004). https://harvest.usask.ca/bitstream/handle/10388/etd-07112005-100045/JMilne_FinalThesis.pdf?sequence=1&isAllowed=y.

W.L. Morton. *Manitoba, A History*. 2nd ed. Toronto: University of Toronto Press, 1967.

Muir, Dorothy. "Winnipeg Women." *C-O-A-C-H* (December 1932).

Muir, Shirley and Penni Mitchell. "Winnipeg Journalist Have Always Led the Way." *Manitoba Historical Society* 70 (Fall 2012). http://www.mhs.mb.ca/docs/mb_history/70/womenjournalists.shtml.

The Municipality of Grassland. "Our Heritage: Grassland Heritage Photo Album—Hartney," http://www.virtualmanitoba.com/grassland/photos/hartney/index.html.

The Municipality of Grassland. "Our Heritage: Special Places: Hartney: The Town of Hartney," https://www.virtualmanitoba.com/grassland/specialplaces/hartney.html.

Neufeld, Teyana. "Hartney 1882–Present." Southwest Manitoba: Turtle Mountain-Souris Plains Heritage Association. http://vantagepoints.ca/stories/hartney/.

Oldfield, Sybil, ed., *International Woman Suffrage—Jus Suffragii*, II (Nov 1914–Sept 1916). London: Routledge, 2003.

Parker, C.W., ed. *Who's who and Why: A biographical dictionary of notable living men and women in Western Canada Volume 2*. Vancouver: Canadian Press Association, Limited, 1912, 47. https://open.library.ubc.ca/collections/bcbooks/items/1.0355313#p46z-5r0f:.

Parker, C.W., ed. *Who's Who in Western Canada: a biographical dictionary of notable living men and women in Western Canada*. Vancouver: Canadian Press Association, Limited, 1911, 109. https://open.library.ubc.ca/collections/bcbooks/items/1.0348960#p111z-4r360f:.

Parkinson, Hazel McDonald. *The Mere Living: A Biography of the Hartney District*. Altona: D.W. Friesen & Sons Ltd., 1957. https://digitalcollections.lib.umanitoba.ca/islandora/object/uofm%3A2235091#page/1/mode/2up.

Perfect, Mary Brewster. "One Hundred Years in the History of the Rural Schools of Manitoba: Their Formation, Reorganization and Dissolution (1871-1971)." (Winnipeg, University of Manitoba Master of Education, 1978).

Perry, Anne Anderson. "Winning the Franchise." *The Grain Growers' Guide*. (7 July 1920), (1503)19.

Philistia, "Mrs. Lillian Beynon Thomas," *The Canadian Courier*, Vol. XIV. No. 22 (Toronto: Courier Press, Limited, November 1, 1913) 23.

Phillips, G.G. *The Rise and Fall of a Prairie Town: A History of Lauder Manitoba and the Surrounding District*, Volume 3. Ottawa: Gordon G. Phillips, June 1977. https://digitalcollections.lib.umanitoba.ca/islandora/object/uofm%3A2386467#page/1/mode/2up.

Plett, Lynette Sarah. "How the Vote Was Won: Adult Education and the Manitoba Woman Suffrage Movement, 1912-1916," (Winnipeg: University of Manitoba Master of Education Thesis, 2000). https://mspace.lib.umanitoba.ca/bitstreams/d592bfe3-dcc9-4964-8f09-05e192e97d34/download.

Roberts, Barbara. *A Reconstructed World: A Feminist Biography of Gertrude Richardson*. Montreal and Kingston: McGill-Queen's University Press, 1996.

Sangster, Joan. *One Hundred Years of Struggle: The History of the Vote and Women in Canada*. Vancouver: UBC Press, 2018.

Saskatchewan Grain Growers' Association. *The Women's Section: Past Present Future*. Regina: The Saskatchewan Grain Growers' Association Limited Women's Section, 1923.

Saskatchewan Grain Growers Association, Women's Section. *Yearbook, 1916*.

Sawatzky, Roland. "Manitoba's First Petition for Women's Suffrage and the Demography of Activism," *Prairie History*, 2022 (9), 38.

Schreiner, Olive. *Woman and Labour*. New York: Frederick A. Stokes, 1911.

Siamandas, George. "Lillian Beynon Thomas: Writer and Social Reformer." *The Winnipeg Time Machine*. http://timemachine.siamandas.com/PAGES/people_stories/LILLIAN_BENYON_THOMAS.htm

Simon Fraser University Digitized Collections. "Lillian Beynon Thomas." https://digital.lib.sfu.ca/ceww-705/thomas-lillian-beynon.

Skene, Reg. "Harriet Walker". In *The Canadian Encyclopedia*. Toronto: Historica Canada, 16 December 2013. https://www.thecanadianencyclopedia.ca/en/article/harriet-walker

Strathy, Kerrie A., "Saskatchewan Women's Institutes: The Rural Women's University, 1911-1986," (Saskatoon: University of Saskatchewan Department of Communications, Continuing and Vocational Education Master of Continuing Education Thesis, 1987). https://harvest.usask.ca/handle/10388/6705.

Strong-Boag, Veronica. "Introduction." *In Times Like These*, Nellie L. McClung. 1915; Toronto and Buffalo: University of Toronto Press, 1972, vii.

Swann, Michelle and Veronica Strong-Boag, "Mooney, Helen Letitia (McClung)." In *Dictionary of Canadian Biography Online*. http://www.biographi.ca/en/bio/mooney_helen_letitia_18E.html.

Taylor, Georgina M. "'Ground for Common Action': Violet McNaughton's Agrarian Feminism and the Origins of the Farm Women's Movement in Canada" (Ottawa: Carleton University Department of History Doctor of Philosophy Thesis, 1997). https://www.collectionscanada.gc.ca/obj/s4/f2/dsk2/ftp03/NQ26870.pdf.

Taylor, Georgina M. "Homemakers' Clubs and Women's Institutes." In *The Encyclopedia of Saskatchewan*. Regina: Canadian Plains Research Centre, 2006. https://esask.uregina.ca/entry/homemakers_clubs_and_womens_institutes.jsp.

Thieme, Katja. "Language and social change: the Canadian Movement for Women's Suffrage, 1880-1018." Vancouver: The University of British Columbia Department of English Doctor of Philosophy Thesis, 2007). https://open.library.ubc.ca/soa/cIRcle/collections/ubctheses/831/items/1.0100685?o=1.

Thieme, Katja. "Uptake and Genre: The Canadian reception of suffrage militancy." *Women's Studies International Forum* 29.3 (2006), 279-88. https://www.sciencedirect.com/science/article/abs/pii/S0277539506000173.

Vanasse, André and Darcy Dunton. *Gabrielle Roy: A Passion for Writing, English Translation*. Montreal: XYZ Publishing, 2007.

Virtual Manitoba. "Pivotal Events in Hartney and Region: An Illustrated Timeline," https://www.virtualmanitoba.com/grassland/events/HartneyTimeline.pdf

Watters, Reginald Eyre. *A Checklist of Canadian Literature 1628-1960*. Toronto: University of Toronto Press, 1959.

Welton, Michael. "Pioneers and Progressive Pedagogues: Carrying the University to the People of Saskatchewan, 1905-1928." *Canadian Journal for the Study of Adult Education* 17.2 (2003), 59. https://cjsae.library.dal.ca/index.php/cjsae/article/view/1857/1617.

Women's Institutes of Saskatchewan. *Legacy: A History of Saskatchewan Homemakers' Clubs and Women's Institutes, 1911-1988*. Saskatoon: Saskatchewan Women's Institute, 1988.

Woodsworth, James S. *Strangers Within Our Gates or Coming Canadians*. Toronto: The Missionary Society of the Methodist Church of Canada, 1909.

INDEX

Lillian B. Thomas,

Lillian Beynon Thomas signature from her will, April 20, 1954
SOURCE: SURROGATE COURT OF THE EASTERN JUDICIAL DISTRICT OF
THE PROVINCE OF MANITOBA, APPLICATION FOR PROBATE, RE: LILLIAN
BEYNON THOMAS, DECEASED, OCTOBER 10, 1961, #63222.